THE HEBREW IMPACT ON
WESTERN CIVILIZATION

THE HEBREW IMPACT ON WESTERN CIVILIZATION

אבגדהוז
חטי
כלמ
נסעפצקר
שת

Abridged Edition

Edited by DAGOBERT D. RUNES

THE CITADEL PRESS
SECAUCUS, N.J.

Second paperbound printing, 1976
Published by Citadel Press
A division of Lyle Stuart, Inc.
120 Enterprise Ave., Secaucus, N. J. 07094
Manufactured in the United States of America
Copyright 1951 by Philosophical Library, Inc.
ISBN 0-8065-0532-X

Preface

THIS BOOK is a book of propaganda. It has the mission to bring intelligence about the work and the life of the Hebrews pro paganis. The pagans for whom this volume is intended are the many, many people in whose midst the Hebrews have lived for thousands of years. The Jews had to learn the ways of their harborers in order to live, but seldom did the princes and the people of the West give more than a passing glance to their strange Asiatic guests.

For almost eighteen hundred years—with few and brief exceptions—the Jews of the Western World were confined in high walled corrals, the gates to which were rarely opened and then only by the kings, knights and crusaders who combined the infernal spectacle of slaughtered, defenseless Jewish men and women with their instinct for robbery, together with a remarkably recurrent Christian theology of vengeance on the descendants of those who allegedly had executed the son of God.

During these many hundreds of years of their ghetto life, the mind of Israel and the art of Israel and the courage of Israel were pining away in a captive's existence, chained to frustration by intolerant and bigoted nations. The Great Show of the world was closed to them. On rare occasions only was it possible for some—and few—to break out and to storm into the whirl of events.

Then, two hundred years ago, there rose the American rebellion against a king and his disciples, and the jubilant Dare, so vehemently sparked in America, flamed up in France and from there spread over most of the Western World. The same spirit that drove tyranny from American soil and corruption from France, the same spirit smashed the ghetto walls of Europe and set the Jew free.

It is actually with the American and French revolutions that the real life and influence of the Israelites in the Western World begins.

If what the Jews have done for Europe and America in these few hundred years appears gigantic, the statement of it here is no exaggeration, as the scholar can quickly discover, and it is not overstressed, I am sure, by any of the contributors, of whom some are Jews and some are not. It is rather related purposefully so that those who disapprove of an act or person of a Jew may balance such acts and persons against the magnitude of Jewish Drama on the other scale.

It is with the Christians among whom Jews reside as it is with the human heart: they are rarely aware of the Jew unless he hurts them. His silent and constant work for their welfare—one would almost think it doesn't exist.

And still, their every church is a monument to the Jew Jeshu ben Joseph and his Apostles:—Saul, whom they named Paul; and Shimon, whom they named Peter; and Levi, whom they named Matthew; and so on. It is true—if it is—that many of those who knew Jeshu (whom we call, after the Greek, Jesus), did not take him for the Messiah (in Greek: Christos) but many of them did, and they all, as well as Miriam (Mary), (and her sons whom she bore after Jeshu) were Jews. The whole ancient church of Christendom is Jewish in origin, Jewish in concept (Messiah) and Jewish in followship; and if there were many who wished his death, there were many who wished his life to be unending.

When Christianity made its great reforms in the 16th and 17th centuries, it opened the pages of the Old Testament and drank from the Hebrew fountain of wisdom. The Hebrew testament was the light and the guide by which not only the Puritans but also the other great armies of pioneers and settlers worked, lived and governed. In the later years our greatest statesmen and reformers, men like Thomas Jefferson, Benjamin Rush, Abraham Lincoln,—they held the Hebrew Testament to be the Truth forever.

THE HEBREW IMPACT ON WESTERN CIVILIZATION

The Western World has pulled some sordid jokes on the Jew. For almost two thousand years they stopped him from owning land, and then they accused him of refusing to work it; they stopped him from bearing arms, and then they called him a coward; they kept him from their schools and laughed at his ignorance; they kept him from public office and the right to vote, and then they called him subversive and disloyal; they stopped him from engaging in anything but small trade, and then they referred to him sneeringly as an unmitigated tradesman; and some of the grand lords in the manors of the Medieval Ages used the Jews to administer their loan business, and then they called them usurers.

This book will show to those who wish to learn that the Jew is a diligent farmer, an heroic soldier, a loyal servant of his people and an ardent scholar.

Many of the facts quoted in this book may startle even the well-read. How many people know, for instance, that half of the German Nobel Prize winners were men of Jewish descent? Six hundred thousand Jews of pre-war Germany produced as many Nobel Prize winners as sixty million Germans, the *Herrenvolk* that showed its gratitude to the men who so tremendously helped in their growth by massacring the Jewish people of Europe. Six million souls in six years! A million Jews a year were hunted down by German nationals in every corner of Europe, dragged to the executioners, choked to death in sealed trains or gassed in torture chambers and burned in huge bread ovens. This is how one Christian nation repaid its debt to the people of Israel. And of the millions of the Teutonic malefactors, the axemen as well as their millions of helpers and their multi-millions of Jew-denouncers and Hitler-heilers, all but an ugly few are alive and kicking the same bloody boots in goose-step.

Perhaps it would be better to forget the Hitler monstrosities. The Western World is somewhat embarrassed about its indifference towards Teutonic inhumanity. Perhaps we Jews would like to forget too. Forget the joyful victory marches in every town and hamlet of Germany when their last Jew was safely squeezed into the awaiting freight car, to die of asphyxiation with the other hundred members of his tribe, men, women and infants, living for minutes and minutes without a breath of air, body after body collapsing, so closely packed that the dead would hang against the shoulders and backs of those still living, and at the point of destination, hours away, the whole sordid mess of human cadavers would be shovelled into huge stoves by their German tormentors.

We would like to forget those things. We would like to forget the cultured German officers who so carefully lined up three children in a row that they might kill them with one bullet instead of three . . . we would like to forget the German scientists who vivisected our mothers and sisters and daughters in cannibalistic fashion . . . we would like to forget the group of German scholars that succeeded in making soap out of Jewish body fat, and later sold it to the Jews at exorbitant prices, for burial purposes. . . . We would like to forget those things, but the Germans don't forget. They haven't forgotten the glory and the strut of their Jew-killing heydays, even though they go to church on Sundays, and to the Salzburg festivals and the Passion play in Oberammergau. And though by all candid reportage they may have some doubts as to Hitler's political craftsmanship, there is no doubt today in their black hearts, after all has been shown and told, that they enjoyed this spirit of Jew-killing and regret nothing more than that it stopped.

And the Christian nations of the Western World speak to these Teutons as if they were humans! Some even join them in their festivals and their cultural activities, which are typical German intermezzos between wars and assassinations. . . .

Perhaps the world needs to know more about the Jews.

Perhaps they ought to know that were it not for Jewish discoverers in medicine, millions of their children and people might have perished. Perhaps this book will help to show that in these two thousand years of unwanted neighborness the Jew has contributed a goodly share for the betterment of this, our society, for which thanks were few on the record, and humiliations many.

This book will show only some of the Jewish contributions to Western culture. Space did not permit its dwelling upon many other aspects which must be left missing from this volume. But there is enough, I feel, to demonstrate our case— that the Jews have done their share and more than their share in building the culture of the West. They have given of their heritage a full measure, and given it diligently—to science and literature, statesmanship and art. How the Christian world has repaid them—I leave that evaluation to the reader. I hope my contributors have succeeded in showing the Hebrews to the Western World in their true light, in their deeds. And by their deeds you shall judge them.

D. D. R.

Table of Contents

THE HEBREW IMPACT ON
WESTERN CIVILIZATION

Hebraic Foundations of American Democracy

By ABRAHAM I. KATSH

Introduction

EVEN a most cursory study of early American life reveals the vast influence on it of the Scriptures and the Hebrew language. The New World as an extension of the Old absorbed much from its cultural roots. The importance of the Bible in day-to-day living in Europe was transferred with appropriate changes to the new soil. The earliest settlers were men who carried their Bibles both in their hearts and hands.

The Scriptures which have come down to us today in Hebrew have importance in half a dozen fields. Their historical significance is too obvious to need expansion here. The far-reaching effect of Biblical law and lore is sometimes amazing. Consider for instance, the number of uses to which the Ten Commandments have been put. Much in many Occidental and Near Eastern philosophies stems from the Bible. Whole non-Jewish theologies of today derive their authenticity from, and have their roots in the Old Testament.

The influence of the Scriptures on literature is all-embracing. Writers in all ages and in all places have drawn on it both as a source of material and as a model for style. The simplicity, brevity, and clarity of the Old Testament in the original Hebrew is a monument to the men who compiled it. Consider for a moment the question of vocabulary. Shakespeare, thought by many to be the finest poet of the English language, employed approximately 20,000 different words. Milton to realize his epics required 10,000. But the vast panorama of Biblical thought and emotion is conveyed in little more than 6,000!

Unfortunately, this point gives rise to one of the prime difficulties in dealing with the Scriptures. The style and flavor of biblical language is, in essence, untranslatable. Indeed one might go so far as to say that in another language some phrases are virtually unintelligible. What meaning has this quotation to the reader who has no knowledge of Hebrew as we find it in the English translation? "And thou shalt call me Ishi, and shalt call me no more Baali." (Hosea ii, 16)

Time, repeated translations from one language to another, actual misinterpretation of words, misunderstandings, all have played their part in contributing to the confusion. For example: The first part of verse two in the Song of Deborah (Jud. 5, 2), has been rendered by many scholars in the following ways: ". . . when men let grow their hair in Israel,"[1] "Because the leaders took the lead in Israel."[2] "When the people willingly offered themselves."[3] There is little standardization of meaning here; little agreement on the actual equivalents for the Hebrew words.

Numerous other examples can be cited. The same English word "ark" is used to denote the craft in which Noah sailed-out the flood and the receptacle that held the Five Books of Moses. The terms are wholly different in Hebrew. The phrase "voice of the turtle" has in recent years become increasingly popular. Much of the bewilderment that arises from the anomaly of the voice of a mute animal could have been forestalled had the phrase been rendered "voice of the turtle-dove," a more accurate reading of the Hebrew. Moses is often depicted with horns, notably in Michelangelo's masterpiece, because the Hebrew word, *qrn*, used to describe Moses can be translated either "ray of light" or "horn." The ancient writer was obviously pointing out a ray of light about the great leader's head, not a horn.

W. L. Roy wrote "The Bible can never be understood, unless through the medium of the language in which it was

originally written, and the spirit by which it was dictated ...
Hebrew is so pregnant and rich in sense that no translation
can do it justice."[4] Careful examination of what has been done
to scriptural text in translation bears this out.

The value of Hebrew to Christian and Jewish scholars alike
has been well documented. Luther, in speaking of the 45th
psalm, said: "I am acquainted with a sufficiency of Hebrew
to be able to combat all my enemies, the knowledge of which,
though small, I prize above millions of gold." Roger Bacon,
always an advocate of precise and pure thought, on more than
one occasion expressed his zeal for the language. With extraordinary acumen for his times he felt that all translations of
the Bible had become hopelessly corrupt. The Puritans and
the Quakers to whom we owe so much that is basic to our
concept of democracy both highly cherished the Old Testament and Hebrew as a language. For the inspiration and but-
tressing of their religious and political views they drew freely on this great source.

Throughout all the history of the United States the story
has been much the same. Time and time again men have returned to the spirit of the Hebrews. Much of the contribution
of England to the colonies was in terms of this spirit. Indeed,
in the Occident at any rate, wherever men read they are almost certain to be touched in some degree by it. To vivify this
the writer in the coming pages presents in some measure the
contributions of the Hebraic spirit to the English-speaking
peoples as a whole and to America in particular. For conve-
nience this study has been divided into the following subdivi-
sions: (a) The Influence of the Bible, (b) Early Popularity
of the Hebrew Language, (c) Influence of the Judaic Spirit,
(d) Legislation, (e) Polity, and (f) The Literature of England and America.

Both the language and the message of the Bible are very
much alive even today. Both—one through the other—are
equally potential as forces that may well help to restore some

order to our age of chaos. And perhaps, as never before in world history, has there been such a need for order.

FOOTNOTES

1 *Holy Scriptures*, Jewish Publication Society.
2 J. A. Bewer, *The Literature of the Old Testament in its Historical Development*.
3 E. S. Bates, *The Bible as Literature*.
4 W. L. Roy, *A Complete Hebrew and English Dictionary*, pages 736-7.

A.—THE INFLUENCE OF THE BIBLE

ALTHOUGH the influence of Jewish culture on Western civilization is generally recognized by scholars, the majority of people are unaware of any such contributions. Of course, this influence was not wholly one-sided. As the Jews exerted considerable influence on non-Jewish elements, so they too were influenced by others.

In the modern world the most exemplary link between Judaism and Western civilization is the Bible. Specifically the Jews were concerned with the Old Testament; the Histories, Laws and Psalms, the words of the Prophets, all of which they created out of their own experiences.[1] In its pages are found the whole duty of man, the constant outcry of the prophets for peace, the elevation of man to the height of his potentialities.

Despite our current emphasis on science and our ability to "disprove" certain bald statements in the Bible, its precepts remain as valid today as they have ever been. Matthew Arnold, the classic minded author of *Dover Beach*, in speaking of this point said; "To the Bible men will return; and why? Because they cannot do without it. Because happiness is our being's end and aim, and happiness belongs to the righteous, and righteousness is revealed in the Bible."[2] Philo is quoted as saying that: "The laws of Greek legislators are continually subject to change; the laws of Moses alone remain steady, unmoved, unshaken, stamped as it were with the seal of nature herself, from the day when they were written to the present day, and will so remain for all time as long as the world endures. Not only the Jews but all other people who care for righteousness adopt them . . . Let all men follow this code and the age of universal peace will come about, the kingdom of God on earth will be established."[3]

The Bible has been put to every conceivable use. It has been translated with varying success (but always with remarkable devotion) into upward of one thousand languages. One can readily go along with Norman Bentwich when he says: "The Bible is the one book which appears to have the capacity of eternal self-adjustment."[4] It can not be regarded merely as the dead record of an ancient people. Rather should we think of it as a living literary possession of the modern world. Time and time again the moral feelings of men have been deepened, strengthened, and one might go so far as to say even created by the Hebrew prophets. Into this account of the welding of a relatively weak federation of tribes into a homogeneous and dynamic entity is the whole story of the fashioning of man from his feeble beginnings to vast civilizations. Here are the materials with which man toughened the fibre of his character, emancipated himself from the bondage of idolatry and nothingness to moral triumph and spiritual excellence.

Despite the almost constant ill-treatment suffered by the Jews in most of their contacts, their culture left permanent marks wherever it touched. Beginning with their initial exilic period, the original Babylonian captivity, when they were for the first time forcibly exposed to undesirable influences, through the period of the early Samaritans, Ethiopian Africa, Babylonian and Persian Asia and down to their wanderings in Christian and Moslem Europe, the Old Testament has been carried by the Jews. Their conception of morality, godliness, and ethics left its mark quietly but firmly. As they moved they carried their particular usage of the Scriptures with them and so not only transplanted it to ever new and fertile soil, but also strengthened their own ideas about monotheism, morality, and ethics.

During the Dark Ages, when all cultures slept, the Jews by nature and instinct observant and restless, kept alive what little knowledge was vouchsafed to them and constantly expanded theirs. The era abounds in names that would do honor to any people; Gabirol, Halevi, Maimonides, Rabbi Gershom, Eldad the Danite, and the inveterate traveler, Benjamin of Tudela, to name but a few. But this is not the place to treat the accomplishments of individual men no matter how worthy they might have been. How can one summarize the importance and consequences of the work of men like Saadia Gaon, Jona Marinus or Abraham Ibn Ezra. Utilizing their brilliant command of languages, they laid the foundation for much of the subsequent Biblical criticism that has been so important a part of the work of Christian scholars.

Indeed, during all of the Middle Ages, Hebrew scholarship flourished among enlightened Latin Christians. As early as the thirteenth century disputations between Hebrew and Christian scholars arose concerning the exact meanings of the Hebrew text of the Old Testament. The result of the first great public hearing was what has been called "a vast bonfire of Hebrew books,"[5] a phenomenon not unknown in more recent times.

But to others, Hebrew writings and Hebrew as a language was something to be treated with respect and diligence. Robert Grosseteste, bishop of Lincoln and teacher of Roger Bacon, was a pioneer in this field. Bacon himself repeatedly stated that a knowledge of Hebrew was necessary for proper comprehension of science, theology, and philosophy. Bacon went so far in this belief to work on a Hebrew grammar. He was a Franciscan friar and so characteristic was his attitude of the order as a whole that "when in a thirteenth or fourteenth century manuscript we find any evidence of Hebrew knowledge we may suspect a Franciscan origin."[6]

There was considerable activity during the Middle Ages in the translation of the Bible from Hebrew into other languages. Several attempts were made from Hebrew to Latin; one of them a rare example of interlinear technique. Some fragments have been found of an Italian version based on the

Hebrew. But by far the most interesting are those in Castilian. A number of people—all of them Christian—worked on them. One such example had an interesting history. "When the Jews were expelled from Spain at the end of the fifteenth century they took with them to the Eastern Mediterranean the language of the country of their birth . . . These people needed a Bible and it was first printed for them in Ferrara in 1553."[7]

The transition out of the Dark Ages was in great part due to the scholarship of the Moorish Arabs, "and they were solely indebted to the Jews who interpreted Greek literature to them."[8] The work, the debt, the perseverance was extraordinary. Schleiden sums it up as follows: ". . . we find that during the intellectually dark and slothful Middle Ages, the Jews were the preservers of agriculture, of all large industries, the cultivation of silk, dyeing and weaving works. It was they who carried on an international trade which was and ever will be necessary for the well-being of all nations. (They) left no branch of science or learning untouched, ever searching and developing, and at the end of the Middle Ages handing over the results of their long and arduous labors to the nations who were only then commencing to wake up."[9]

As world attitude changed, the Jews were treated accordingly. As the Middle Ages gave way to the Renaissance, they were able to assume a new position in the emerging world with little effort. The Age of Enlightenment still found them adhering to the old truths. Industrialization affected them as a people almost not at all. Great individuals rose from their ranks as they always had in the past. Now we have emerged into the Atomic Age, and here, too, is valid the basic contribution of the Jews to civilization. As man has pushed back the horizons of learning, he has sought to apply the principles which for over 2000 years have guided him.

Expression and explanation of this opinion is found in every literature but in none more profoundly than the English.

Were one to eliminate from English literature whatever it owes to the Bible and Hebraic writings, the remainder would be "barely recognizable."[10] The extent and influence of English literature is almost inestimable. It is the direct expression of a people that have spread out from their small island to every corner of the world carrying their particular institutions and beliefs. Where the English have gone they have taken their literature. As a result ". . . could the Bible be erased from the consciousness of those peoples, it would forfeit well-nigh half of its influence over the world."[11]

But the English language has been repaid for this service ". . . by an elevation, a picturesqueness, and an affluence of beautiful sentiments which confers . . . a great advantage over those which, whether from national incompatibility, or the impediments created by sinister interests have been more or less debarred from this treasury of grandeur."[12]

All modern literatures have borrowed unsparingly from the Scriptures and subsequent Hebrew literature and commentaries. But in the case of English literature there has been so thorough an assimilation that the Hebrew Patriarchs and Prophets often seem to have been rendered into people born on English soil.

Let us begin to narrow down the scope of our observations to matters of more immediate concern to the subject at hand, the Puritans. These stern and devoted self-styled saints had a great deal to do with the establishment of much that can be called "typically American." What influenced them, therefore, can be said to have influenced America. Prime among their source books was the Old Testament. Living as they did in the wilderness, the Puritans found there not only history and morality but also a far-reaching theology. To them, the Book was not a mere narrative of days gone by but a Scripture-in-life, meeting their daily needs and aspirations.

Think what we will about their narrowness and bigotry, there is probably nothing more valuable, memorable, weighty or even commendable about the Puritans than their religion

[9]

and in that they were almost solely influenced by the Old Testament. "The whole Old Testament is vital and commanding with examples of the Puritan spirit. . . . They with their more virile temper, their experience of hardship, and their secluded homes in the wilderness, saw in the ancient Testament not history only, theology, or praise, but the glory of man reflecting and celebrating the glory of God. It was a Scripture in life which smote and stirred their strong emotion. Not merely as to Deborah under the palm-tree, or to Ezekiel by the river of Chebar, was the majesty of the Eternal manifest to them. The whole Hebrew economy bore its radiance, and declared its effect; an economy stern, sublime, working for freedom because binding to God; training men to be careless of the world with its lusts, that they might be champions for the kingdom unseen. This was the lambent cloud of glory which filled all Puritan temples when the ancient Scriptures were opened within them."[13]

The Puritans found the whole of their religion in the Bible. Ecclesiastical rules and traditions played only a minor part. (This last can be used in direct refutation of the generally accepted idea that the Puritans established a theocracy.) A chief guide for the actions was the Old Testament. To them it contained ". . . the only and the perfect Rule of Faith."[14] It is interesting in this connection to quote the following: "God declares it to be a sinne for the godly to leave the worship of God for the wickednesse of those that come unto' it We know that the sinne of the sonnes of Ely was so great, that men abhorred the offerings of the Lord: but in so doing it is said, that the Lord's people did transgresse, even unto a cry. Surely, this truth will not easily bee outfaced; yet some of them to avoid it say, that no marvell if morall wickednesse did not pollute the Jewish worship, because God required only ceremoniall cleannesse then. But how false this is, appears by God's Covenant with *Abraham* where God requires *Sincerity;* by the morall law which was God's *covenant*: by God's requiring then, truth in the *inward part;* by his injoyning sacrifices for morall transgressions as well as ceremoniall: by his signifying of pollution by morall uncleanesses: and by threatening of morall sinnes, and *abhorring all ceremoniall* service when men sinned morally against God."[15]

The idea of covenant between God and man warrants investigation for a moment. This subtle agreement capable of so many and such diverse interpretation is first mentioned in Genesis. There are numerous other references. The Puritans time and time again drew on it, referred to it, worked it into their dealings both religious and secular. The first major Pilgrim document, the so-called Mayflower Compact, employs the word. "We whose names are underwritten . . . having undertaken . . . a voyage to plant ye first colonie in ye Northerne parts of Virginia, doe by these presents solemnly & mutually in ye presence of God, and one of another, covenant & combine our selves together into a civill body politick . . ."[16]

They felt that their Church was in actuality a continuation of the covenant between God and the Jews. This theme was hammered out from every pulpit. John Stevens in a church in New Marlborough, Massachusetts, said: *"The Christian Church so called, is only a continuation and extension of the Jewish church."*[17] With unconscious and unexpected humor William Brattle drove this home with: "The covenant of grace is the very same now that it was under the Mosaical dispensation. The administration differs but the covenant is the same."

The Puritans built up a body of law about the covenant, interpreted previously existing laws in terms of it, and derived a great deal of their power from it. As Thomas Jefferson Wertenbaker says: "But whatever its origins the covenant gave to each congregation an independence which would have been impossible had it been constituted by any superior human authority. It made of it, in the words of Ames and Cotton and other Puritan leaders, a Church responsible not to bishops or assemblies or kings, but to God Himself."[18]

This idea certainly stemmed from a very palpable relationship with the Old Testament. It should not be assumed from this, however, that the Puritans were the only sect to find refuge in the New World who drew inspiration from the doctrine of the covenant. The dour and hard-hitting Scotch Presbyterians who came in such large numbers between 1730 and 1770, settling in the upland areas some hundred miles inland from the coastal developments, held firmly to their own ideas about the meaning of the covenant. Theirs was an austere life following the principle of John Knox. To them the Bible was law. "They were brought up on the Old Testament, and in the doctrine of government by covenant."[19]

Morality, not ceremony, was the vital teaching here. The accent was always placed on moral conduct rather than on ritual alone. "Three-fourths of human life are conduct. Hebrew Scriptures deal pre-eminently with conduct. Their influence, at any rate on the English-speaking portion of our Western civilization, is three times as important as the influence of the Greeks."[20] It would appear from this that one might say that the civilization of Great Britain was influenced by Hebrew Scriptures and by Greek philosophy at a proportion of three to one respectively. John Cowper Powys feels that the Bible is to us what Homer was to the Greeks; that the words of the Bible have become a magic touch that ". . . throws across the passing details of each individual life the undying beauty of the life of humanity."[21]

It would be easily possible to trace Hebraic influences in the life of the Puritans before they came to these shores. One brief instance will suffice. When Scrooby Congregation left Leyden in Holland for a new land they fasted. "It then became necessary to decide who should go, that such might prepare themselves. 'They had . . . a sollemne meeting and a day of humiliation to seeke ye Lords for his direction: and their pastor tooke his texte, I Sam. XXIII: 3, 4. "And David's men said unto him, see we . . . etc." From which texte he taught many things aptly, and befitting the present occasion and condition, strengthening them against their fears and perplexities, and incouraging them in their resolution.' "[22]

Once in America such procedure was retained. "In the beginning of 1620 they kept a solemn day of prayer, when Mr. Robinson delivered a discourse from I Sam. XXIII: 3, 4 in which he endeavored to remove their doubts, and confirm their resolution."[23] Even as late as 1744 Massachusetts held a day of fasting and prayer when England passed the Intolerance Acts. We find that President Adams called a day of fasting during the Napoleonic Wars. The link with the Old Testament-inspired preparation in Holland was direct and evident.

Time after time the Puritans outrightly identified themselves with the Israelites as they toiled and wandered in the wilderness. Consider this brief poem from a life of Roger Williams.

> "Like Israel's host, to exile driven,
> Across the floods the Pilgrim fled;
> Their hands bore up the ark of Heaven,
> And Heaven their trusting footsteps led,
> Till on these savage shores they trod,
> And won the wilderness for God."[24]

When the Pilgrims reached America, a bitterly persecuted people, they drew sharp parallels between themselves and the Jews. They drew constantly on the Bible and their own experience to renew the similarities. Its philosophy soon came to permeate their very beings. Like Israel of old, the Pilgrims were able to regard themselves as the elect of God and throughout the Revolutionary War visualized themselves as fighting against their enemies who were to them Philistines or Amalekites.

Not unlike the recitation by the Jews of the Haggadah on Passover night, they too recited: "Ought not, and may not the children of these fathers rightly say, our fathers were Englishmen, which came over this great ocean, and were ready to perish in this wilderness; but they cried unto the Lord; and

[13]

he heard their voice, and looked on their adversity; Let them therefore praise the Lord, because he is good and his mercy endureth for ever; yea, let them who have been the redeemed of the Lord, shew how he hath delivered them from the hand of the oppressor, when they wandered in the desert wilderness out of the way, and found no city to dwell in; both hungry and thirsty, their soul was overwhelmed in them. Let them there confess before the Lord his loving kindness, and his wonderful works before the children of men."[25]

It was from the days of the Puritans that the Psalms rooted themselves permanently in the affection of most English-speaking people. They considered the Psalms which they sang while going into battle, as the deepest expression of their noblest ideals, a source of encouragement and inspiration. They used them constantly in a literal translation in public worship. When Isaac Watts' version of the Psalms reached the Colonies they were at once widespread hearings. This was doubtless due to the affection in which their originals were held. "The introduction of these Psalms . . . provoked considerable controversy, but they were soon in general use everywhere."[26]

The first book printed in America was the *Bay Psalm Book*. Its title page reads: "THE WHOLE BOOKE OF PSALMES Faithfully TRANSLATED into ENGLISH Metre. Whereunto is prefixed a discourse declaring not only the lawfulness, but also the necessity of the heavenly Ordinance of singing Scripture Psalmes in the Churches of God. . . . Imprinted 1640."[27]

How closely the Puritans identified themselves with the Israelites is hard to over-emphasize. This identification becomes manifest when we realize that they actually thought of themselves as a new Israel, fighting in a land of wickedness and paganism to exterminate those who were on the side of Satan. The Puritans' lot became the lot of Israel. If Egypt had been to Israel a "land of bondage," so was England to the Puritans. Like the Israelites they commemorated, in the Scriptural text, their plight. On the title page of the first edition of

"New England's Memorial" appears the biblical text: ". . . and thou shalt remember all the way which the Lord thy God led thee this forty years in the wilderness."[28]

In searching the Scriptures for a text relevant to their own particular needs the Puritans soon discovered the general similarity between themselves and the ancient Israelites. They firmly believed that the Hebrew prophets spoke to them as directly as they had spoken to the Hebrews. The life of the Israelites as related in the Bible served as a mirror, according to the ministers of the time, in which they could see reflected their own activities. "From the beginning of the enterprise the leaders were conscious of a similarity between New England and the Jews: 'Let *Israel* be the evidence of the *Doctrine,* and our glass to view our Faces in', said the ministers, while the irreverent Peter Folger threw the idea into satirical verse,

New-England they are like the Jews,
As like, as like can be."[29]

Not only was it possible to draw parallels between narrative actualities but in fundamental doctrine the Puritans returned to the Israelites. In this they differed most sharply from the majority of the older Christian theologies. To the Puritans the outstanding moral of the Old Testament was that a nation as well as an individual could be in covenant with God, and therefore a nation could be constrained by its own assent to obey the laws of God. "If wee keep this covenant," Winthrop assured his people, "wee shall finde that the God of Israell is among us, but if wee deal falsely with our God . . . wee be consumed out of the good land wither wee are goeing."[30]

The Bible was in all instances and for all occasions the ultimate source of knowledge and precedent. They believed in it utterly and with a kind of rigorous literal-mindedness. They regarded it only in terms of the unchangeable. "That the Bible is the inspired word of God rested for the Puritans upon absolute conviction."[31] It was the measure for everything. This Miller and Johnson have sharply summarized in

[15]

these typical words: "When both sides agree that these are the words of God, and the question of faith is concerning the meaning of the words, nothing is an article of faith, or a part of religion, but can be proved by reason to be the sense and intention of God. Reason is never to be pretended against the clear sense of scripture, because by reason it is that we came to preceive that to be the clear sense of the Scripture . . . We do not test the Bible by nature, but nature by the Bible."[32]

Failure to abide by the strict interpretation of the Old Testament was punishable with whipping. "If any 'Christian, so called,' spoke contemptuously of the Scripture, or of the holy penmen thereof, they were to be punished by fine or whipping. Laws were also passed punishing those who violated the Sabbath. . . . One of the most prominent traits was a conscientious adherence to what they believed were the teachings of the Sacred Scriptures. To them the authority of God was most supreme. Believing as they did that the Bible was his revealed will, they made that their exclusive guide in matters of faith and practice. Creeds, characters and customs were all tried by this unfailing test, and all was rejected which, in their opinion, did not stand this ordeal. Laws and regulations adopted by them, which, at the present day, are stigmatized as singularities, were, in many instances, the legitimate fruits of their strict adherence to the teaching of the Bible."[33]

If Israel had its Pharaoh, so had the Puritans one in the person of King James I. The Atlantic Ocean was to them the Red Sea. America was the new Canaan and Washington and Adams, their Moses and Joshua.

These analogies should not in any way seem strange coming from a people who so constantly drew the Old Testament into their lives. This reference to politics in no way equals in intensity the official acts of the colony of Connecticut. "The Mosaic Law was adopted in the Connecticut Code of 1650; while half the statutes in the Code of 1655 for the colony of New Haven contain references to the Old Testament, and only three percent to the New."[34]

Comparisons with Moses and Joshua for Puritan leaders were very common. For example, in Cotton Mather's *Magnalia Christi Americana* we find the following paragraph in regard to John Winthrop of the Massachusetts colony: "Accordingly when the *noble design* of carrying a colony of *chosen people* into an *American* wilderness, was by *some* eminent persons undertaken, *this* eminent person was, by the consent of all, *chosen* for the *Moses,* who must be the leader of so great an undertaking; and indeed nothing but a Mosaic spirit could have carried him through the *temptations* to which either his *farewell* to his *own land,* or his *travel* in a *strange land,* must needs expose a gentleman of his education."[35]

In Davis' book is recorded the saying on the tomb of John Cotton:

> "But let his mourning flock be comforted,
> Though Moses be, yet Joshua is not dead;
> I mean renowned Norton; worthy he
> Successor to our Moses is to be,
> O happy Israel in America,
> In such a Moses, such a Joshua."[36]

John Norton was herein called a Joshua and, in his turn, when Norton died, an elegy was written by Thomas Shepard:

> ". . . Oh that mine eyes a fountain were of tears!
> I'd day and night in mourning spend my years.
> My father! father! Israel's chariots thou,
> And horseman wert! Sons of the prophets now."[37]

William Bradford too was often called Joshua. When after his death, Thomas Prince was chosen governor of New Plymouth, it was said of him: "At such a time and when the condition of this colony was such as hath been declared, God was pleased to mind it, even in its low estate, and when he had taken unto himself not only our Moses, but many of the elders and worthies of our Israel, he hath not hitherto left us without a Joshua, to lead us in the remaining of our Pilgrimage."[38]

[17]

In the use of invective the Puritans frequently employed Biblical expressions and allusions. The famed heretic, Anne Hutchinson, was to them a "Wretched Jezebel." A coachman driving recklessly was often called "Jehu." While they uttered with contempt the names of the unpraiseworthy characters of the Old Testament, they cherished the names of those they exalted and perpetuated them by naming their offspring after them. Thus the names Daniel, Jonathan, Esther, Enoch, Ezra, Rachel and many others were constantly used among them while there was a conspicuous absence of names commemorating the Christian saints. In short, "They discarded the old English names and those of the saints and confined themselves to names taken from the Scriptures, especially from the Old Testament."[39]

Names of colonies, cities and settlements were likewise chosen from Hebraic Scripture. The names Salem (peace), Bethlehem (house of bread), and others will bear witness. The name Nahumkeik, given, according to Cotton Mather, to a plantation settlement in 1628 was not, as is generally believed, of Indian but rather of Hebrew origin. The name, argues Mather, is composed of two Hebrew words: Nahum (comfort, or console) and Keik (Heq—a haven). "And our *English* not only found in it an *Haven of Comfort,* but happened also to put an *Hebrew name* upon it; for they called it *Salem,* for the *peace* which they had and hoped in it; and *so it was called* unto this day."[40]

Mather was preoccupied with Hebrew to an extraordinary degree. Words and phrases in the language are interlaced into everything he wrote. In the First Book of *Antiquities* the Introduction begins with the Hebrew words *'Im yirzeh ha-Shem*; chapter six starts with the words *ba'ale nefesh*, and in the Sixth Book the title begins with the Hebrew words meaning *liber memorabilium*. In the second volume of the *Magnalia* appears the following: "The Jews tell us of *kilyah* or a *scare-crow* upon the top of the *temple*, which kept off the fowls from defiling it. . . . The same practice was used for candidates for admission to the church—only defilers of the temple were kept out."[41] In speaking of the first ministry when they left England, Mather refers to them as *Hasidim Rishonim* (our first good men).[42] As to the conduct of the magistracy, he states that it was according to Jewish wishes *Beáhavah Veyir'ah, cum mansuetudine ac Timore.*[43]

The Puritans bent the Book to serve their own peculiar needs—often in almost arbitrary fashions. Often they resorted to a primitivism contradictory to the very spirit of the second Isaiah. "For this it is they and not Hebraism that must bear the blame. But their errors in this respect must not be allowed to obscure the positive advantages they obtained from their familiarity with the Scriptures. The legacy of Judaism was to them a real inspiration, and they have handed it on to their posterity in an intensity of religious devotion and a passion of moral fervor for which the whole world is still in their debt."[44]

FOOTNOTES

[1] James Henry Breasted, *Ancient Times*, page 335.
[2] Matthew Arnold: *Literature and Dogma*, page 308.
[3] Norman Bentwich: *Philo-Judaeus*, page 106.
[4] *Ibid.*, page 104.
[5] Edwyn R. Bevan and Charles Singer, *The Legacy of Israel*, page 295.
[6] *Ibid.*, page 301.
[7] *Ibid.*, page 310.
[8] M. I. Schleiden: *The Importance of the Jews for the Preservation and Revival of Learning during the Middle Ages*, page 54.
[9] *Ibid.*, page 55.
[10] Cecil Roth, *The Jewish Contribution to Civilization*, page 16.
[11] Richard Garnett, *English Literature, an Illustrative Record*, Vol. I, page 204.
[12] *Ibid.*, page 204.
[13] R. S. Storrs, *The Puritan Spirit*, pages 52-3.
[14] *The Second Part of a Reply to the Vindication of the Subscribing Ministers by a Committee of the Non-Subscribing Ministers*, page 12.
[15] Robert Abbot, *A Trial of Our Church-Forsakers*, pages 127-8.
[16] *Bradford's History "Of Plimoth Plantation"*, page 110.
[17] *Sermons on Important Subjects collected from a number of ministers, in some of the northern states of America*, page 62.
[18] Thomas Jefferson Wertenbaker, *The Puritan Oligarchy*, page 59.
[19] Frederick Jackson Turner, *The Frontier in American History*, page 103.
[20] John Cowper Powys, *Enjoyment of Literature*, Introduction.
[21] *Ibid.*, page 12.

22 W. De Loss Love, Jr., *The Fast and Thanksgiving Days,* pages 61-2.
23 Belknap, *American Biography,* Vol. II, page 171.
24 Romeo Elton, *Life of Roger Williams,* page 2.
25 John Davis, *New England's Memorial,* page 36.
26 P. Marion Simms, *The Bible in America,* page 52.
27 *Ibid.,* page 111.
28 Davis, *op. cit.,* title page.
29 Perry Miller, *The New England Mind,* page 475.
30 *Ibid.,* page 477.
31 *Ibid.,* page 20.
32 Perry Miller and Thomas H. Johnson, *The Puritans,* pages 49, 54.
33 Joseph Banvard, *Plymouth and the Pilgrims,* pages 204, 231-2.
34 Paul Masserman and Max Baker, *The Jews Come to America,* page 69.
35 Cotton Mather, *Magnalia Christi Americana,* Vol. I, pages 109-10.
36 Davis, *op. cit.,* page 255.
37 *Ibid.,* page 301.
38 *Ibid.,* page 272.
39 C. E. Whiting, *Studies in English Puritanism from the Restoration to the Revelation 1660-1688,* page 445.
40 Mather, *op. cit.,* Vol. I, page 63. The influence of Judaic culture went far beyond the bounds of technical scholarship and professional training for theologians. One has only to look at some of the names of the towns of the United States: Salem, Canaan, Zion, Hebron, Bethlehem, Sharon, Palestine, Jaffe, Goshen, Beth-el, Carmel, Eden, Jordan, Jericho, Rehoboth, Pisgah, Nimrod, Shiloh, Gilead, to see that the intellectual and spiritual geography of the founders of the colony was derived as much from Hebrew culture as from their immediate experience in the Old World or the New. A. I. Katsh, *Hebrew in American Higher Education,* pages 61-65.
41 *Ibid.,* Vol. II, page 244.
42 *Ibid.,* Vol. I, page 213.
43 *Ibid.,* page 130.
44 Bevan and Singer, *op. cit.,* page 431.

B.—EARLY POPULARITY OF THE HEBREW LANGUAGE

One can easily deduce from the wealth of material in the foregoing discussion that since Hebrew names, proverbs, excerpts and interjections, to say nothing of the generalized use of Hebrew thought, played so great a role in American Colonial life, the Hebrew language itself had to occupy a correspondingly prominent position in Colonial education. The study of Hebrew long ranked high in popularity among the clergy of New England. Cotton Mather records in the second volume of the *Magnalia Christi* that at the second session of the Synod of the Elders and Messengers of the churches an article was drawn up to provide for the study of the Old Testament in the original Hebrew, ". . . the native language of the people of the God of Old."[1]

Early American education was tightly linked with religious studies. Indeed, the main purpose for most early institutions of higher education was the provision of the requisite number of clergy. Most of them were in the service of a specific denomination and most, at any rate in New England, drew their inspiration from Puritan sources. Hebrew, therefore, played its part.

"Not only was Hebrew considered the foundation for an exact understanding of the Old Testament, but it was then as later thought to be the mother of languages; a knowledge of it therefore was believed to advance learning in the best sense."[2] An early president of King's College which later became Columbia University said: "As soon as a lad has learned to speak and read English well, it is much the best to begin a learned education with Hebrew . . . the mother of all languages and Eloquence."[3] Many of the leading citizens of the age were distinguished Hebrew scholars. Among them John Eliot, Isaac Addington, Ethan Allen, both Mathers, father

[21]

and son, William Bradford, Charles Chauncey, Joseph Green, John Dunster and Samuel Sewall can be cited as particular examples.

One must remember that, as has been pointed out, the first book published in the Colonies was the so-called *Bay Psalm Book,* a rendering of the Psalms into English from the original Hebrew by Richard Mather, John Elliot and Thomas Welde. This joint labor was later submitted to President Dunster of Harvard who drawing on his own extensive knowledge of the language revised and polished the translations.

Little wonder that in such an intellectual climate, Harvard, the first American institute of higher learning, established in 1636 and endowed by John Harvard in 1639, followed the English cultural tradition so deeply rooted in the Bible, and included the language of the Bible as an essential course in its curriculum on a level with Latin and Greek. Many generations of students at Harvard devoted one day each week for three years to the study of Hebrew and allied tongues. In addition to the texts in grammar and syntax, the books of the Old Testament were the principal study material used.

The College regarded Hebrew as a key to the textual study of the Bible. It had been founded on principles of Scriptural influence. In all matters of administration, the leaders ". . . were agreed in declaring the Scriptures, as the *direction* of all. . . . It is *not* the opinion of *men,* but the *Scripture* which must decide the controversy."[4]

Samuel Eliot Morison has this to say about the historical basis of this insistence on the study of Hebrew. "Authorities on the history of education have too readily assumed that colonial students were forced to study Hebrew and Greek simply in order to read the Bible. As regards Hebrew, that may well have been the real reason, though the *good* one assigned in an early commencement thesis was that Hebrew is the mother of languages. This theory that Hebrew was the archetype of all western tongues, was common in the Renaissance; the great English Hebraist, John Selden, among others, be-

lieved it. A smattering of that language was then supposed to
be a classical education in England; Sir Humphrey Gilbert had
it on the program for his proposed academy for young gentlemen of the court and even in the late eighteenth century,
President Samuel Johnson of Columbia declared that Hebrew
was part of a 'gentleman's education.' Wilhelm Schickard,
professor at the University of Tübingen, prepared especially
for his pupils a Hebrew text with the attractive title (in
Latin) 'The Hebrew Sun-dial, or advice as to how the elements of that Holy language may be sufficiently apprehended
by College students in a space of 24 hours.' "[5]

Further historical evidence comes directly from Mather.
"The reader knows that in every town among Jews, there was
a *school,* whereat children were taught the reading of the *law*;
and if there were any town destitute of a *school,* the men of
place did stand excommunicate, until one were erected: besides and beyond which they had *midrashoth,* or *divinity-
schools,* in which they expounded the law to their disciples.
Whether the churches of *New-England* have been duly careful or not about *their* other *schools,* they have not been altogether careless about their *midrashoth;* and it is well for them
that they have not."[6]

Freshmen at Harvard began with Hebrew. The first textbook was Wilhelm Schickard's *Horologium Hebraeum* (Hebrew Sun-dial) mentioned above by Morison. Several other
formal texts for grammar were used. One of these was the
Martinius of Navarre grammar; another a general grammar
by Christian Ravis. John Harvard's initial contribution of
books to the college library included several commentaries on
the Old Testament. There still remain twelve Bibles from the
year 1651 which contain inscriptions by their original owners.
Time and time again interest in the language manifests itself
in baccalaureate theses. Some subjects covered at one time or
another include: "*Aleph* with the function of a point has the
sound of all vowels," "By contracting their sentences the Hebrews enlarge their meaning," "Points received on both sides

of a letter remove *sheva*," "*Benoni* (the participle) takes the place of the present, which is wanting in Hebrew."[7]

A custom inaugurated at Harvard in 1655, and continued for many years, called for the mention by all students except Freshmen, of a verse from the Hebrew original of the Old Testament into Greek, as a part of morning prayer. In 1735 the college sponsored publication of a Hebrew grammar prepared by Judah Monis, a converted Jew. Monis, a colorful character of Portuguese Marano extraction, was the first full-time Hebrew instructor in any American college. Though he was converted to Christianity through the efforts of Increase Mather, all through his life he was referred to as "Rabbi".

In 1782 the first concessions concerning the study of Hebrew were made in the Harvard curriculum. At that time students were formally allowed to substitute French for Hebrew provided they obtained special permission. For over a century and a half, until 1817, the commencement exercises at the college included a Hebrew oration which during the early years was concerned solely with questions of syntax and grammar but which later was extended to broader and more varied topics.

Yale, established in 1701, followed the same tradition. Its seal at the very outset depicted an open Bible with a Hebrew inscription spread across its pages, *Urim Vetumim*. But feeling as they did that Hebrew was the province of advanced students, the founders "In charity to their successors who might be less familiar with the language of scholars . . . happily added a translation in the vernacular: *Lux et Veritas*".[8] From the very beginning Hebrew was a required subject.

Ezra Stiles, who surely ranks as one of the most learned men ever to hold a college presidency, was during his entire lifetime an ardent Hebraist and philo-semite. He set the standards during his day, making the knowledge of Hebrew an integral part of a scholar's liberal education and a requisite for a minister. When elected president of Yale and Professor of Ecclesiastical History, he voluntarily took upon himself the teaching of Semitics. In his diary Stiles records: "From my first accession to the Presidency 1777-1790, I have obliged all the Freshmen to study Hebrew. . . . This year I have determined to instruct only those who offer themselves voluntarily and that at Subsecivis Horis only with omitting any of the three daily classical Recitations to their Tutor. Accordingly of 39 Freshmen, 22 have asked for instruction in Hebrew, and these accordingly I teach. IV.P.M. Mondays, Wednesdays, and Fridays. I have besides several of the other classes at other times."[9] Stiles "drilled his pupils especially in one of the Psalms which he thought 'would be the first we should hear in Heaven.' He would have been ashamed if any graduate of Yale should be entirely ignorant of the holy language when he got to heaven!"[10]

In 1781 the commencement address at the University was delivered by Stiles in Hebrew. He based his remarks on a verse from Ezra (VII, 10). "For Ezra had prepared his heart to seek the law of the Lord, and to do it, and to teach in Israel statutes and judgments." He went on to evaluate the study of Hebrew and referred to it as ". . . a glorious language which throws more light on the Old Testament than all the Commentators." Throughout his life Stiles persisted in his enthusiasm for the language. For him it was indispensable for a properly balanced liberal education.

The popularity of Hebrew at Yale continued for many years and towards the end of the 19th century Professor William Rainey Harper's students were said to have filled the largest of the lecture halls. Harper, a colorful personality, was a brilliant Hebraist. As one of the founders and later first president of the University of Chicago, Harper made the study of Hebrew a national fad, establishing summer courses, institutes, and correspondence courses. It is said that he had so much mail in connection with his instructional activities that the salary of the local postmaster had to be raised.[11]

Samuel Johnson, the first president of King's College, now Columbia, gave expression to the sentiments of intellectuals of his time when he referred to Hebrew as "being essential to a Gentleman's education." Johnson was the most scholarly American of his time and with Jonathan Edwards, another student of Hebrew, he "takes rank as one of the two really powerful and constructive American philosophers of the 18th century." Johnson had a passionate love for Hebrew and demanded a knowledge of it from all King's College tutors. He studied Hebrew in his early years, at the Guilford Grammar School in Connecticut and later taught his children and his grandchildren the rudiments of the language. He also wrote *An English and Hebrew Grammar, Being the First Short Rudiments of Those Two Languages Taught Together, to Which is Added a Synopsis of all the Parts of Learning.* A son of a successor to Johnson, Clement Clarke Moore, who graduated from King's College in 1798 at the head of his class, composed a *Compendious Lexicon of the Hebrew Language* in two volumes, a work which is presumed to be the first of its kind in this country. In his middle years he taught Hebrew and Greek to students of the General Theological Seminary, established by the Protestant Episcopal Church through his efforts. In 1859 the Seminary established the Clement Clarke Moore professorship of Hebrew. It is interesting and a little ironical to note that Moore is now known almost exclusively as the author of the ever popular *A Visit from St. Nicholas.*

King's College and the Philadelphia Academy, now the University of Pennsylvania, were exceptions to the usual pattern of the early colleges which served as theological seminaries. The curriculum of the Philadelphia Academy, on the instance of Benjamin Franklin, was not limited exclusively to the classics, but was broadened to include many other subjects such as applied mathematics, science, natural history, international law and modern languages. Yet one of the seven professorships in the institution in 1782 was in Hebrew and Oriental languages. In 1792, a combined professorship of Hebrew, Oriental languages and German was established. About a century later, in 1885, the noted Jewish scholar, Dr. Morris Jastrow, Jr., was at the head of the Semitics Department. Dr. Jastrow also distinguished himself as the University librarian.

Dartmouth, organized before the outbreak of the Revolution, as an institution to train missionaries to evangelize the Indians also followed the Hebraic tradition of the older American Colleges. Professor John Smith, who was appointed to the chair of Oriental languages as a very young man, prepared a treatise on Hebrew grammar in his junior year, in 1772. In 1803, he published a grammar for the use of his students. Hebrew was said to be as familiar to him as his native tongue. Professor Benjamin Hale, who was professor of medicine at Dartmouth in 1827, also held "recitations in Hebrew," for two years "not perhaps" as he put it "much to the profit of my classes but because I happen to be fresher in that study than any college officer."

The pattern set by the early institutions was followed by the colleges in America until about the Civil War. In addition to Harvard, Yale, King's College, the Philadelphia Academy, other great institutions of higher learning founded in the eighteenth century, including William and Mary in Virginia, Rutgers and Princeton in New Jersey, and Brown University in Rhode Island, were conducted with a religious or classical motif, and regarded Hebrew as a major subject in the course of study. It is of interest to note that Harvard, Yale, King's College, the Philadelphia Academy, Brown, Princeton and Johns Hopkins are among the schools which have been teaching Hebrew without interruption since their inception.

It has been said to fully understand a poet one must dwell in his homeland. But in actuality this is only a secondary qualification. A primary one is the poet's language. For it is through his language that one finds the expressive spirit of his thought and creativity. As has been pointed out, one can not fully appreciate the Hebrew Scriptures in any translation —even the best. This attitude in the Puritans was perhaps best exemplified in William Bradford's attempts to master

[27]

Hebrew. "The French tongue he (Bradford) could also manage; the Latin and the Greek he had mastered but the Hebrew he most of all studied, because, he said, he would see, with his own eyes, the ancient Oracles of God in their native beauty."[12] This spirit died hard in American colleges—if indeed it ever actually did. The revival of interest in Hebrew in widely divergent universities in recent years would argue that it did not.[13]

Though we have thus far concentrated our observations on American colleges it should not be assumed that it was only the institutions of higher learning which were interested in Hebrew. Not only in colleges but in lower schools as well was Hebrew offered as a language. Miller and Johnson point out that it was taught at the Boston Latin School in the seventeenth century. In an act dated 1695 providing for the establishment and building of a free school in St. Andrew's parish, a clause was inserted which read; "Along with instructions in reading, writing, Latin, Greek . . . arithmetic . . . the scholars were to receive instruction in Hebrew."[14]

John Davenport, himself a Hebraist and a colleague of John Cotton, "was directly instrumental in introducing the study of Hebrew in the first public school of New Haven, an action which was in part inspired by a bequest in the will of Governor Hopkins; according to the records of the colony, the instructor was appointed June 28, 1660."[15] It was this early and continuing interest in the language that enabled most colleges to require their freshmen to study it. Some basic work had been done before their arrival at the higher level.

This avid study of the language brought forth many first rate scholars of Hebrew. Increase Cotton knew the language well enough to deliver discourses in it. As has been pointed out many times, his son, Cotton, was much interested in the language and wrote a relatively scholarly dissertation on Hebrew punctuation. John Udall translated Peter Marinius' Hebrew Grammar and compiled a Hebrew dictionary, *The Key of the Holy Tongue*. At the first Harvard commencement an oration was delivered on the topic "Hebrew Analysis, Grammaticall, Logicall and Rhetoricall of the Psalms."

It might be interesting at this point to list the rules and precepts at the College as they were listed in this discourse.

> "*The fifth day reads Hebrew, and the East-*
> *erne Tongues*
> *Grammar* to the first yeare houre the 8th
> To the 2d. *Chaldee* at the 9th houre,
> To the 3d. *Syriack* at the 10th houre,
> Afternoone
> The first practice in the Bible at the 2d. houre
> The 2d. in *Ezra* and *Daniel* at the 3d. houre"[16]

At commencement questions were asked of the students by the examiners who ". . . did heare their Exercises; which were . . . and Hebrew Analysis grammaticall, Logicall and Rhetoricall of the Psalms. . . ." The questions asked concerning Hebrew were: "Haebrea est Linguarum Mater," "Consonates et vocales Haebreorum sunt coaetaneae," and "Punctationes chatephatae syllabam proprie non efficiunt."[17]

There were many other serious students of the language. The work and influence of Ezra Stiles have already been noted. John Dunster was called upon to work on the *Bay Psalm Book*. Others have been mentioned.

The position of Hebrew in the Puritan world can perhaps best be understood from their concern with the *Bay Psalm Book*. The book, an original translation of the Psalms from the Hebrew text into English, was the first printed in the Colonies. Copies are now reckoned among the rarest treasures of Americana and as such bring tremendous prices. The purpose of the publication was to replace the Sternhold and Hopkins version then in popular use. This rough rendering of the Psalms frequently sacrificed literal translation for the sake of poetic effect. The inaccurate reading of the text troubled Puritan conscience and this was to be rectified with the publication of the *Bay Psalm Book*.

In a similar spirit, Cotton Mather wrote: "But of all the more than twice seven versions, which I have seen it must be affirmed, that they *leave out* a vast heap of those rich things, which the Holy Spirit of God speaks in the original Hebrew; and that they *put in* as large an Heap of poor things which are entirely their own. . . . I am therefore strongly of the opinion, that the *Poesie* of the Ancient Hebrews, knew no *Measure,* but that of the unknown Music, wherein it was to be accomodated. Our Psalms in the Hebrew, are not so much *metrical* as *musical.*"[18]

While the Puritans regarded the Old Testament as the supreme authority they did so on the basis of the original Hebrew rather than the Latin Vulgate. From this stems their reverence for Hebrew as the holy language. God spoke to them much as he did to the ancient Hebrews. As was natural He spoke the ancient tongue. They adopted not only their version of the spirit of the Old Testament but the letter of it as well. The most famous of grammar school texts was *The New England Primer,* better known as Milk for Babes which was based largely on Biblical narratives. (Seven million copies of this remarkable book were published before 1840 alone!) The alphabet was taught by means of verses. From "A—in Adam's fall we sinned," to "Z—Zaccheus, he did climb a tree, His Lord to see."[19]

There was a sufficiently widespread interest and knowledge of Hebrew in the Colonies at the time of the Revolution to allow for the circulation of a story that ". . . certain members of Congress proposed that the use of English be formally prohibited in the United States, and Hebrew substituted for it."[20] Whether or not there is any basis of fact in this story has never actually been determined but that is relatively of little moment. The important thing is that the people of the time thought it logical enough to circulate.

The instances that have been previously mentioned indicate the prominent place of Hebrew in the early academic life of this country and the esteem in which it was held by the pioneers in American collegiate education, religious thought, and general scholarship. The decline in the study of Hebrew in American institutions of higher learning may be attributed to many and varying factors. Almost immediately after the Revolutionary war, following the growing tradition of separating church and governing bodies, education in general was shifted from religious to a political basis. It was now regarded as essential to liberty and the preservation of the state; and higher education, too, began to reckon with this broader aim, rather than merely with the training of ministers. Moreover, the rapid and extensive growth of the natural sciences impelled the universities to broaden their curricula to meet the growing demand for professional, technical, and scientific courses. The older colleges, now endowed by men of wealth, expanded their facilities and established schools of engineering and law, medicine and science.

The new tendency was reflected in the utilitarian educational philosophy advocating the application of knowledge to everyday affairs, and derogating the value of the study of the classics for mental discipline, or of learning for its own sake. Education, according to this doctrine, was to provide for a useful and happy life. In this pragmatic view Hebrew and the classics played a very minor part.

The colleges which greatly increased in number during the 19th century, and the state universities established during that period followed the new mode and did not provide for Semitic departments; they did offer courses in Bible, but these were given in the English translation as a part of English literature, rather than as sacred text, as formerly. A knowledge of Hebrew was, of course, not considered essential for either teacher or student in this type of course.

A number of American universities during the 19th century transferred their early function of training for the ministry, with its attendant courses in classics and Hebrew, to theological departments or schools. In most instances, universities assigned their courses in Hebrew to the Semitic or Oriental language departments which were associated with their graduate divisions, thus restricting these studies to a more limited number of students. The poor methods of teaching based on the traditional way of conjugating the verb *Qatal, Qatalti* were enough to "kill" interest in any language, and this contributed further to its decline. The secularization of the universities and colleges also resulted in a departure from the custom of appointing clergymen to the presidencies of universities—a practice which had strengthened the religious tone of the institutions and created an atmosphere favorable towards Hebrew. As we have seen, many of the presidents were themselves Hebrew scholars and had also served as instructors in the courses.

The content of the Hebraic studies was meager and with the diminution in enrollment, the universities permitted the Semitic departments to lapse, particularly in those schools where the original endowment for the chair was depleted. Because of the lack of financial support, several institutions such as New York University in 1923, Cornell University in 1938, Buffalo University in 1940, and Wilson College in 1941 discontinued their Hebrew and Semitics departments with the death or retirement of the individual professor in charge.

In the case of New York University this situation has since changed. A course in Modern Hebrew was introduced by the writer in 1934 in the Division of General Education on an experimental basis. Three years later, in 1937, this course was incorporated, by Dean E. George Payne, into the accredited curriculum of the School of Education of the University. Success of this course led to the introduction of additional courses and in 1944 the first Chair of Modern Hebrew Culture and Education in an American institution of higher learning was established. The department of Modern Hebrew Culture and Education now sponsors two curricula, one in the language proper and one in general Hebrew culture. It thus enables students to pursue a course of study leading to the baccalaureate, masters and doctoral degrees majoring in Hebrew, Jewish culture or Jewish education.

This pioneering work was a source of inspiration to other colleges and universities. In the last few years seventeen institutions of higher learning in the country introduced in their curricula departments in Modern Hebrew as well as courses in Hebrew culture as a living dynamic civilization. There are also 199 colleges and universities which teach Hebrew as a Semitic tongue. Harvard and Columbia have had endowed chairs in Jewish philosophy and in Jewish history for some time.[21]

FOOTNOTES

[1] Mather, *op. cit.*, Vol. II, page 183.

[2] Miller and Johnson, *op. cit.*, page 698.

[3] Anita Liebman Lebeson, *The Pilgrim People*, ms.

[4] Mather, *op. cit.*, Vol. II, page 53.

[5] Samuel Eliot Morison, *Puritan Pronoas*, pages 41-2.

[6] Mather, *op. cit.*, Vol. II, page 7.

[7] Samuel Eliot Morison, *Harvard in the 19th Century*, page 205.

[8] Charles Seymour: From an address delivered in New Haven, Conn. February 13, 1949.

[9] Lee Friedman, *Rabbi Haim Isaac Carigal*, pages 36-7.

[10] Seymour, *op. cit.*

[11] Abraham I. Katsh, *The Teaching of Hebrew in American Universities*, page 577.

[12] Davis, *op. cit.*, page 270.

[13] Abraham I. Katsh, *The Study of Hebrew Language, Literature and Culture in American Institutions of Higher Learning.* Some of the material used in this section is based upon pages 1-13 of the book.

[14] *Publications of the American Jewish Historical Society*, Vol. V, page 56.

[15] L. I. Newman, *Jewish Influence on Christian Reform Movements*, page 636.

[16] *New England's First Fruits with Divers other Special Matters concerning that Country*, pages 29-35.

[17] *Ibid.*, pages 29-35.

[18] Miller and Johnson, *op. cit.*, pages 678-80.

[19] *The New England Primer*, pages 10-14.

[20] H. L. Mencken, *The American Language*, page 79; Supplement I, page 138.

[21] A. I. Katsh, *op. cit.*, pages 40-58.

C.—INFLUENCE OF THE JUDAIC SPIRIT

"The priceless jewel of Hebrew religious development, a pure ethical idealism of the prophets, was not lost to the religious experience of Israel, but was rather preserved for her and for all ages and all races through the ritual legalism of the priests. The world's richest treasures of religious and moral truth are the gifts and fruitage of Jewish ethical idealism."[1] Such is the opinion of one scholar on the far-reaching influence of the spirit epitomized in the Old Testament.

Relating it more specifically to American life we find that mastery of Hebrew only served to intensify the Puritan roots in Jewish ethical idealism. By knowing the language they were more easily able to acquire the spirit and meaning of the Old Testament. This particular idealism as they chose to interpret and use it, not only dominated their theology but reached over into the patterns of everyday life. It helped them to discipline their minds. It fortified their will. It confirmed in divine terms the principles for which they stood. And these were the factors which enabled them to survive. Perhaps as much as any more practical factor, their belief in their divinely inspired mission enabled the Puritans to triumph over the difficulties which had defeated preceding colonists. It gave them a hardihood and a tenacity of purpose, a will and courage which were sorely needed to withstand the rigors of life in the wilderness that was America during the early years of the seventeenth century.

Life in general was modeled as much on the Hebraic pattern as was possible for them under the circumstances. When occasion for a holiday arose, they drew their inspiration from Jewish models. The first Thanksgiving celebration in 1621 was not a joyous holiday but rather an imitation of a Jewish fast day. It was a purely religious service with the emphasis on fasting rather than on feasting as has become the custom in more recent years. "Let us, we beseech you (all you that love Zion) your prayers, and helpe in heaven and earth for the furtherance of this great and glorious worke in our hands; great works need many hands, many prayers, many tears."[2]

In their commonwealth there was, according to the historian Fiske, "the same ethical impulse which animates the glowing pages of the prophets and which has given to the history and literature of Israel their commanding influence in the world."[3] The foreword to the 1656 revision of the Pilgrim code carries this idea forward with this comment: "It was the great privilege of Israel of old and soe was acknowledged by them, Nehemiah the 9th and 10th that God gave them right judgments and true Lawes. They are for the mayne so exemplary, being grounded on principles of moral equitie as that all Christians especially ought alwaies to have an eye thereunto in the framing of their politique constitutions. We can safely say both for ourselves and for them that we have had an eye principally unto the aforesaid platforme in the framing of this small body of Lawes."[4]

An interesting parallel can be noted here. The government of the Puritan colonies was not, strictly speaking, in the hands of the ministers. In this sense they never actively achieved a theocracy. There is little doubt, however, that they aimed at one. Laws and regulations were determined for them. The "saints" were merely given the privilege of confirming them. For this they drew again on the numerous examples of such procedure in the Old Testament. They were more concerned with the religious ideals involved than with any concept of political or even social democracy. And Millar Burrows has said of the Hebrew ideal that it "was not democracy but theocracy. The days when 'there was no king in Israel,' when 'every man did that which was good in his own eyes,' were regarded in retrospect, not as a time of hateful anarchy, but as a time when God ruled his people directly."[5] The Puritans looked for this situation again in the new Canaan of America.

"Now Puritanism was, in essence, the rebirth of the Hebrew spirit in the Christian conscience. It was the Hebrew religious genius come to life to wage battle for God and soul-
freedom, once more to impress upon the world the sovereignty
of God and the holiness of life. . . . The most drastic reforms
which Puritanism introduced in the church polity, when it
broke away from the Anglican episcopacy, lay in the decen-
tralization of the Church, the abolition of the hierarchy, and
the bridging of the gap between the minister and the laity.
In all of these directions, Puritanism paralleled or unconsciously followed Jewish precedent. Every Synagogue was an
independent entity; formal ranking and grading of the rabbi-
nate was unknown; and the rabbi, like the Puritan elder—
the order should be reversed—laid no claim to supernatural-
ism in any form. Learning, piety, interpretation of God's will
as revealed in the Law—a source open to all—these were the
essential qualifications for spiritual authority in Judaism as in
the Puritan Churches. In both institutions, the religious head
was chosen by the people."[6]

This is a rather striking similarity. Despite the fact that
President Neuman sees in it a model for all religious leadership, both the Jews and Protestants have often been criticized
for it. Actually, it allowed participation on the part of church
members in matters both of dogma and church government.
Herein lay the crux of the objections. Yet, in more than one
fundamental have the Puritans, consciously or unconsciously,
followed the Jewish ethical tradition of idealism. Like the
Jews, the Puritans began observance of the Sabbath at sun-
down of the previous day; and would not, within the full
twenty-four hours of the day, shave, have their rooms swept,
beds made, dishes washed, any cooking done, or perform
work of any kind.

There is a good deal of evidence on many of these points.
Whiting states quite flatly: "The Puritans treated it (Sunday)
as the Jewish sabbath; no work was to be done, no amuse-
ments to be indulged in, it was a day of prayer and worship."[7]

Gregory gives us this picture of the Puritan Sabbath. "From sunset on Saturday until Sunday night they would not shave, have rooms swept, nor beds made, have food prepared, nor cooking utensils and tableware washed."[8] There is more than a superficial resemblance here to the traditional Hebraic observation of the Sabbath. Indeed, were it not for the difference in the day (the Jews observing Saturday rather than Sunday) one might be tempted to call the imitation exact.

Again, as in the orthodox Jewish Synagogue, in the Puritan Churches, the sexes were separated. John Cotton on a Sabbath day would not even study for a sermon for fear of "wearisome labour to invention or memory."[9] Banvard states: "The peculiarities of some of the forms of legislation were occasioned by their imitation of ancient Jewish customs. Thus, in New Haven the members of the constituent committee were called the 'seven pillars hewn out of the house of Wisdom,' and Rhode Island performed for one or two years a 'Jewish masquerade.' Their language was quaint, because interlarded with the phraseology of Scripture. They disapproved of wigs, veils, and long hair. They were equally opposed to immodest and extravagant apparel because both were alike at variance with the simplicity and purity inculcated by the Bible. They were precise in their manners, because, as one of them said, they had 'a precise God to deal with.' They repudiated crosses and beads, surplices and prayerbooks. To their minds, these were too intimately allied to Rome. They denied the superiority of the bishops over other orders of ordained ministers. With them all the ministry occupied the same official privileges and powers. They maintained that the Church was independent of the ministry; that every church possessed the right of electing its own pastor; that no power outside of themselves, whether king or archbishop, had any right to impose upon them a minister, contrary to their wishes. In ecclesiastical and civil government they were republicans—the majority ruled."[10]

There is a decided turning away here from the complicated

hierarchy which the Church had become and a resurgence of the vastly more independent spirit which marked the ancient Israelites. Though the power of the ministry remained tremendous in civil affairs (this point making of the Puritans republicans but not democrats) the people had a say in the choice of their ministers. The spirit of exhortation had returned to religion and the voices of the prophets were heard again calling for the correction of sins in government as well as in religion. In all of this the Bible served as the model.

In fine, the state, civil laws, the Sabbath, the general rules of conduct and behavior, justice and equity, both in act and in thought ("They rejected trial by jury, that being no part of the Mosaic law."[11]) had to derive their sanction from the Old Testament in which the Puritans believed "God had revealed for all time in its entirety all true religion, a revelation absolute and final."[12] As a consequence of this repeated and devoted use of the Bible, this highly conscious emulation of Biblical models, this infiltration of the general spirit of Hebraism, it is safe to say with Simms that: "The American people owe more to the ancient Hebrews than to any ancient people. More than to either the Greeks or the Romans, because to the Hebrews we owe our ethical and spiritual ideals."[13]

FOOTNOTES

[1] Frank H. Ridgley, *Jewish Ethical Idealism,* page 88.
[2] *New England's First Fruits, op. cit.,* page 21.
[3] Abraham I. Katsh, *Biblical and Hebraic Mortar in American Structure,* page 9.
[4] Newman, *op. cit.,* page 658.
[5] *Science. Philosophy and Religion*: Second Symposium, page 400.
[6] A. A. Neuman, *Relation of The Hebrew Scriptures to American Institutions,* pages 6, 12.
[7] Whiting, *op. cit.,* page 442.
[8] J. Gregory, *Puritanism in The Old and in The New World,* page 318.
[9] Mather, *op. cit.,* Vol. I, page 253.
[10] Joseph Banvard, *op. cit.,* pages 318-26.
[11] J. Gregory, *op. cit.,* page 293.
[12] James Ernst, *Roger Williams,* page 89.
[13] Simms, *op. cit.,* page 222.

D.—LEGISLATION

We have previously considered the importance of the Hebraic elements in the Mayflower Compact. This document was by no means, however, the sole instance of such an instrument. The covenant of the Salem colonists is replete with a spirit that directly reflects the Old Testament. It reads in part: "We covenant with the Lord and with one another, and doe bynd our selves in the presence of God, to walk together in all his waies, according as he is pleased to reveale himself unto us in his Blessed word of truth."[1] There are echoes here of the prophetic and legislative portions of the Hebrew Scriptures. A similar spirit prevailed among the colonists at New Haven when, in 1639, they assembled at a general meeting to discuss the setting up of a civil government that would be in accordance with the wishes and uses of God.

In a sense one might say that this meeting marked the inception of the peculiar type of legislation that the English colonists fostered in America. The general form of the meeting was something they evolved for themselves, but in drawing up their legislation they followed closely the models of Hebraic law. The set-up of the legislators was also based on a Hebraic pattern. "When the great God of heaven had carried his *peculiar* people into a *wilderness* the theocracy wherein he became . . . the Lord of Host, unto them and the four squadrons of the *army*, was most eminently displayed in his enacting of their *laws*, His directing of their *wars*, and his electing and inspiring of their *judges*. In some resemblance hereunto, when *four* colonies of Christians had marched like so many *hosts* . . . into an American *wilderness*, there were several instances wherein that *army* of *confessors* was under a *theocracy*; for their *laws* were still enacted, and their *wars* were still directed by the voice of God, as far as they understood it, speaking from the *oracle* of the *scriptures*."[2]

[39]

To comprehend better the attitude of the colonists one must study the individual attitudes of their leaders and the cumulative effect of their general concern with the Scriptures. These men were all highly revered and honored. Their influence extended to every facet of life in the colonies. They were successful in leaving their imprint on business, politics, theology, morals, and in the case of Roger Williams, the actual extension of the settlements to new and untried areas. It naturally follows that those things which were of concern to men like Williams, William Bradford, John Davenport, were of concern to the whole colony. These leaders leaned heavily upon the Scriptures in practically all their undertakings. "John Davenport came to New England 'resolved . . . to drive things . . . as near to the precept and pattern of Scripture as they could be driven.' "[3] And Hugh Peter, in his public letter of 1646, requested to ". . . keep a window open to more light and truth."[4]

An interesting parallel was drawn by John Davenport from biblical narrative in a letter to Alexander Leighton. He wrote: "How much better would it beseeme us to combine together in an holy league against the common Adversary, according to Joab's agreement with Abishai, if the Aramites be stronger than I, thou shalt helpe me, and if the children of Ammon be too strong for thee Ile come and succor thee, then thus to resemble those servants of Saul and David, under the command of Abner and Joab, each of which caught his fellow by the head, and thrust his sword into his fellowes side so they fell downe together?"[5]

Roger Williams, who in many of his speeches suggests an Old Testament prophet, in his *Queries to Parliament* in 1643 remarked: "Yea, one Scripture in the mouth of a mechanic before any decree of the whole council . . ." is expected to be ". . . a far greater light than yet shines."[6]

To return for a moment to the widespread influence of John Davenport, it is worthwhile revealing that, when at the

Restoration of 1660, Major Generals Goffe and Whalley and Colonel Dixwell fled to the colonies and were pursued from New York, they found a refuge in the Massachusetts and Connecticut colonies. To insure the safety of the refugees Davenport undertook to preach publicly from a text appropriate to his sentiments in the matter. "Take counsel, execute judgment, make thy shadow as the night in the midst of the noon day; hide the outcasts, betray not him that wandereth. Let mine outcasts dwell with thee; Moab, be thou a covert to them from the face of the spoiler." (Isaiah XVI, 3-4) The sermon had its desired effect.

At the first assembly of the colonists in New Haven in June of 1639, Davenport asked whether the ". . . . Scriptures do hold forth a perfect rule for the direction and government of all men in all duties which they are to perform to God and men as well as in the government of families and commonwealth as in matters of the church?"[7] No one even bothered to debate the point with him. The thesis was irrefutable. Upon further questions of like import it was voted unanimously that the word of God as revealed in the Bible was to be the only rule to be observed in executing the duties of government in the plantation.

Before selecting any officials, the several Biblical verses dealing with the council of elders established by Moses were read. These verses ranged through Exodus, Deuteronomy, and first Corinthians. The high standards of justice and equity, the care with which the elders were to be selected—but not forced upon the people—were rehearsed in order to serve as a pattern for their own actions. In matters of crime and the administration of justice a prisoner was always reminded that: "He that hideth his sin shall not prosper, but he that confesseth and forsaketh his sins shall find mercy." (Proverbs XXVIII, 13)

It was a fundamental thesis, not subject to dispute or refutation, that ". . . the judicial law of God given by Moses and

[41]

expounded in other parts of the Scripture, so far as it is a hedge and a fence to the moral law and neither ceremonial nor typical nor had any reference to Canaan, has an everlasting equity in it and should be the rule of the proceedings."[8] This spirit is clearly evident in all of the legislation of 1639 and in the subsequent law reinforcements in 1642 and again in 1644.

The Massachusetts settlers, headed by Cotton, in 1684 also based their administration on the Scriptures. "The government might be considered as a theocracy, wherein the Lord was judge, law-giver, and king; that the laws of Israel might be adopted so far as they were considered God's people in a covenant with him; that none but persons of approved piety and eminent abilities should be chosen rulers; that the clergy should be consulted in all matters of religion; and that the magistrates should have a superintending and coercive power over the Churches."[9]

In Massachusetts, as in New Haven before it was formally joined to Connecticut, English Common Law was largely neglected and textual rulings from the Old Testament substituted for it. Some of the resentment the Puritans felt towards English Law undoubtedly was the result of their extremely unpleasant experiences with it before they sailed for the New World. But by far their more significant regard grew from their long established concept of a direct covenant with God. For more than ten years the administration of justice in Massachusetts during the Confederacy of the four colonies (Massachusetts, New Haven, Connecticut, and Plymouth; Rhode Island having been excluded for its radical and separatist views) ". . . . was without the security of either a system of statutes, or of any recognition of the authority of the Common Law. The law dispensed by the Magistrates was no other than equity, as its principles and rules existed in their own reason and conscience, instructed by Scriptures."[10]

In a great many of the laws framed by all of the New

England colonies there was constant reference to the Bible. "The choice of magistrates, legislation, the rights of inheritance, and all matters of that kind were to be decided according to the rules of Holy Scripture."[11] Ever since the bold and shocking work of men like Robert Browne, the Puritans had declared the sanction of the Mosaic legislation for their own regulatory laws. While still in England they had rejected the authority of both the established church and the magistrates. Their authoritative statute book was the Pentateuch and directly from this was drawn the first formal code of laws framed at the request of the General Court of Massachusetts.

"When, in 1646, the General Court found it necessary to convoke a public assembly of the elders they did so protesting, however, that 'their lawful power *by the word of God* to assemble the churches or their messengers upon occasion of counsel' is not to be questioned, and therefore the said assembly of elders, after having 'discussed, disputed and cleared up *by the word of God* such questions of church government and discipline . . . as they shall think needful and meet,' is to report to the General Court, 'to the end that the same being found *agreeable to the word of God,*' it may receive from the said General Court such approbation as is meet. . . . Not only the church synod is to judge what is 'agreeable to the holy Scriptures' but the civil government takes it as its own duty to make sure that the resolutions of the synod are really in accordance with the Scriptures and only then to give their approbation."[12]

In 1641, a Body of Liberties was framed. In a proposed draft consisting of forty-eight laws, forty-six of them were drawn from the Old Testament, and only two from the New Testament. In 1648 a new code, based on the previous one was adopted and published. This code, though never formally adopted in a legal sense, was considered by the legislative body as the general standard. The virtual unity of the source of these laws led Gregory to say with understandable exaggeration: "For their sumptuary laws and regulations the Puritans of New England pleaded the sanction of the Mosaic legislation. The Bible was their statute book, the law of Moses their fountain of authority. The first code of laws drawn up at the request of the general court of Massachusetts was taken entirely from the Old Testament."[13]

An interesting test case is cited by James Truslow Adams wherein the court was divided in a complicated dispute concerning the ownership of a cow.[14] A question of precedence was raised. Was it possible for a small number of judges to hamper lawfully the decision of a large number of deputies? Winthrop wrote a treatise on the subject claiming that: ". . . were the magistrates forbidden to veto the action of the deputies, the colony would not be a democracy, and *there was no such government in Israel.*"[15]

It was not only occasionally or incidentally that the Mosaic rulings played an important role in Northern Colonial legislation. They were used as supreme authority when any occasion arose that required the citation of a precedent. They were a source of power which, not only no one would dare to question or refute, but which were willingly and reverentially accepted as supreme authority. There was no question of the imposition of an outside code of laws but rather a willingness to abide by these Biblical rulings. In them, the colonists felt, was to be found democracy as they understood it. Thus from these halting beginnings did Hebraic law and legislation extend and prevail in the colonies. Eventually they found a place in the more unified laws of the separate colonies, and, still later, in the system of constitutional law that governs today.

FOOTNOTES

[1] Ezra Hoyt Byington, *The Puritan as a Colonist and Reformer,* page 81.
[2] Mather, *op. cit.,* Vol. I, page 131.
[3] John Wingate Thornton, *The Historical Relation of New England to the English Commonwealth,* page 38.
[4] *Ibid.,* page 38.

5 I. M. Calder, *Letters of John Davenport,* page 24.

6 Thornton, *op. cit.,* page 38.

7 Ernst von Dobschutz, *The Influence of Bible on Civilization,* page 153.

8 *Ibid.,* page 156.

9 Hannah Adams, *An Abridgement of the History of New England,* pages 21-2.

10 John Gorham Palfrey, *The History of New England,* page 279.

11 Gregory, *op. cit.,* page 292.

12 Dobschutz, *op. cit.,* pages 158-9.

13 Gregory, *op. cit.,* page 324.

14 James Truslow Adams, *The Founding of New England,* pages 208-11.

15 *Harvard Classics,* Vol. 43, page 90.

E.—POLITY

The full import of the Hebraic influence on early American life and its subsequent passage down the years to the present can only be grasped in all its completeness if one examines the statistical data compiled from the various codes of the New England Colonies. To use as an example the code of 1655 which was drawn up in New Haven: there were in it 79 statutes of government. Of these 50% contained Biblical references; 47% from the Old Testament and the remaining 3% from the Christian Gospels. In essence, any body of legislation derives from the underlying body of polity* which motivates it. One might say that formal law is the outgrowth of polity. And in the particular case of the United States (though the example could be applied to other countries) there is an outstanding parallel between the basic idea of the Old Testament and the law of the land as exemplified in the Constitution.

"The government of the United States . . . is based upon a . . . unique principle. The Declaration of Independence, endorsed and enforced by the Constitution, states that governments are not laws unto themselves, that they can not create right, that they are accountable to a Higher Power. It asserts that governments exist to 'secure these rights'—the 'unalienable rights' with which men 'are endowed by their Creator.' It recognizes 'the laws of nature and nature's God' as a Higher Law binding on all governments. . . . The Declaration of Independence thus affirms the duty of the government to uphold the Right and rights as ordained by Divine Law. And it declares that the citizen is obligated in obedience first to the Divine Law, and that he should defend it against the encroachment of even his government."[1]

*Polity (according to Webster), the form, constitution, system, or fundamental principles of government of any political body or other organization; the recognized principles on which any institution is based.

As we have seen the "Divine Law" and the "Higher Law" which so much concerned the men who framed both the Constitution and the Declaration of Independence was in effect the restoration of the ancient God of the Hebrews. The use of the phrase "laws of nature and nature's God", of course represented the preoccupation during the latter half of the sixteenth and the early part of the seventeenth centuries with the concept of God, Nature and Reason. "The sermons of the century are filled with it—proving the existence and goodness of God from the intelligence which the delicately adjusted mechanism of Nature everywhere exhibited."[2]

Thus it can be seen that there runs through the deeper meaning and higher purpose of our two prime instruments of government a constant regard for principles and theocratic ideas based largely on protracted study of the Old Testament. Though the actual words of the Scriptural text were not used, the spirit was present in a marked manner. Henry M. Field, a distinguished Christian clergyman, summed the matter up as follows: "Perhaps it does not often occur to readers of the Old Testament that there is much likeness between the Hebrew Commonwealth and the American republic. . . . At the bottom there is one radical principle that divides a republic from a monarchy or an aristocracy, and that is the natural equality of men . . . which is as fully recognized in the laws of Moses as in the Declaration of Independence. Indeed, the principle is carried further in the Hebrew Commonwealth than in ours, for there was not only equality before the law, but the laws aimed to produce equality of conditions in one point, and that is a vital one; the tenure of the land, of which even the poorest could not be deprived, so that in this respect the Hebrew Commonwealth approached more nearly to pure democracy."[3]

As we have had occasion to mention before the government of New England was as near an approach to a theocracy as the world had witnessed since the ancient Jewish state. Great diversity of opinion has persisted in all attempts to determine the exact form of government in Massachusetts. Wertenbaker sums the matter up as follows: "When the historian seeks a name for the Massachusetts type of State he encounters difficulties. The use of the word 'theocracy' has been criticized. In a theocracy, it is argued, the clergy are rulers, whereas in Massachusetts the ministers, even though they had a deciding voice in picking the electorate, did not themselves hold civil office. The word 'commonwealth' is also open to objection, since it is defined as 'a State especially viewed as a body in which the people have a voice' or as 'a State in which the sovereignty is vested in the people,' or 'a government chosen directly by the people,' and none of these definitions fits the society established in Massachusetts."[4]

To the early English settlers on the Northern reaches of the American Continent worship was not merely a passion but a final objective in itself. "It had been as unusual for a right New England man to live without an able ministry as for a smith to work his iron without a fire."[5] In the original conception of the Puritan's Bible State one of the cornerstones was to be an attempt to introduce into the theocracy of New England the minute control and punctiliousness of the laws which had governed the ancient Jewish theocracy in its wandering in the wilderness between Egypt and old Canaan. To the Puritans, their period of uncertainty, of trial, of violent conflict with the elements and the savage inhabitants of the land was in every way comparable to the trials of the Israelites in the desert.

Stemming directly from this identification with Israel was one of the main objections raised to the idea of a king. From the very beginning, the Puritans abhorred the idea of kingship. To them he was the embodiment of the forces of Satan working against their new Canaan. The clergy very early took up this idea and constantly hammered away at it. All throughout the seventeenth century struggles between Massachusetts and the throne over the all-important charter for the Colony, the ministry called out against the king. Moses had been extremely reluctant to allow any monarchic considerations to enter the government of Israel and the modern Israel would follow his example! Samuel had nothing but ill-will when called upon by the elders to establish a monarchy. The prophets of New England would follow his tastes. Long after the clergy had lost its power, after devastating inroads had been made into the government by the elite, the Congregational ministers kept up the battle. There was no king but God! They had so completely assimilated the Old Testament idea that, though virtually without effect and out of touch with the world of eighteenth century realities, they still opposed a concept they felt out of keeping with the Scriptures.

Though the ideas had come originally from the pulpit, the masses of people in New England turned willingly to the Old Testament for their political ideas and governmental procedures. They found there what was for them full justification for their antagonism to any idea of absolutism, to the principle of divine right. Samuel's distaste for monarchy was often the starting point for the clergy in advocating the separation of the colonies from England. Jonathan Mayhew, a leading clergyman and often referred to as the father of true civil and religious liberty in America, in a sermon delivered in Boston on May 23, 1766 on the repeal of the Stamp Act declared: "God gave Israel a king (or an absolute monarch) in his anger, because they had not sense and virtue enough to like a free commonwealth, and to have himself for their king— where the spirit of the Lord is there is liberty—and if any miserable people on the continent or the isles of Europe be driven in their extremity to seek a safe retreat from slavery in some far distant clime O let them find one in America."[6] With these ideas in mind, Mayhew fought not to table the idea of a pure democracy.

It became clear that Moses' warning and Samuel's admonition against monarchy played a considerable part in actuating the polity of the Colonies at the crossroads of their life during the third quarter of the eighteenth century. Hebraic idealism had inspired many of the practical considerations which spurred the patriots to challenge monarchy in a decisive way and to offer their blood in the Revolutionary War. Monarchy was termed by Jonathan Mayhew "unbiblical and unHebraic." And so it was for the clergy. To the masses it had become more succinctly "unAmerican."

Of striking interest is the draft for the seal of the new United States which was drawn up by Franklin and Jefferson. It showed Pharaoh, with a crown on his head and a sword in his hand, sitting in an open chariot and passing through the divided waters of the Red Sea in pursuit of the fleeing Israelites. Moses, beams of light protruding about his head, stands on the shore extending his hand over the sea and causing it to overwhelm Pharaoh and his men. Underneath was the motto: "Resistance to tyrants is obedience to God."[7] The general plan and spirit of this draft by two of the fathers of our democracy convey unquestionably the weight of Hebraism in their thinking.

The Puritans viewed their stand as a fight in the name and cause of God against mere human tyranny, for the vindication of the rights of man against despotism. This idea was often expressed by the preachers of the Gospel who, as we have seen, had no small part in stirring up and keeping alive the reaction that culminated in the break with England. W. E. H. Lecky wrote: "It is at least an historical fact that in the great majority of instances the early Protestant defenders of civil liberty derived their political principles chiefly from the Old Testament."[8]

Basing their work on the general idea behind Lecky's statement quoted above, many scholars have felt that this led certain Puritan leaders to be tolerant towards the Jews. Investigation does not bear this out for the vast majority but in connection with radical visionaries like Roger Williams it often does. For instance the following statement from Williams: "I humbly conceive it to be the duty of the civil magistrates to break down that superstitious wall of separation (as to civil things) between the Gentiles and Jews, and freely without their asking to make way for their free and peaceable habitation among us. . . . For who knows that but many of the Jewish religion may be clear and free from scandalous offences in their life, and also from disobedience to the civil laws of the State."[9]

Williams' biographer carries this idea forward. "Actuated by the lofty idealism of Williams and the significant Jewish interest in things biblical of the first settlers, Rhode Island paved the way for the recognition of the rights of the Jewish people in all American colonies."[10]

But to return to a more general consideration of polity. Once the concept of democracy as a form of government had gained practicing adherents, it was a natural and inevitable step that the laws governing the democracy be drawn from the source most familiar and revered. The Old Testament was, of course, one such inspiration. The government the founding fathers evolved was one based on practical experience. It was not at the outset (with the exception of New England) ". . . the conscious creation of far-seeing statesmanship but of adventurous, hard-working, home-loving men and women of the middle and lower classes of society of the British Isles and of Europe who were endowed with extraordinary initiative, tenacity of purpose, and resourcefulness in meeting as individuals the problems of frontier life." The Bible had become an integral part of that frontier. Its precepts and intentions had seeped deeply into the lives of the people. Its influence, as we have seen, was present in a dozen fields. It was, in short, part of American thinking.

"As a political *modus vivendi* . . . democracy presupposes a moral basis and background. Democracy is moral before it is political. That people may rule, there must prevail among the people justice and righteousness and a passion for liberty for oneself and one's brothers. Without these virtues a people, even when living under a democracy in form, will find itself living under tyrannous masters in fact."[12]

THE HEBREW IMPACT ON WESTERN CIVILIZATION

This philosophical statement is a double tribute to the early settlers of New England and to the English pioneers in the interior regions. Firstly, by their lives they proved that they possessed the prerequisite love of liberty for true democratic government and were, therefore, like Israel in its oppression, free within slavery. Secondly, the Puritans upon entering America were like Israel under Joshua at the River Jordan, fully prepared for an ideal theocracy. It is everlastingly to the credit of the men and women of early America that, as they came to realize that the exacting principles of a theocracy were not feasible in their infinitely practical world, they were able to supplant the rigid code of one with the more liberal laws of the other, always retaining the moral forces which motivated their initial move. The thesis in both polities came from the same source, the Old Testament.

FOOTNOTES

1 Dan Gilbert, *The Biblical Basis of the Constitution*, pages 77-8.

2 Carl Becker, *The Declaration of Independence*, pages 77-8.

3 Quoted in Masserman and Baker, *op. cit.*, page 108.

4 Wertenbaker, *op. cit.*, pages vii-viii.

5 Gregory, *op. cit.*, page 317.

6 Oscar S. Strauss, *The Origin of The Republican Form of Government*, pages 119-20.

7 *Ibid.*, page 140.

8 W. E. H. Lecky, *Rationalism in Europe*, Vol. II, pages 281-3. In connection with Lecky it is, perhaps, in place to note that the phrase "Hebraic mortar cemented the foundations of American Democracy" quoted by so many scholars and attributed to Lecky, is not to be found in any of his writings.

9 Ernst, *op. cit.*, page 350.

10 *Ibid.*, page 351.

11 Lawrence Henry Gipson, *The British Empire Before the American Revolution*, Vol. I, page 32.

12 Louis Witt, *Judaism and Democracy*, page 7.

F.—THE LITERATURE OF ENGLAND AND AMERICA

We have discussed the influence of Hebrew both directly and indirectly on the morality, legislative procedure and contents, and general polity of early American life. We shall now turn to the position of Hebrew in English and American literature.

In England, as in America, the Bible has long been recognized as the best selling book. Its popularity is an accepted fact. Perhaps more than any other book, it is constantly read and reread. Some people have, by virtue of their frequently repeated readings, committed whole chapters, even books, to memory in the exact phraseology. Until well into the nineteenth century and the spread of mass-produced cheap books, the Bible was frequently the only book that was owned in many homes. It was well-thumbed and finger-stained. It was the record of living and dying, of marriages and divorces. It was passed on from father to son, as much a part of the physical inheritance as the spiritual. And this reverence for the book was by no means confined to one class. All men knew it. All men were exposed to it. Through direct personal contact in addition to the more formal efforts of the clergy, familiarity grew. In this way, the English language and through it English literature acquired so many phrases and idioms grounded in or directly quoted from the Bible.

In his book *Mithridates* (1555), Conrad Gesner indicated that when Hebrew, as an Oriental language, joined Greek and Latin, linguists began to observe it with peculiar interest. Among the scholars of the time it was an irrefutable hypothesis that since the Old Testament was written in Hebrew, that tongue must have been the earliest of mankind; that by philological analysis Hebrew was the mother language from which all other living languages sprang, "... a theory which has found adherents down to Gesenius in recent times."[1]

Modern philological research has forced the abandonment of this idea in favor of a more general and inclusive picture. There is no doubt, however, that Hebrew is an extremely ancient tongue, one of the very oldest in the Semitic group, and the only one to have maintained an active position. Its influence on the languages spoken near it started extremely early in its development. As far back as the second millennium B.C., several Hebrew words are found in the letters of Tel El Amarna in Egypt. The exact position of Hebrew in the development of the Semitic languages has never been determined. Many scholars have accepted Hebrew as the most ancient. More recently, it has been suggested that Arabic preceded Hebrew. Others give precedence to either Aramaic or Assyrian. One thing is fairly well agreed upon: that the present Semitic languages are all dialects of one common ancient language.

But these fine points are of concern more to the philologist than the social historian. In any event, for purposes of this study, it may flatly be stated that Hebrew is the oldest of the ancient Semitic languages to exert a continuing influence on modern languages. This is equally true of Hebrew literature. This projected, long-range influence has reached our present English and American literature primarily through the agency of the Scriptures. Biblical precepts, injunctions, nobility of thought, and matchless eloquence are the source of much that is great in English and American literature.

If one wishes to study English literature from its beginnings there is little doubt that an intimate acquaintance with the Bible is an excellent preparation. Caedmon, who is often referred to as the father of English poetry, won early fame for his paraphrases of Biblical tales. The Anglo-Saxon Chronicle of King Alfred the Great was modeled on the Hebrew Chronicles and was prefaced with a copy of the Decalogue and other verses of the Mosaic law. The works of Shakespeare—a unique treasure to fall so early in the history of a national literature—are replete with references to Biblical characters with direct quotations from the Bible. (There are, for instance, eight different cases in which Shakespeare uses the story of Cain and Abel.) Shakespeare's England, despite repeated endeavors to exclude the Jews, was in many ways influenced by Hebraic thought. The Talmud had seeped deeply enough into the general culture to provide writers like Shakespeare with inspiration on many occasions.[2]

Moving on to classical poetry, the case can best be exemplified in the work of John Milton. Speaking of Milton's three great narratives, Whiting says: ". . . Milton was much more successful with the Old Testament story than with the new. *Paradise Lost* is an infinitely greater work than *Paradise Regained* and *Samson Agonistes* is so great because blind, captive Samson is, in one sense, none other than blind John Milton, who had been so great, and had fallen so low."[3] The Bible was, in a sense, the basis for most of the major work of Milton. He studied Hebrew at an early age (probably while still in grammar school) and made it a part of him. He was able to paraphrase in a highly poetic manner many of the Psalms. He referred to "the great task-master," "Babylonian woe," "cherubim and seraphim," "the sons of morning and fountain of light." There is hardly a place in his writing where a Biblical spirit and Biblical diction do not shine through.

At a later date, though Biblical influence is not lacking in the poetry of Shelley, Keats and Tennyson, it is perhaps Robert Browning who best epitomizes late Hebraic learning of any considerable extent. Browning's "intellectual subtlety, the metaphysical minuteness of his argument, his fondness for parenthesis, the way in which he pursued the absolute while he loaded it into a host of relatives and conceived the universal through a multitude of particulars, the love he had for remote and unexpected analogies, the craft with which his intellect persuaded him that he could insert into his poems thoughts illustrating legends and twisted knots of reasoning which a fine artistic sense would have omitted were all Jewish as the Talmud."[4] His acknowledgment of his Hebraism is found in his own words. Speaking of his use of Hebrew phrases in the body of poems like *Jochanan Hakkadosh* he said: "The Hebrew quotations are put in for a purpose: as a direct acknowledgment that certain doctrines may be found in the Old Book which the Concoctus of Novel Schemes of Morals put forth as discoveries of their own. I have put those into English characters with the proper pronunciation that you may see they go properly into English verse."[5] The stern moralizing of *Rabbi Ben Ezra* is too well known to require repetition at this point.

In the field of prose, Thomas Hardy might serve as an example. His plots are motivated by the Bible; his characters bear Old Testament names. There is a conscious imitation of the beautifully idiomatic prose of the Bible. In *Far From the Madding Crowd,* the characters plainly speak the speech of the Scriptures. In *Jude the Obscure,* Bath Sheba speaks the ironic words of Hebrew vengeance, "burning for burning," "wound for wound," "strife for strife." In *The Mayor of Casterbridge* the characters are strikingly similar to Biblical narrative.

"All our English literature is saturated with its (the Bible's) imagery; reference and echo are everywhere. It underlies the pomp of Milton, the vigor of Johnson, the limpid flow of Wordsworth, the rhythms of Ruskin, the eloquence of Macaulay, the severe, swift ease of Arnold, the roll of Hooker and Browne, the perfect periods of Dryden, the rugged fire of Carlyle, the companionability of Emerson, the clarity and repose of DeQuincey, the chastity of Whittier, the music of Tennyson, the conviction of Browning, Bacon, Jeremy Taylor, Charles Wesley, Southey, Newman, Webster, Froude, and so many, many more answer the trenchant mastery, the polychromatic vividness, the purged and exalted, the liquid and pellucid style of the book that bred them."[6]

When we turn to American literature the same picture is repeated. In the earliest native efforts scriptural influence and evidence is obvious. The one truly creative center of the early colonies was New England. Here the austerity of Puritan belief ruled out self-expression in any but divine channels. Painting and music they regarded as either frivolous or actually the work of the devil. Most of the very early writers like Roger Williams, Nathaniel Ward, John Cotton, and Thomas Morton must still be regarded as English rather than American writers.

With the growth of the first native-born into productive maturity the all consuming subject became religion. (The concern of their elders for matters of government strangely disappeared for a while or, at best, became subservient to the interests of God.) Even in their diaries everything was related to their faith. Samuel Sewall's *Diary* is replete with Old Testament references. By using and extending the story of Joseph and his brethren he wrote in *The Selling of Joseph* what "... was probably the first published attack on slavery in America."[7] The use Cotton Mather made of the Bible has been too often mentioned in these pages to require detailed repetition at this point. Wigglesworth, Edwards, John Hull, all wrote with an eye to the Scriptures.

Their books were circulated widely. When in June of 1774 dissatisfaction with the rule of the British Parliament had spread through the colonies and Virginia was in a turmoil, it was decided to call for a day of fasting and prayer to protest the closing of the Boston harbor. The leadership of New England in such matters was acknowledged as Thomas Jefferson was sent "... rummaging for precedents and Puritan forms."[8] These he found and promptly expressed with a fury suggestive of Jeremiah. The purpose of the fast day, he explained, "... was devoutly to implore the divine interposition in behalf of an injured and oppressed people."[9]

It must be pointed out in reference to Jefferson that when Benjamin Franklin first told him of the slogan "Resistance to tyrants is obedience to God," it was then ascribed to one of the regicides of Charles I. It is, of course, a quotation from the Book of Maccabees. Jefferson at once adopted it as his own motto and later in 1776 urged that it be used on the great seal of the newly proclaimed United States.

As time passed and the stresses of the Revolution relaxed literature (as all of life) took a more secular turn. But for many the Bible still pointed the way. Leon Spitz, with just-ifiable pride if slight exaggeration, calls Bryant the ". . . first of America's great poets," and goes on to say that he ". . . has shown the way to the Bible."[10] His ideas were basic, simple, the common knowledge of all. In a deeper sense, however, he reverted to the past. "His metaphysics was predominantly that of the Old Testament: God is the Creator and His works and His purposes are good."[11]

In the conflict over slavery that tore the Union apart for so long, the Bible was used by both sides to bolster arguments. Theodore Weld in 1837 published *The Bible Against Slavery* in which he used Old Testament texts extensively to prove the evils of the South's "peculiar institution." This was answered by a host of articles and pamphlets originating with the slaveholders proving the validity of slavery with Scriptural texts. The climax of this verbal battle was probably *Domestic Slavery Considered as a Scriptural Institution,* published in 1845, an exchange between Richard Fuller, a prominent clergy-man from South Carolina, and Francis Wayland, then presi-dent of Brown University. Both men predicated their argu-ments on the Word of God as they felt it had been revealed in the Bible.

One of the most literate converts to the cause of the Abol-itionists was John Greenleaf Whittier. Through all of Whittier's impassioned anti-slavery poetry burns a fierce light of Biblical inspiration. Spitz says flatly: "Whittier may justly be crowned The American Bible Poet."[12] His Puritan ancestry is clearly marked in much that he wrote. Though he abandon-ed the faith of his fathers for Quakerism, he took with him the stern New England regard for the validity of Scriptural text. Take away from Lincoln's Gettysburg address the bibli-cally flavored words and phrases, writes Auerbach, "and much of the solemn music has died out forever from this inspiring Batt.e Hymn of consecration to the Republic." Numerous biblical phrases and words from the Hebrew language have become an integral part of our daily speech and vernacular.[13] "We simply cannot estimate the effect of the Biblical influence on English—in style, imagery, and narrative technique, in moral and even political concepts. What, for instance, would have given so persuasive expression to the egalitarian ideas of Cromwell's followers if they had not been able to present them in a guise of a reversion to the simple, healthy ideals of the ancient agricultural com nonwealth in Palestine? Even the idiom of characteristic Hebrew expressions, shining through the King James translation, has repeatedly affected English stylists. A recent example is Pearl Buck, who perhaps unconsciously has recourse to Biblical style in trying to convey alien culture of quite a different kind, namely, the Chinese. Many speakers, pamphleteers, orators and moral allegorists have made use of the technique of balanced metaphor, so characteristic of the Hebrew poetic books like the Psalms, without being aware of its origin."[14]

This detailed enumeration of works and authors could easily be brought step by step down to the present. But certainly enough has been presented to make clear the point that, in the development of the literature of America, the Bible in general and the Old Testament in particular has been a constant and potent force. In all stages of our development, in periods of peace and times of troubles our authors have turned to the Scriptures for inspiration and guidance. Many of our ideas of government, of morality, many of our turns of speech, many of our customs have their origins in the Bible. It loomed large in the life of the early New England settlers. It is an active force to-day. One of the most persistent and sensational best-selling books of recent years is the work of a rabbi, Joshua Loth Liebman. Dr. Liebman, drawing heavily on his experience as a teacher and clergyman, brought together the ancient world of the Bible and the modern era of psychology and psychoanalysis. The unbroken continuity of interest in this great flowering of Hebraic genius made this synthesis inevitable.

FOOTNOTES

1 H. Thomas Rack, *A History of Classical Philology*, page 398. See also Lynn Thorndike, *University Records and Life in the Middle Ages*, pages 297-8.

2 Haim Shechter, *The Influence of Talmudic and Midrastic Literature on Shakespeare* in "Areshet" (Hehers) pages 394-399.

3 Whiting, *op. cit.*, page 442.

4 S. A. Brooke, *The Poetry of Robert Browning.*

5 Judith Berlin Lieberman, *Robert Browning and Hebraism*, page 85.

6 Henry Kendall Booth, *The Background of The Bible*, page 260. See also David Daiches, "The Influence of the Bible on English Literature", pages 1114-1132, *The Jews, Their History, Culture and Religion*, Vol. III, edited by Louis Finkelstein.

7 Bernard Smith, *The Democratic Spirit*, page 15.

8 Dumas Malone, *Jefferson the Virginian*, page 172.

9 *Ibid.*, page 172.

10 Leon Spitz, *The Bible, Jews, and Judaism in American Poetry*, page 6.

11 *The Cambridge History of American Literature*, Vol. I, page 266.

12 Spitz, *op. cit.*, page 6.

13 Katsh, *Hebrew in American Higher Education*, pages 54-61.

14 Margaret Schlauch, "General Values of Study of Hebrew", pages 7-8. *Proceedings of the Hebrew Panel*, (Mimeograph), edited by A. I. Katsh. Much of the material used in this study is based on the author's *Hebrew in American Higher Education*, pages 4-18; 26-54.

BIBLIOGRAPHY

BEVAN, EDWYN R. and SINGER, CHARLES, *The Legacy of Israel.*

BEWER, J. A., *The Literature of the Old Testament in Its Historical Development.*

DAVIS, JOHN, *New England's Memorial.*

ELTON, ROMEO, *Life of Roger Williams.*

GREGORY, J., *Puritanism in the Old and in the New World.*

KATSH, A., *The Study of Hebrew Language, Literature and Culture in American Institutions of Higher Learning.*

LECKY, W. E. H., *Rationalism in Europe.* Vol. II.

MALONE, DUMAS, *Jefferson the Virginian.*

RACK, H. THOMAS, *A History of Classical Philology.*

RIDGLEY, FRANK, *Jewish Ethical Idealism.*

SCHLEIDEN, M. I., *The Importance of the Jews for the Preservation and Revival of Learning during the Middle Ages.*

SIMMS, P. MARION, *The Bible in America.*

STORRS, R. S., *The Puritan Spirit.*

THORNTON, JOHN WINGATE, *The Historical Relation of New England to the English Commonwealth.*

WERTENBAKER, THOMAS JEFFERSON, *The Puritan Oligarchy.*

The Jew in Modern Science

By A. A. Roback

FOREWORD

The treatment of the various parts in this chapter which I have been commissioned to do is by no means exhaustive even in regard to mathematics, although from the reader's angle it may seem as if too much has been made of this science, while chemistry has been almost cramped.

My object has been to approach each subject not in a uniform manner but in accordance with its significance and destiny. Mathematics has been surveyed more in detail in order to show what (space permitting) might be done with the other disciplines. Were this method extended even to the physical and natural sciences alone, nothing short of a few volumes would be required to carry the idea through. The unevenness, which, no doubt, will be recognized by the trained eye, is, therefore, advised. The author said to himself "Let me show how at least one of the sciences should be covered." As to the others, each has its own story to tell, but we cannot do the same for all, since my own assignment is but one of many; and a single volume is to encompass all the contributions. Besides, physics lends itself to subject-treatment, while mathematics is more the product of individuals. Physics forms almost a drama centering around the discoveries of electricity, relativity, and nuclear fission, with its political angles. Chemistry, if surveyed on the same scale as mathematics, would need hundreds of pages, hence only the highlights have been flashed.

Some of the minor sciences, if sciences could be designated as such, have been glossed over—again, as the newspapers would explain "for technical reasons". Perhaps "mechanical reasons" would be less ambiguous here.

In spite of the strenuous efforts to obtain certain dates, I found the various reference works inadequate. Particularly is this true in regard to dates of deaths. There is no dearth of Jewish encyclopedias, yet *the* Jewish encyclopedia is still to be compiled. The omission of important names in science is altogether too frequent. It is sad to reflect that the Jews, who deserve a national biographical dictionary at least as much as any other people, have none, although Salomon Wininger's *Grosse jüdische National-Biographie* has been of some value, its many hundreds of errors and omissions notwithstanding. Furthermore, this work has been out of date for many years.

Even the general reference works are unsatisfactory. The wars have been instrumental in reducing to a minimum all international coöperation in the compilation of data on scholars and scientists, and the various biographical dictionaries tend to stress either politicians and public men or their own intellectual celebrities.

The academic lexicons and other reference works have fallen into neglect and it is no longer possible to verify simple biographical facts as in pre-war years.

I have tried to verify the Jewish lineage of scientists in every possible way, and if a slip has been made in this direction at rare intervals, let us remember that the number of unidentified Jewish scientists, and therefore not included here, would surely more than make up for the exaggeration.

INTRODUCTION

THE world at large, and this is true even of educated circles, is still prone to think of Jews in terms of old clothes or manufacturing, or as money lenders, peddlers, storekeepers, and on the highest level, as professionals, either as clever physicians or shrewd lawyers. The clothing industry and the movie industry represent to many a "well-informed" person the empire of the Jew.

Indeed, perhaps the foremost historian of science of our day once admitted to me—or was it a boast?—that he never considered the origin of a scientist, and that it was a revelation to learn that this mathematician or that physicist was Jewish; yet he was well aware that Galileo was an Italian, that Copernicus was a Pole, that Huyghens was Dutch, and that Vesalius would have been classified today as a Belgian. In other words the attitude is: let us forget nationality—when the famous man is a Jew. If the Jew should happen to be a financier, then he is euphemistically referred to as an international banker or broker.

When liberal scientists are gently rebuked for this inconsistency, they—that has at least been my experience—merely laugh mischievously or are mildly amused. There are anti-Semitic scientists who are more genealogically minded; and once they are successful in uncovering the Jewish skeleton in the scientific closet, the man is paged in the *semi-Kürschner Lexikon,* a sort of academic laundry bag for such unfortunates as have been contaminated by owning a non-Aryan grandfather or grandmother, and therefore must be kept apart until the stain is washed or stamped out after generations of dilution with pure "Aryan" blood, if there is any such article in civilized countries.

[64]

THE HEBREW IMPACT ON WESTERN CIVILIZATION

The name Albert Einstein has done much to focus attention on the possibility that a Jew might be a great scientist; for even the newspaper reader has heard the name and has associated it with the most seen and least known of peoples. Perhaps a few other names have since been singled out as those of Jewish scientists, but, in general, the ignorance of even the upper classes in this regard is appalling and requires some stimulant in the first place, and perhaps a sedative afterwards. . . .

Every time someone writes about the Jewish contribution to science, there is a reaction to it of an ambivalent nature. It seems as if the writer is boasting or attempting to show off the Jews. Frequently a non-Jew is assigned to the task of singing the Jew's praises. Ada Sterling's *The Jew and Civilization* has been motivated by such scruples; and every intelligent Jew knows what a farrago of truth and fiction that book is— a miscarriage of the plan to disseminate information about the Jews.

The usual attitude toward a biographical collection of Jewish celebrities is to ask: What purpose does it serve? Suppose we know that the Jews have contributed their quota and more to the world's culture, what benefit will accrue to anyone? Should we not be content in the awareness that the Jews are constantly furthering science without bothering about comparisons, statistics, etc.?

The famous Emile Meyerson once attempted to persuade me that as Jews we should do no stock-taking of this sort, that we are doing our share in advancing the cause of progress; and that should be sufficiently gratifying. My answer was that if all nations were willing to refrain from recording the exploits of their individuals as national achievements, I should of course, subscribe to his view but since (as in the matter of disarmament, where every country is anxious to have the others disarm while making her own military programme more and more elaborate) every national group is doing its utmost to claim as many distinguished men and women as its own, there is no reason why the Jews should relinquish their privilege and cede their notables to other nationalities.

There is, however, a more cogent argument for the research in question. Unless we took the trouble to bring together all the Jewish philosophers, scientists, literary men, artists, philanthropists, etc., under one rubric we should never learn just how we stand in this regard. For all we know, we might be extremely backward in the domain of science or art, particularly as the masses still believe that Jews are shrewd businessmen, financiers, money lenders, and nothing more. Every ignoramus of a Hitler, every brigand of a Goebbels and every mountebank of a Streicher might come forward with the challenge, as indeed these sorry specimens of humanity did, to show our intellectual credentials. If no bookkeeping is done, there can be no records to present, and as time goes on, the problem becomes more and more complicated. Even today it is by no means easy to establish the Jewish descent of some of the most renowned scientists of their generation, e.g., the great astronomer, Herschel.

The case is somewhat similar to the hue and cry raised against the teaching of Greek and Latin. If these subjects are not taught on the ground that they are not practical and that the students forget all they learn about these languages, it must yet be urged that certain authorities will be needed to interpret the cultures of the Greeks and Romans, that translators will always be in demand for the rendering of the best of these cultures into other tongues, and should the study of Greek and Latin be discontinued in the advanced schools and colleges, where are we to obtain our experts and authorities, our translators and interpreters? Similarly, unless we make an effort to collect all the data about Jewish leaders in every walk of life, we shall be groping and floundering, and the libels of anti-Semitic writers will seem even to the educated close to the truth.

As a matter of fact, the belittling of Jewish achievement in the sphere of the abstract and theoretical is of frequent occurrence in the writings of Jew-baiters from Apion down to the Nazi race investigators of 1933. Has not Voltaire repeated parrot-like Apion's charge that the Jews have never invented or discovered anything? And has not the British renegade, Houston Stewart Chamberlain, who became a lackey of the last Emperor of Germany, ruminated the same chaff without bothering to examine the issue fairly?

Compilers of Jewish biographical data and historical writers often make the mistake of citing the activities of Jews during the Mediaeval period, or dwelling on a relatively insignificant fact, to the exclusion of contemporary achievements. While we are all interested in the fact that Levi ben Gerson's *Jacob's Staff* which he invented in 1325, was used by Columbus in the discovery of America, it is a good deal more consequential to turn to the illustrious scientific productions of our own generation. To be sure, individuals like Levi ben Gerson deserve even greater credit than the Michelsons and Lippmanns who had at their disposal the finest laboratories and observatories and moved in an academic atmosphere, yet it is not the man we are judging but his results.

At a time, when the Jews were to be counted not in the millions, but in the thousands and when over half of them scarcely lived, but merely existed in a cage-like ghetto, we could hardly have expected them to produce Newtons and Galileos, but since the nineteenth century with the comparative emancipation of the Jews a change has been wrought in their cultural status; and scientists of Jewish parentage were remaking the world.

It would take reams and reams of paper to set down the accomplishments of Jews in every branch of science. There are the mental sciences, the social sciences, the medical sciences, and the physical sciences, with mathematics forming a sort of foundation for the whole structure. In every group and in every single branch we find Jews pre-eminent. If Voltaire's perverse remark that "all their thoughts are about money" were true, so many Jews of ability would not turn to such an unprofitable pursuit as science, but instead would enter business. Thousands and thousands of Jews have worshipped at the shrine of science, in many cases enduring privation and taunts, for the sole reason that they were idealists and wished to help humanity and realize their own powers.

In Jewish reference works our subject has been handled frequently but with varied success, never on such a large scale, as in the present volume, although possibly more comprehensively as to names. One might list a few thousand names of Jews engaged in science either as contributors after a fashion or as teachers, or as research workers, but the weighing of values is a requisite if the compendium is to be an adequate and reliable summary.

BASIC PROBLEMS

At the very outset, we are confronted with the questions: when does modern science begin? What is to be subsumed under science? To what extent, if any, should the sons of converts or demi-Jews be included?

It is not the purpose of the author to pack the scientific pantheon. At the same time, we cannot afford to ignore some significant facts in our investigation.

There are numerous other queries which crop up, and which will at least be adverted to even if the answers can at most be tentative or hypothetical. Matters such as the predilection of the Jews for some particular branches or phases of science, or the possible physiological substratum of special endowments, may also be reasonably tackled; but first of all, there is the question of the growth of Jewish achievement in science within the past century or so—a growth which has been steadily increasing until it has reached a stage of the phenomenal.

Writers of considerable vogue have often contrasted the Jews and the Greeks as to scientific prowess. I shall not allude to Houston Stewart Chamberlain in whose *Foundations of the Nineteenth Century,* the Greeks are unfavorably compared with—of all people—the Persians, and are even rated an "ignorant people". Carlyle, however, and Buckle, who show a supreme contempt for the attainments of the Jews, should have known better, and Voltaire had he lived in the twentieth century could not have brought himself, prejudiced as he was, to write *"Les juifs n'ont jamais rien inventé",* adding that all their thoughts were about money—a beautiful example of the projection mechanism operating in the great petty Frenchman.

It is true, nevertheless, that in antiquity the Jews did not cultivate scientific pursuits. Their tradition was along different lines. They were intent upon laying the foundations of justice, humanitarianism, world peace, and spiritual values rather than discovering laws of nature. The desert was not likely to bring into being academies and lyceums.

It is during the diaspora, and, nevertheless, in connection with the *Torah,* that numbers and measurements, the stellar bodies, and bodily organs and functions begin to take on a special coloring for the students of the law of God and man. Science in the Talmud is, of course, only observational and fragmentary, but as one of my collaborators will doubtless prove, in this symposium, it is unjustified to suppose that ancient Jewish thought was entirely devoid of scientific tendencies.

The mediaeval period is not within my scope either. Suffice it then to say that where there was so little accomplished in general, the Jews, who were constantly living in mortal fear, lest they be banned or burned, enjoying a breathing spell now and then between one crusade and another, now perishing by the sword of the Crusaders, and now by the fire and fury of the Moslems, could hardly be expected to busy themselves with evolving scientific principles. The Talmudic tradition absorbed what little time was left in respite after the harrowing experiences of pillage and exile, let alone ghetto restrictions reminiscent of conditions under the Nazis, at their worst. The least facilities were missing; for when the Talmud would be burned periodically, what availability was there of books along general lines for the denizens of the compounds in which the Jews were forced to live?

Notwithstanding, luminaries like Ibn-Gabirol, Ibn-Ezra, Maimonides, Gersonides, and others did arise who conquered adversity and carved out a niche for themselves in the secular hall of fame. When we compare their wretched existence with the secure, leisurely, and comfortable lives of the scholastic monks, we can only marvel at the works they have wrought.

As we approach the Renaissance or the Revival of Learning (disregarding the pronunciamento of T. S. Eliot and his co-horts to the effect that there was no such Revival, in other words that the Dark Ages were just flooded with light) Jew-ish scholars and savants begin to emerge more distinctively in some countries, where they had been able to achieve a mod-icum of ease—Spain, Portugal, and Italy. It was not long, however, before the Holy (Sic) Inquisition swooped down upon the "infidels"; or else some Prince or Duke would make short shrift of his Jewish subjects, and either a painful double life had to be led or an equally painful baptism had to be submitted to, or as in the case of a genius like Abarbanel, a forced march out of the country had to be undertaken.

Under such conditions, inhibitions would set in, the daily tension would cramp every impulse, and worse still, all the brilliant work of crypto-Jews such as Pedro Nuñes, whose treatise on the Sphere (Lisbon 1537) was rated "one of the scientific glories of Portugal" and Joseph Vecinho, who was, besides court physician, a scientific consultant in the court of King Manoel, particularly in the field of navigation, which was so important for Portugal at the time of Columbus, would redound to the credit of the Portuguese alone. Vecinho's grandchildren, in the following century, taking up residence in Italy, practiced Judaism openly.

Of a perhaps greater calibre was Vecinho's teacher, Abra-ham Zacuto, an astronomer who taught at the University of Salamanca, but after the wicked edict of 1492, fled to Portugal, whence, five years later, he was compelled to make his escape again to North Africa, unless he became an apostate. Zacuto is well remembered because of his conference with Columbus, who used his nautical tables, thanks to which the great discoverer not only was able to reach further than his destination, but dumbfounded the natives by "wishing" on them an eclipse, as predicted on the basis of the tables, and saving the day for himself and his little band of adventurers. Zacuto's astrolabe was of great assistance to another explorer, Vasco da Gama who was on the most friendly terms with this early Jewish scientist.

It is one of the most tragic ironies that the countries which profited most from Jewish genius were the very ones to treat the Jews cruelly and to "kill the goose that laid the golden eggs". Germany might have easily won the war, if the scientists she had practically exiled had, in consequence, not been giving invaluable aid to the Allies. We shall see later the part they played in the atomic drama.

As we draw closer to the era of Emancipation, the interest of the Jews in matters scientific increases, but for the most part, it is in the forensic studies of the rabbis that we find some raw ore; for what grains these masters in Jewish lore could have gleaned through autodidactic channels would hardly have contained more than textbook material which may have been pioneer work centuries previously. The celebrated gaon of Wilno, Elijah, managed to set down a number of reflections on astronomy (upon which the Talmudic masters would have come by way of their preoccupations with the calendar, new moon, computations in regard to the holidays) geometry, trigonometry and algebra, but in spite of his fabled mental powers, there appears to be nothing of the originality characteristic of those who have made mathematics their life work.

I

WHICH SCIENCES ARE FAVORITES WITH THE JEWS?

The question as to Jewish preference for any one science will be answered variously by different writers. If the Jews are only a religious group and represent no biological or anthropological entity, but adopt the tradition and adjust themselves to the facilities of the country in which they happen to reside, then *cadit quaestio.* Indeed, environmentalists and specificists, will probably deny that there are special national endowments or even proclivities. According to them, the individual might be conditioned in youth or even childhood in divers ways, and as a nation or any other group consists of individuals, certain traditions might prevail in a certain country, due to the founding of a school, or the attraction of noted teachers, or special encouragement by a government through stipends, or the particular needs of a given territory (agricultural or maritime, or military requirements) in which case the Jews, who, aside from Israel, are cast in the same environmental mould as the rest of a given country, would naturally be expected to follow the general trend. Nor are Jews supposed to have any scientific traditions of their own.

This, curiously enough for environmentalists, materialists, and mechanists is a deductive approach—from the general environment to individual output. The empirical method would be to view the individual cases of each group for the various sciences so that we might establish what uniformity or deviations there are.

It is true, is it not, that some sciences, whatever the reasons therefor, have been more steadfastly cultivated in some countries rather than in others. Do the Jews fall in line in every instance; do they turn the scales and actually dominate that field, or do they stand off and evince a different leaning? Any scientific worker who is both ethnically alert and *au courant* with the facts must have been able to observe certain tendencies in one direction or another; and I think it may safely be concluded that the Jews of the past century have excelled in two general fields of science which are disparate and yet in a sense they complement each other, *viz.*, mathematics and medicine. Mathematics is the most fundamental and most speculative of sciences (unless philosophy is accorded the honorific of *scientia scientarum*) while medicine is perhaps the most practical science, since there is not a soul, or perhaps, better, body, which does not enlist its services at one time or another; and therefore it may be called the most urgent in life, even if mathematics should prove just as necessary in shaping the conditions of living.

Mathematics, as the most abstract of sciences, and healing, as the most concrete, make a good combination in which the head and the heart arrive at their highest functions; and although medicine was even many centuries ago bringing emoluments to its practitioners, and particularly influence, although to Jewish physicians, occasionally, as in the case of Lopez, Queen Elizabeth's personal friend and counsellor, it had brought cruel death following torture, the prime impulse was doubtless to allay suffering. Perhaps medicine, until modern days, could scarcely be considered as anything more than an art based on experimental common sense and intuition rather than on experimental procedures.

Why should mathematics have had such a great appeal for the Jews, assuming, of course, that they have distinguished themselves in this science more than in others? Furthermore, in mathematics, are there specific branches for which the Jews have a special penchant? This may be posed with every other large field of science. It would be possible even to institute an investigation on the relative strength in a given science on the part of Jews in various countries, e. g., France, Germany, England, Russia. Many are the factors to be considered in such a piece of research—opportunities, the proportion of the Jewish population, tradition, and quality of the members of the group. It has been often remarked that each country has the Jews she deserves. Is the obverse of this proposition worth looking into, *viz.,* that Jewish merit is commensurate with the people among whom they sojourn? Certainly what has happened in Germany would tend to disprove such a generalization. If anything, it may be concluded emphatically that wherever and whenever the Jews have rendered conspicuous service to the culture of the country, as in Spain, Portugal, and Germany, they have been made the scapegoat up to the point of extermination.

In spite of the Nazi infamy toward the Jewish scientists every close observer of German intellectual life for the past fifty years is impelled to descant with admiration on the subject of Jewish intellectual activities in Germany.

"Take away the Jews—and Germany is destitute"—is the way ex-Ambassador Gerard has expressed it in his *Four Years in Germany.*

First of all it might have been the great Frenchman, Ernest Renan, who, in his *Recollections of Infancy and Youth,* gave expression to this fact in the following passage "Germany, after devoting herself entirely to military life, would have had no talent left if it were not for the Jews, to whom she has been so ungrateful".

Renan wrote his appreciation in 1883, while ex-Ambassador Gerard, who certainly knew all the ins and outs of Germany, had occasion to remark, thirty-five years later: "Germany boasts of her *Kultur,* her learning, that she is pre-eminent in philosophy, literature and art. But that is not true. It is not they—but the Jews. Take away the Jews from all branches of her culture and Germany is destitute".

Renan's opinion was seconded by an equally famous man, though in a different field of endeavor. In 1884, Sir William Osler wrote: "Should another Moses arise and preach a Semitic exodus from Germany, and should he prevail, they would leave the land impoverished far more than was ancient Egypt by the loss of the jewels of gold and jewels of silver, of which the people were spoiled. . . . There is not a profession which would not suffer the serious loss of many of its most brilliant ornaments, and in none more so than in our own." (i. e. medicine)[1]

How prophetic the passage from Sir William Osler sounds today. Little did that illustrious physician realize in 1884— just about 65 years ago—that the hypothetical event would come true, but not because another Moses preached a Semitic exodus! Certainly the most bizarre mind could not for a moment have imagined that a band of hoodlums would create an exodus or wreak the destruction of their precious ornaments in the most truculent manner conceivable.

One thing which has been puzzling me is this: with all the millions of Jews killed off and still more millions forced to assimilate in every respect, largely through conversion to Christianity, the comparatively small number left by far exceeds its quota in practically every sphere of civilization. The ancient Greek legend of the phoenix seems to be applicable to the Jews rather than to the Greeks.

It is not in a spirit of pride or ethnocentricity that this matter has been brought up, but rather in a scientific vein. It is a problem like any other problem to be solved outside the bounds of emotion, just as the genius of the ancient Greeks during the fourth century B. C. has yet to be explained. The facts cry for justice, but the cry is a *vox clamantis in deserto*. Yet another matter suggests itself: is there a national equation with the Jews, dispersed as they are, as in the case of other peoples, as has been argued by the present author,[2] or is all science strictly universal, the Jewish contribution partaking of this general attribute? If the Jews do offer a separate slant, then, is there a common denominator which can be detected as applying to the scattered groups in different lands through the generations?

The following pages can but allude to the possibilities. Regrettably, the whole field of collective psychology has been allowed to lie fallow, while mechanistic doctrines bolstered alike by behaviorist in psychology, materialist in the historical and philosophical framework and environmentalist in the so-ciological sphere, have cluttered up the approach with compli-cated terms and oversimplified theories which, when exploded, take refuge in other theories, equally oversimplified and equally fantastic. In many instances these allies will shut their eyes to the hard facts often because they are not inclined to discern the particulars. They will first treat the Jews as an ethnically mixed group, and therefore nondescript or at least undifferentiated from the dominant group, and in consequence will asseverate that there is nothing to look into except the assumed ecological processes, conditionings, adjustments, ac-culturations, etc. In large part, the scientific smugness, if not priggishness, is due to the ignorance of origins. If as Pasteur has so pointedly remarked: "in the sphere of observation, chance will favor the prepared mind", then how much more necessary is it to be prepared at least by keeping one's mind open to the facts that almost stare us in the face?

It is these facts which I have tried to collect for decades, so that the chain could be forged out of the links, and when a German, Frenchman, or American would ask me why I bother accumulating such insignificant data, I ask him in return whether such data on Germans, Frenchmen, or Ameri-cans are more significant, and if so, why, except that in the one case it is a political majority and in the other it is a po-litical minority. What is it, then, but a fascistic method in science? During the Hitler regime we were all shocked to find Nobel Prize men, scientists of world renown accommo-dating their scientific temper to the raving doctrines of an ignoramus and his cohorts, which goes to show that although science is objective, scientists who have made wonderful dis-coveries, laboratory champions are not necessarily champions of truth and justice, that a certain dissociation holds in some whose intellectual endowments and character traits are not in harmony *ab initio*.

And yet the procedure of such studies as have been sug-gested does not require elaborate techniques. No interferometers, no cyclotrons need be constructed for such purposes. First, the enumeration of outstanding contributions by those of Jewish antecedents is essential, which means that the investigators must be familiar with ethnic origins; and then comparison with non-Jewish productions, both quantitatively and qualitatively, is apt to establish the preliminary results, which must be checked against methodological fallacies.

The present work, a sequel to others of a similar nature, is the first step in this direction; and it is toward that end we begin with Jewish achievement in mathematics.

II

MATHEMATICS

In our survey, it is meet perhaps to begin with mathematics, not only because Jews have enriched it so considerably even in the Middle Ages when, aside from the treatises written in Hebrew, according to the authoritative testimony of Ibn Ezra, the modern notation referred to as Arabic numerals was brought to Moslem dominions from India by a Jewish scholar, while another, Ibn Daud, later relayed the information from Moslem soil to Christendom via Spain.

It will scarcely serve any useful purpose to make an inventory of the individual works treating of mathematics during the past four centuries covering the period of my present assignment. We are primarily interested in the highlights, the pioneers, the spearheads of a new movement or trend in science. While it is true that given the same opportunities many an obscure writer in Hebrew might have been a director of a university institute or a laboratory instead of turning out an autodidactic lucubration which has gone over the ground of others, nevertheless, in our realistic world, we must reckon with the accomplished and universally recognized facts —all the more so as space is restricted, and the subject is so extensive that comprehensiveness is out of the question.

What is particularly enlightening is the upswing of Jewish

scientific achievement in our own century; and despite the Nazi attempts to undermine its progress, Jewish research and discovery has been in the ascendant for the past fifteen years.

There are many names which become stereotyped because of the accumulated weight of their mention in compendium after compendium, while those of worthier bearers, contemporaries of ours, have not had the chance of being bruited around. Another handicap is the difficulty, almost impossibility, of a compiler of data in so many different fields doing justice to the various representatives as to their relative merit, so that for the most part the same amount of space is allotted to each. To some extent this defect will be noticeable here too, but at least a conscious effort will be made to ameliorate, if not remedy, the situation.

There are other snags too, *e. g.,* the paucity of genealogical data and sometimes even the attempt to conceal the Jewish origin of some scientists. One of the foremost French mathematicians of the seventeenth century, Ozanam, has been repeatedly spoken of as of Jewish descent, and probably the greatest mathematician Russia has produced, Lobatchevsky, a co-discoverer of non-Euclidean space, was also alleged to have been born into a Jewish family.

There is nothing doubtful about Carl Gustav Jacobi (1804-1851) who in his short life has packed in a century of original thought along different lines of mathematical theory: Homogeneous functions, spatial functions, calculus of variations, elliptic functions and, not least, the theory of numbers.

Leo Koenigsberger's large volume on Jacobi gives us a full-size and many-sided picture of the man who, although not as great as Gauss or Euler, was much gentler than the former, who reminds one of a dictator, and more influential than the latter. Had he lived longer (he died at the age of 46) he might have approximated them in mathematical stature.

Jacobi's works were published in 7 volumes by the Prussian Academy of Science after his death. The editor, K. W. Borchardt, one of Jacobi's most brilliant students and a mathematician of note and also Jewish, did not live to complete his task, which was carried out by the famous Weierstrass. His message to the widow of Jacobi on publication of the set was a high tribute to her husband, whose qualities of the heart endeared him to all his students, first at Koenigsberg and later in Berlin, which thanks to him had begun to compete with Goettingen as a mathematical centre. There is, in addition to the large biography and monographs on his mathematical labors, a little book entitled *C. G. J. Jacobi als Politiker,* which describes some interesting episodes at the Prussian Academy in connection with his liberalism.

Transfinite Numbers

A second mathematical giant of the nineteenth century, more concentrated and more influential, although not at so many points, was Georg Cantor[3] (born in St. Petersburg, in 1845 and died at Halle in 1918) who may be looked upon as the man who established the mathematics of infinity, thus bringing into the science not only a new dimension but a new mode of thinking. The great mathematician, Gauss, had, by his authoritative decree, once and for all, as it seemed to his contemporaries and the succeeding generation of mathematicians, given the *congé* to the concept of infinity in mathematics except as a mere limit, not as a thing allowing of definite relations (Adolf Fraenkel *Einleitung in die Mengenlehre,* p. 1), half a century before. It was left to Georg Cantor not only to dispute this doctrine, but actually to supplant it in favor of a decidedly broader view which represents transfinite numbers on an equal footing with the finite. Euclid's axiom, 'The whole is greater than its part', with which we are all familiar, must be further qualified in the light of the new mathematical system and thus becomes only an axiom applicable to finite collections only, not an absolute and universal one.

[79]

Cantor, like his younger and more famous contemporary in mathematical physics, Albert Einstein, was obliged to contend against a host of great minds until his voice was heard. In the '80's of the last century, after dealing with the negative views regarding the possibility of infinite numbers set forth by philosophers from the time of Aristotle, Cantor put his finger on the weak spot and declared 'All so-called proofs of the impossibility of actually infinite numbers are, as may be shown in every particular case and also on general grounds, false in that they begin by attributing to the numbers in question all the properties of finite numbers, whereas the infinite numbers, if they are to be thinkable in any form, must constitute quite a new kind of number as opposed to the finite numbers, and the nature of this new kind of number is dependent on the nature of things and is an object of investigation'.[4] This observation was the first step to the establishment of a mathematics of classes, aggregates or types, and to the conception that in the realm of number we are dealing with types of order, and that every class or aggregate is a 'totality of definite elements which can be bound up into a whole by means of law'.

What two other celebrated Jews, viz., Lazarus and Steinthal, have accomplished in psychology by their pleading that the mental properties of a group of people are not to be confused with the characteristics of the individuals who go to make up the group—Cantor has accomplished in mathematics, and it is not an idle compliment when Bertrand Russell, acknowledged as the foremost mathematical philosopher of our time, says in the introduction of his *Principles of Mathematics*—the work on which his reputation rests—'In mathematics my chief obligations, as is indeed evident, are to Georg Cantor and Professor Peano'.

Hebrew Symbols in Higher Mathematics

While a student, I once had occasion to look into a ponderous and highly technical work of Bertrand Russell (*Princi-*

ples of Mathematics), probably the clearest philosophical mind of our generation; and was struck by a very familiar symbol. At first I thought that the resemblance between the particular symbol and the first letter in the Hebrew alphabet was but a coincidence. But no, a moment's scrutiny convinced me that the character was identical with the first letter of the Hebrew alphabet.

The next question was: Did Russell first introduce the aleph into mathematics, or was there a Jewish hand in it? Naturally the latter hypothesis seemed more reasonable, though we know that often Jewish scientists will go out of their way to conceal their ethnic origin, and might likely draw on a Sanskrit or Chinese source, when in need of a new symbol, in preference to a Hebrew one. In this instance, however, the reasonable turned out to be the likely explanation; for it was actually Georg Cantor who introduced the *aleph* into his special brand of mathematics, the mathematics of infinity; and, curiously enough, in the *Annuario del Circolo Matematico di Palermo*, a biographical handbook for mathematicians, the *aleph* placed, in agate type, before the name of some of the members, denoted that they were—not Jews, but distinguished enough to be incorporated as life members.

Whether this introduction could be considered an intrusion by Judaeophobes, or whether the Nazis and their ilk looked upon this as a Jewish conspiracy in the abstract region of mathematics, the *aleph* is here to stay. Let us now see what the *aleph* represents in mathematics.

Cantor makes this symbol designate a class of transfinite numbers, the smallest of which would be denoted by *aleph*-zero and would consist of the totality of finite cardinal numbers. The series may be drawn up endlessly by placing at the bottom right of the aleph various symbols, first of all, in Arabic numerals, then in Greek, such as *nu* and *omega*—and even then the series of classes is not exhausted.

But Cantor was not the only mathematician to make use of Hebrew characters. Another shining light in this respect was James Joseph Sylvester, about whom more will be said later in various connections.

In his remarkable treatment of what he called syzygetic relations, he introduces Hebrew letters from *aleph* to *Kaph* to designate the references to his articles or sections in that paper. It is scarcely a coincidence that two mathematicians of Jewish descent have reverted to the alphabet of their ethnic group in order to express their needs in symbols.

The other symbol which may be regarded as a Hebrew character is a sort of inverted C, but which a Jew would easily recognize as a *kaph,* though it is hardly likely that Peano, who has introduced the symbol into mathematics, had taken it from that source. Originally, of course, the Roman C was merely an inversion of the Phoenician letter, which, in Hebrew, is called *kaph.* But it is noteworthy that in mathematics, this symbol stands for 'implies', and the *kaph* is the most suitable letter to designate the relation of implication; for it is used in the sense of 'like' very frequently.

But why stop at symbols, alone, from the Hebrew, when we can pick up a volume edited by one of England's most illustrious astronomers, of Halley-comet fame, and find many words, *i.e.*, technical terms in Hebrew? For it was Edmond Halley who translated into Latin the *Spherics* by Menelaus of Alexandria from a Hebrew version of an Arabic translation, made perhaps from a Syriac rendering of an imperfect Greek original Ms. Costard, in his preface, published after Halley's death, tells us also of the version of Isaac ben Khunain; and Max Krause's edition of the *Spherics* preserves that translation,[5a] while Halley's was based on that of Jacob ben Makhir, the Provençal grandson of the famous translator of Maimonides, Samuel Ibn-Tibbon. It was around 1273 that ben Makhir completed his version. Thus we see that Hebrew figured in England as late as the eighteenth century, and unlike Arabic which was acquired comparatively late in life, Hebrew was, with Halley, a subject he had taken up at Oxford in his teens; for at the age of 22, this genius had already been elected a Fellow of the Royal Society.

Some of the illustrious names associated with both mathematics and physics, like that of Heinrich Hertz, will appear in their more familiar realm, viz. physics, while others will be referred to under astronomy or engineering. For the time being, we shall endeavor to stick closely to the sphere of mathematics, following a politico-geographical plan, for the most part; and since modern mathematics was mainly cultivated in Germany, we shall start with that country, as, indeed, we have already made the first approach with Jacobi and Cantor. In some cases, the mathematicians were born in Russia or Poland but have received their training and laurels in Germany.

GERMANY

One of the great losses to science was the early death, at the age of 29, of F. G. M. Eisenstein (1823-1854) who, according to the greatest of all modern mathematicians, Gauss, as expressed in a letter to Alexander Von Humboldt, "belongs to those talents who are born but once in a century". To what extent he was esteemed by the *princeps* of mathematics is evidenced by the fact that Gauss edited and published Eisenstein's collected writings, chiefly on algebra and the theory of numbers, in 1848.

J. G. Rosenhain (1816-1887), professor at Koenigsberg, established the *Abelian* and *theta* functions toward which another Jewish mathematician, Jacobi, had given the first impetus.

Leopold Kronecker (1823-1891) elder brother of the physiologist, Hugo Kronecker, taught, at the University of Berlin, algebra and the theory of numbers receiving his chief attention. The Russian Academy of Science published his collected works. Kronecker was the champion of natural numbers—the integer was to him a sort of god-arithmeticist. For this reason he took unkindly to Georg Cantor's revolution in constructing a world of transfinite numbers.

His successor, in a sense, was Immanuel Lazarus Fuchs (1833-1902) who became Rektor of the University of Berlin for a period. The theory of linear differential equations is largely associated with his name.

Leo Koenigsberger (1837-1922) whose work lay in the treatment of elliptical functions and differential equations was a pupil of Jacobi and his ardent admirer. The science of mechanics also took his attention, and his voluminous biography of Helmholtz showed that he had broader interests than many mathematicians. His large biography of Jacobi has already been alluded to.

One of the earliest to establish the theory of invariants, which was developed by another Jew, Sylvester, proves to be Siegfried Heinrich Aronhold (1819-1884) who demonstrated the existence of invariants S and T, of the ternary cubic, while Paul Gordan (1837-1912) who was Professor at Erlangen "showed with the aid of symbolic methods that the number of distinct forms for a binary quantic is finite".

Hermann Schapiro's life (1840-1898) could be read as a novel. Here was a young Lithuanian Jew who, after serving as a rabbi, chanced to look into a work on mathematics. Immediately the urge to study overwhelmed him. He first went to Odessa, and after much hardship managed to reach and study in Berlin, whence he was compelled to return to Odessa, but again set out for Germany, studying at Heidelberg and receiving his Ph.D. at the age of 40. As a *Privatdocent* at Heidelberg, he could not support himself and his family, so he took to repairing watches. His work in co-functions and algebraic iterations was only a portion of the planned project, but it was sufficient to prove his worth as a mathematician. Meanwhile, however, he became interested in problems of Jewish nationalism and Zionism, became the patron of Jewish students from Russia and subsequently the promoter of an idea, which, three years after his death, became known as the Jewish National Fund to provide for the purchase of land in Palestine. The new flourishing Hebrew University was also his brain child, absurd though it seemed in his day. His great mathematical gifts were, in a sense, dissipated on propaganda; and yet his dream came true, although he did not live to see it.

Jacob Rosanes (1842-1922) was equally grounded in algebra and geometry. This Galician-born Jew, of an old Sephardic family, even became the Rektor of the University of Berlin, and before that he was made Privy Councillor.

Alexander Brill (born 1842), who was professor for many years at Tübingen, is often mentioned in histories of mathematics.

Eugen Netto (1846-1919) who, after teaching at Strassburg and Berlin, became full professor at Giessen, was well-known for his studies on substitutions and combinations.

Adolf Hurwitz (1859-1919) ranked high in the theory of functions and especially elliptical functions. His work in this sphere was revised and enlarged by R. Courant, while the Technical College at Zürich published his collected papers in 1932-1933.

Friedrich Schur (1856-1941) working on finite transformation series, has not neglected his analytic geometry, and ranks as a mathematician of considerable eminence. While he hailed from Prussian Poland (the lively town of Krotoschin) his more original namesake, Isai Schur, was born in Mohilev, Russia (1875) and became full professor in Berlin, in 1920, after publishing some remarkable work on the theory of aggregates, integral equations, and functions. He was the last Jewish professor in the University to be ousted under the Nazis. Subsequently, he taught at the Hebrew University in Jerusalem, dying in Tel-Aviv in 1941. At the time of his death, he was working on a book which was to revolutionize the science.

Ludwig Schlesinger (1864-1933) although born in Hungary

and for a time teaching in Budapest, published altogether in German, largely in the field of linear differential equations and automorphous functions.

Hermann Minkowski (1864-1909) while not possessing the originality of a Jacobi or Cantor, was held in great esteem at such seats of learning as Bonn, Koenigsberg and Goettingen, where he died in the prime of life. Minkowski's formulae, as we shall have occasion to mention later, were helpful to Albert Einstein in the formulation of his epoch-making theory. Minkowski, who was born in Russia, but left in order to study in Germany when he was in his teens, specialized in the theory of numbers.

The theory of numbers was, together with the theory of functions and aggregate series, the chief interest, aside from art and music, of Alfred Pringsheim (1850-1941) the father-in-law of Thomas Mann.

Felix Haussdorff (Paul Mongré) (1868-   ) was professor at Bonn, and was one of the first to recognize the scope of Cantor's work by basing his own theory of dimension on it.[5]

Edmund G. H. Landau (1877-1938) who was professor at the University of Goettingen, left German soil in 1934 and took up the duties which were offered him years earlier at the Hebrew University, where he had previously helped establish a mathematical institute.

Leon Lichtenstein (1878-1933) was more versatile than most mathematicians, specializing along the lines of astronomical mathematics. He was spared the humiliation of dismissal by dying before Hitler came into power.

Felix Bernstein (1878-   ) who was Professor at Goettingen assisted his former teacher, Georg Cantor, by supplying the important principle of equivalence, which smoothed the path of the aggregate theory.

We can point to the contributions of Max Noether of Erlangen (1844-1921) on singularities of curves, Rudolf Lipschitz (1832-1903) of Bonn and Ferdinand Joachimsthal (1818-1861) at Halle and Breslau, Louis Saalschütz (1835-

1905) of Koenigsberg, Paul Epstein (1871-   ) who was professor at Strassburg and brought out a compendium of higher mathematics; Meyer Hamburger of the Technical Institute in Charlottenburg, and scores of others who have made a mark in mathematics, but then it would require ten times as much space as is at our disposal.

Only those who are conversant with Jewish biography will appreciate to what extent German mathematics is in large part Jewish mathematics, even if the mathematicians themselves renounced their faith and became converts to Christianity. Any history of mathematics—and the most comprehensive historian of mathematics is, again, a Jew, viz., Moritz Cantor, who has taken about 4000 pages to tell the story—will show how the progress of new mathematical movements depended on the Jews. So inextricably intertwined are the Jewish names with each other, as well as with the general group, that if the former were eliminated, the gaps in mathematical advancement would seriously affect the science.

Here is reproduced part of a page in Cajori's *History of Mathematics* with the names of the Jewish mathematicians capitalized (by myself). Germany, France, and England are represented in this passage, but in the final analysis, most of those mentioned are Jewish.

In the *American Journal of Mathematics* are memoirs on binary and ternary quantics, elaborated partly with the aid of F. FRANKLIN, now professor at the Johns Hopkins University. At Oxford, SYLVESTER has opened up a new subject, the theory of reciprocants, treating of the functions of a dependent variable y and the functions of its differential coefficients in regard to x, which remain unaltered by the interchange of x and y. This theory is more general than one on differential invariants by HALPHEN (1878), and has been developed further by J. Hammond of Oxford, McMahon of Woolwich, A. R. Forsyth of Cambridge, and others. SYLVESTER playfully lays claim to the appellation of the mathematical Adam, for the many names he has introduced into mathematics. Thus the invariant, discriminant, Hessian, Jacobian, are his.

The great theory of invariants, developed in England mainly by Cayley and SYLVESTER, came to be studied earnestly in Germany, France, and Italy. One of the earliest in the field was SIEGFRIED HEINRICH ARONHOLD (1819-1884), who demonstrated the existence of invariants, S and T, of the ternary cubic. Hermite discovered evectants and the theorem of reciprocity named after him. PAUL GORDAN showed, with the aid of symbolic methods, that the number of distinct forms for a binary quantic is finite."[6]

It is true that at times Jewish encyclopedias and reference works erroneously include a few names of non-Jews, like Felix Klein, Hilbert, or Hermann Weyl, but probably many more of Jewish descent are not known to be such.

I have a faint suspicion that the famous Ludwig Otto Hesse (1811-1874) was of Jewish origin. The clues? It took some time before he was given a professorship, and in this connection, J. J. Sylvester, himself the victim of prejudice or bigotry, as we shall see later, in one of his many original papers, viz., "On a Theory of Syzygetic Relations" while speaking of the Hessian curve, pauses to interpolate, amidst the intricate reasoning, a temperamental aside which reminds us of a prophetic outburst in these words: "named after Dr. Otto Hesse of Koenigsberg (the worthy pupil of his illustrious master)[7] but who, to the scandal of the mathematical world, remains still without a chair in the University he adorns with his presence and his name". My third clue is the fact that Moritz Cantor wrote the obituary article on Hesse in both a technical journal and also the dictionary of German biography, and he mentions there only one other obituary in a mathematical journal—written by Hamburger. Naturally these may all be coincidences, but such coincidences are worth looking into.

Among the more recent mathematicians who have attained fame are Richard Courant (born in Poland 1888) who after serving as professor at Goettingen and director of the Institute for Mathematics and Mechanics in that place, left Germany in 1933, and after a year at Cambridge University, arrived in New York to head the department at New York University; Richard von Mises, one of the foremost authorities on the theory of probability, aeronautics and the applications of mathematics to physics. On the termination of the First World War, in which he served as a pilot and plane designer, he was dismissed, as a German, from the University of Strassburg; while under the Nazi regime, he was forced to leave under the Aryan clause. After teaching in Turkey for some time, he received a call to Harvard where he is professor in the graduate School of Engineering. Besides his philosophical diversions, von Mises happens to be an authority on Rilke too, having published much on the German poet.

Philipp Frank, who originally was in the general field of mathematics, is now identified with physics where he will appear later in this discussion; Alfred Rosenblatt, formerly of the University of Cracow, later taught in the University of Peru, Lima, dying there in 1947.

Adolf Fraenkel, Director of the Einstein Institute of Mathematics at the Hebrew University; F. W. D. Levi, formerly of Leipzig and recently teaching at the University of Calcutta, are others of some distinction.

Let us take note of the fact that many mathematicians have distinguished themselves primarily in allied fields like astronomy (Schwarzschild) mechanics or physics (Heinrich Hertz) (Arthur Moritz Schoenflies, who was a protégé, or perhaps aide, of Nernst). These will be discussed in their proper sphere.

ENGLAND

England has not been productive of great mathematicians; and, of course, there were few Jews who distinguished themselves in this field as compared with German or Italian Jews, but there is hardly a mathematician in England, after Newton, who could compare in stature with James Joseph Sylvester (1814-1897) the son of Abraham Joseph (the name Sylvester was adopted by James later in deference to an older brother, living in the United States), unless it is Sylvester's collaborator and friend, Arthur Cayley. Sylvester, as irony would have it, one of the most original and influential mathematicians of his day in England, did not receive his bachelor's degree from Cambridge University until long after he had been a professor in several universities—and only for the reason that he was a professing Jew. Besides collaborating with Arthur Cayley in the establishment of the theory of invariants, he covered a vast amount of mathematical territory, such as reciprocants, the theory of forms, matrices and Hamiltonian numbers. In addition, he invented a few geometrical devices, among them, the plagiograph, which reproduces similar figures but turned at an angle to the original. The Royal Society in England struck a medal in his honor commemorating his great service to mathematics, and one of the first recipients of the Sylvester medal was Georg Cantor, who received it in 1904 for his original work in aggregates.

The Cambridge University Press has brought out four huge volumes containing Sylvester's collected writings, under the editorship of Prof. Baker. Sylvester was the sage among mathematicians. Many of his witty remarks appear in a book called *Mathematical Memorabilia.* His verse writing was a hobby which shows his well-rounded personality. In appearance, he resembled a genial rabbi of the old generation, with the polish of an English lord.

The anecdotes told about him would fill a volume. I remember reading once that when he was teaching at Johns Hopkins University, he was invited to dinner at the home of a colleague. Since it began to pour as the mathematician was ready to depart, the hostess insisted that he spend the evening there. Somewhat reluctantly, Sylvester accepted the invitation, but a few minutes later, the household missed him. When he returned he was asked where he had been during the period, and to their astonishment, it turned out that Sylvester had gone out in the rain for his pajamas.

At Johns Hopkins, Sylvester trained a number of students who subsequently became leaders in the discipline. We shall have occasion to refer to him again in connection with the founding of the chief mathematical journal in the United States, when he taught in Baltimore.

Although Benjamin Gomperz (1779-1865) was a mathematician of a different sort, and might be mentioned perhaps more appropriately under another rubric, as an astronomer, he was in fact a pioneer in vital statistics, having worked out the tables of mortuary resistance to the extent that the whole actuary system may be said to date from him.

Selig Brodetsky (1888-   ) formerly professor of applied mathematics at Leeds, and now Chancellor of the Hebrew University in Jerusalem, is prominent in the mathematical phase of aerodynamics, although his leadership in the Zionist movement and other Jewish activities, as well as general professional organizations, has sidetracked him considerably. In his student days in Cambridge he distinguished himself by his attaining the senior wranglership.

Louis Joel Mordell (1888-   ) is professor of pure mathematics at Manchester University.

H. Levy (1889-   ) head of the mathematical department at the Imperial College of Science in London has written prolifically on various subjects but differential equations and the theory of probability have been his mainstay. Like Brodetsky, he takes an interest in Jewish affairs, but is leftist in orientation otherwise.

ITALY

Coming to Italy, we have in the person of Luigi Cremona (1830-1903) who was director of the school of engineering in Rome, and even at one time minister of education, a geometrician of unusual acumen, especially in the synthetic sphere. Cremona's textbook on projective geometry has been translated into many languages and his treatises on graphical calculus and reciprocal figures have also had a wide vogue in academic circles. We shall return to Cremona in another section, since he stood high in another sphere of activity too. At present suffice it to record that he stands out as one of the great geometricians of his generation, and Italy is truly proud of him.

Italy has been especially fortunate in its Jewish mathematicians who, it has been said, constitute 80% of its more conspicuous representatives. Although Volterra was also a physicist and an aeronautic engineer and inventor, his chief contribution lay in his studies on permutable functions and integro-differential functions, which brought him fame throughout the world. He was, however, disposed to make theory the all-in-all, and we find him now revising and modifying theories of elasticity, and now laying the foundations for a mathematics of the social and biological sciences; but from one angle, his character interests us even more, for he was brave enough to refuse taking the Fascist oath in 1931, and thus was dismissed by Mussolini from the University of Rome where he served as professor of mathematical physics for 31 years.

Guido Ascoli (1843-1890) was equally versed in algebra and geometry, and his chair was at the Milan Technical Institute where he has done some important work.

Salvatore Pincherle (1853-1930) whose chief work lies in developing the field of analytic functions was professor at Bologna University where he presided in 1928, at the International Congress of Mathematics.

Corrado Segre (1863-   ) Professor at Turin, was a devoted pupil of Cremona, whose geometrical contributions he brought up to date with researches of his own.

Among the world's foremost authorities on calculus and probability was Guido Castelnuovo (1865-1947) late professor of analytic geometry at the University of Rome. It is my recollection that Castelnuovo was one of the bitterest opponents of Mussolini's Fascism.

Another brilliant name in the annals of Italian mathematics is that of Tullio Levi-Civita (1873-1942). That this beacon should have been given the congé by Mussolini (in consequence of Nazi pressure to enforce the Nuremberg laws in Italy, too) only to find a haven in the Vatican is one of the ironies of science and progress. His work on absolute differential calculus was at the basis of Einstein's relativity theory, and his three volumes on rational mechanics, as well as his *Fondamenti di Meccanica Relativistica,* were hailed as monumental. While he was a member of the Pontifical Academy of Science (Volterra was the only other Jewish member) he was also on the academic board of the Hebrew University at Jerusalem.

One of the most prolific mathematical textbook writers is Giulio Vivanti (1859-   ) who, according to my Italian informant, was listed as a Jew under the fascist restrictions. Vivanti, trained as an engineer, held a chair in mathematics at the University of Messina, then at Padua and Milan, carrying on in several different fields: calculus of variations, theory of analytic functions, infinitesimal calculus, and theory of transformations. Some of his works were translated into French and German. His name appears in the 1948 edition of the Italian *Chi è.*

Federigo Enriques (1871-1942) was known in circles of philosophy largely because of the journal *Scientia* which he founded in 1909; but it was as a geometrician that the mathematical world hailed him when his three volumes on advanced geometry appeared. Enriques worked in several sectors, algebraic functions and mechanics too, but he was not content to stay in the technical field. His highly speculative mind led him beyond to the foundations of all science, to methodology and the theory of knowledge; and his deductions touched upon the theory of relativity. Prior to the Nazi war, he served as the head of the Italian Institute of Mathematics and the Italian Institute for the History of Science.

A geometrician of a high order was Gino Loria (1862-   ) who received gold medals for his ingenious research from the Academy of Madrid and the French Institute. His "side line" was the history of mathematics.

One who might have risen to the heights of a Volterra or a Levi-Civita was the brilliant mathematician, Eugenio Elia Levi (1883-1917) professor of infinitesimal calculus at the University of Genoa, had he not been killed in his 34th year during the First World War; Levi's papers were many and on diverse problems. His brother Beppo Levi (1875-   ) formerly professor at Bologna (theory of functions) is now teaching in Rosario, Argentina.

Equally noted as a geometrician is Beniamino Segre who, after teaching at Rome and Bologna for many years, was removed by the general edict of Mussolini and left for England. His *Non-Singular Cubic Surfaces* was published at Oxford.

For a country which, prior to the Nazi War, harbored only from forty to fifty thousand Jews, Italy might be said to have fared quite well by her Semitic minority, although during the Nazi bond, or better perhaps, under Nazi bondage, she has not done so well by them.

Among the younger Italian mathematicians of prominence is Alessandro Terracini of a Jewish family which has produced a number of notables like the leftist leader and publicist and the scholar in comparative literature (all brothers). Terracini, who has been professor at the University of Turin, is a specialist in analytic geometry (in the tradition of the illustrious Cremona).

FRANCE

In France, mathematics has had a glorious following, but as is well-known, the arts and humanistic subjects have been far better cultivated; and as the saying goes *Wie es sich christelt so jüdelt sich es* is true here. In Italy, we found the Jews outstripping the Italians. In France, the Jewish mathematicians take their place, more in keeping with our expectations.

Georges-Henri Halphen (1844-1889) although not one of the more original minds, and never divorcing himself from his military interests (as an artillery captain in the Franco-Prussian War of 1870, he was decorated) succeeded in becoming one of the most influential mathematicians in Europe and was even a member of the French Academy of Science, in addition to winning honors for his mathematical articles from German learned societies as well. Making allowance for his brief life, he has certainly made a mark for himself.

Probably one of the most recognized mathematicians in France is Jacques Hadamard (1865-   ) who eventually became professor of mathematics at the University of Paris, but lectured in the United States during the Nazi upheavals in Europe. When we consider that this man who looked like an East European rabbi with an expression of tragedy, perhaps the reflection of his feelings during the persecution of his brother-in-law Alfred Dreyfus, had discovered and formulated important theorems in regard to determinants, upon which is based the modern treatment of integral functions, it is no wonder that the University of Goettingen, the citadel of mathematics, bestowed an honorary degree on him. The general theory of functions, calculus of variation, and the field which Georg Cantor had opened up, viz. infinite series, were also his favorite "pastimes". Hadamard took time off nevertheless to devote his energies to Jewish causes.

Some of the lesser known figures are Paul Emile Appell (1855-1930) who was at one time President of the French Mathematical Society, Isaac Auguste Blum (1812-1877) Eugene Cahen (1865-   ) while André Weil (1906-   ) who was professor at the University of Strassburg and is now teaching at the University of Chicago, promises to take his place with Halphen and Hadamard. His work on topological groups and his *Foundations of Algebraic Geometry* have won recognition in mathematical circles throughout the world.

[95]

Among the younger mathematicians attached to French universities, mainly as professors, are S. Mandelbrojt (originally from Poland), J. Frenkel, Paul Lévy, Jacques Lévy-Bruhl and H. Lewy.

UNITED STATES

It is noteworthy that in the United States, there is hardly a university of some standing which does not count at least one Jewish professor of mathematics or even head of the department. Thus at Columbia there are Edward Kasner and Joseph F. Ritt; in Princeton we find the noted topologist, Solomon Lefschetz and also Solomon Bochner, formerly lecturer at Munich; at Harvard, O. Zarisky and Richard von Mises are teaching in different schools; Yale has its N. Jacobson, and Columbia, besides Kasner, counts S. Eilenberg. Hans Lewy and A. Seidenberg are at the University of California. At the University of Chicago, we have I. Kaplansky and the algebraist, A. A. Albert as professors. J. S. Cohen is at the University of Pennsylvania. P. Erdös teaches at Syracuse University; Otto Szasz is a well-known mathematician at the University of Cincinnati; Hans Samelson at the University of Michigan, while at Brown University, which has a strong mathematical department, there are with J. D. Tamarkin, deceased, W. Prager, M. H. Heins and H. Federer; at the Massachusetts Institute of Technology, there are several Jewish mathematicians like Norbert Wiener, Withold Hurewicz, who taught in Holland, before coming to this country, both well-known in their respective specialties; N. Levinson, I. S. Cohen, S. D. Zeldin and others; Johns Hopkins has had a Jewish tradition beginning with the celebrated James Joseph Sylvester, who was succeeded by Fabian Franklin, while at present, we find Abraham Cohen, Aurel Wintner, and Leonard M. Blumenthal carrying on the work; Jacob D. Tamarkin was at the time of his death professor at Brown University; at Cornell, Wallie Abraham Hurwitz has made an enviable reputation for himself nor should we forget M. Kac at Cornell; the late Emmy Noether, who has been mentioned earlier was associated with Bryn Mawr; at the University of North Carolina, A. T. Brauer occupies a prominent place; J. B. Rosenbach, a successful text-book writer, is professor at Carnegie Institute of Technology, and at Duke, Leonard Carlitz occupies the chair in mathematics; at the University of Pennsylvania, Isaac J. Schwatt has served as professor for many years until his retirement, and is I believe succeeded by J. A. Shohat; at the University of Minnesota we find S. E. Warschawski; Louis L. Silverman is head of the department at Dartmouth, and Henry Blumberg is professor at Ohio State University; while at Antioch College, Max Astrachan is head of the department; at Texas University, Hyman J. Ettlinger is professor; and at Oklahoma University, we find Nathan A. Court in the same capacity; R. J. Levit holds a like position at the University of Georgia.

Furthermore there are Benjamin A. Bernstein at the University of California, L. W. Cohen at Kentucky, Jekutiel Ginsburg at Yeshivah College, Tobias Dantzig at Maryland University, M. G. Gaga at Nebraska University; Arthur Rosenthal, formerly of Munich and Heidelberg, is now head of the department at Purdue University; B. Z. Linfield at the University of Virginia; M. Salkover is at the University of Cincinnati; H. L. Slobin at the University of New Hampshire; E. F. S. Weinberg, head of the department at Rollins College; M. Marden is at the University of Wisconsin (in Milwaukee) and at least a score of others who are professors of mathematics in American universities.

In Canadian universities, Jewish mathematicians are not as plentiful but L. Infeld at the University of Toronto and I. Halperin at Queens, in Kingston have made a reputation beyond the Canadian border. Leopold Infeld, in fact, has a place in the section on mathematical physics as a collaborator of Einstein.

Thanks to the exodus from Germany, Central and South America now have their quota of eminent Jewish mathematicians, which means that they nilly-willy are the disseminators of the Science throughout the Western hemisphere, but such countries as Egypt, Turkey, India, and Japan have also benefited to some extent by the Brown Plague. Thus the dictum "One man's meat is another man's poison" may here be adapted to read "the Brown beast's poison becomes the normal man's meat", or the stones which the Nazi masons have rejected have become a magnificent edifice detracting from the erstwhile grandeur which was German mathematics.

RUSSIA AND THE REST OF EUROPE

In Russia, even during the Czarist regime, a few Jews succeeded in attaining prominence in mathematics, naturally paying the price of their credal affiliations. In Soviet Russia, it was not necessary to become baptized in order to advance professionally or professorially, hence some of the foremost mathematicians in USSR are of Jewish parentage. We do not hear much about them because of linguistic as well as political barriers, but the names of Sergey Bernshteyn, who is professor at Leningrad, P. S. Uryssohn, who is professor at Moscow University, Landau, Frenkel, P. B. Frumkin, E. A. Vainrib, G. B. Spivak, G. Y. Liubarsky and Y. L. Rabinovitch are not the only ones of Jewish origin that are outstanding in this field. In the branch known as topology, L. Lusternik (reported to have been killed during the Nazi War) and L. Shnirelman have been regarded as original exponents.

Poland has been, or should have been indebted to the efforts of Samuel Dikstein, Natanson, both of Warsaw and both editors of journals; H. D. Steinhaus, who was the Dean of the mathematical Faculty, at the University of Lwów, and the late Alfred Rosenblatt who taught at Cracow before he emigrated to Lima, Peru, before the German occupation.

Even Roumania numbered a few well-known mathematicians, like David Emanuel and Valcovici, Professors at Bucharest; and in Hungary, Julius König and R. Eötvös, as well as Izidor Fröhlich were editors of mathematical journals. At the present time, Leopold Feier is recognized internationally as a mathematician of considerable achievement.

Several Jews in Holland made distinct contributions to the science, particularly Lobato and Teixeira de Mattos, the latter of a distinguished Portuguese family that settled in Holland after the ban against Jews in their native country. Latterly, the names of D. Van Danzig and Hans Freudenthal (Utrecht) have loomed up on the mathematical horizon.

It would take altogether too much space to set forth the attainments of Jewish mathematicians in Czechoslovakia, in Jugoslavia, and one or two other countries in Europe, but the work of Harald Bohr in Denmark deserves special mention.

Harald Bohr (1887-   ) younger brother of the more famous Niels Bohr, like him, is a professor at the University of Copenhagen, and has been more popular as a football champion in Denmark than as a mathematician; nevertheless his contributions to harmonic analysis and the Fourier series ("Analytic almost Periodic Functions") have placed him among the foremost of modern mathematicians. Harald Bohr maintains some contact with the Hebrew University.

JEWS AS FOUNDERS AND EDITORS OF MATHEMATICAL PERIODICALS*

It is really difficult to know where to begin in enumerating the most important mathematical periodicals which were edited by Jews. The *Journal für die reine und angewandte Mathematik* was for a long time edited by K. W. Borchardt. J. L. Fuchs was editor and, at a later period, Moritz Cantor was co-editor of the *Zeitschrift für Mathematik und Physik*. The latter also founded the *Abhandlungen zur Geschichte der mathematischen Wissenschaften*, was co-editor, from 1859 to 1900, of the *Zeitschrift für Mathematik und Physik,* and was among the founders of the *Jahresbericht der deutschen Mathematiker-*

*The present tense is used, in order to simplify matters. Naturally all the editing of German periodicals by Jews has been in the past . . .

Vereinigung, which later came in the hands of L. Bieberbach, a non-Jew with a vengeance! Otto Blumenthal and G. Faber. Einstein is co-director of the *Mathematische Annalen,* which is edited by Otto Blumenthal. L. Lichtenstein, who originally came from Poland, not only edits the *Jahrbuch über die Fortschritte der Mathematik* but also the *Mathematische Zeitschrift,* of which I. Schur was co-editor. H. Hahn is co-editor of the *Monatshefte für Mathematik und Physik.* Hermann Blumenberg edits the *Allgemeine Vermessungs-Nachrichten,* and von Mises (whose mark of nobility is not disproof of his Jewishness) directs the *Zeitschrift für angewandte Mathematik und Mechanik.* F. Riesz is an editor of the *Acta Mathematica Universitatis Francisco Josephinae,* and Julius Schuster is director of the *Archiv für Geschichte der Mathematik der Naturwissenschaften und der Technik.*

The versatile Ludwig Grossmann founded both the *Mathematisch-physikalische Zeitschrift* and *Die Controle,* an economic review. (See Wininger's *Grosse Jüdische National-Biographie*). On the other hand, Felix Klein, one of the founders of the *Mathematische Annalen,* although apparently regarded as a Jew by the *Jewish Encyclopedia,* was, I am assured indirectly by his Jewish colleagues in Goettingen, of non-Semitic stock.

In Italy, where the most distinguished mathematicians have recently been Jews (V. Volterra, T. Levi-Civita, C. Segre, Gino Loria, and F. Enriques, all in the line of the illustrious Luigi Cremona, the *ne plus ultra* geometrician of his day) the *Annali di Mathematica* has the second and third of the group for editors; the fourth, Gino Loria, is director of the *Bollettino di Bibliografia e Storia delle Scienze Mathematiche*; while the *Periodico di Mathematiche* is being co-directed by Enriques.

Poland, the majority of whose mathematicians are Jews, has to thank Samuel Dikstein for a number of mathematical periodicals and other serials, inaugurated by this versatile and energetic scientist. Not only has he founded, together with Wladyslaw Natanson, the *Prace Matematyczno-Fizyczne,* but has further established the *Wiadomosci Matematyczno-Fizyca,* not to mention his part in editing the large Polish general encyclopedia, *Wielka Encyklopedja Powszechna,* and other publications. It is rumored, too, that Waclaw Sierpinski, co-editor of the *Fundamenta Mathematicae,* is partly Jewish. In Lwów, the *Studia Mathematica* between 1929-1939, until Poland was invaded, had as its editors Stefan Banach and Hugo Steinhaus.

In Hungary, there are very few outstanding mathematicians who are not Jews, the most illustrious of them being Julius König who, together with R. Eötvös, founded the *Mathematische und naturwissenschaftliche Berichte aus Ungarn.* Another mathematician of note is Izidor Fröhlich, a member of the Hungarian Academy, who edits the *Mathematikai es Termeszettudomanyi Ertesitö* ("Mathematical and Physical Index").

In Copenhagen, Harald Bohr, the younger brother of Niels Bohr, (q. v. in the sections on "Physics" and "The Jews and the Nobel Prize"), is co-editor of *Matematisk Tidsskrift.*

France has comparatively fewer Jewish mathematicians than other countries of like culture, and I know of only one Jewish founder of a mathematical periodical in France, and that is Isaac Auguste Blum, who directed the *Bulletin Polytechnique,* from 1844 till his death in 1877, and edited his daily (?) journal *La Science,* which was devoted mainly to mathematics. Yet Paul Levy, as president of the French Mathematical Society, would naturally *ex officio* take a hand in the *Bulletin de la Société Mathématique de France.*

In Holland, two or three Jews, but particularly Teixeira de Mattos (from Portugal) have been prominent in connection with publications like the *Révue Semestrielle des Publications Mathématiques,* but so far as I could discover, they were not officially known as editors.

In America, J. J. Sylvester founded the *American Journal of Mathematics* in 1878 which was, I believe, the first mathematical periodical of any importance to be published in this country, while the lesser B. F. Finkel (who, judging by the name, is of Semitic descent), was the organizer, in 1894, of the *American Mathematical Monthly*. E. Kasner is an editor of the *Transactions of the American Mathematical Society;* A. Dresden is co-editor of the *Bulletin of the American Mathematical Society,* W. A. Hurwitz was editor of the *American Mathematical Monthly,* 1919-1922, and of the *Bulletin of the American Mathematical Society,* 1921-1924; while Abraham Cohen is an editor of the *American Journal of Mathematics;* R. Brauer is editor of the *American Journal of Mathematics* and Nathan Jacobson is one of the editors of the *Bulletin of the American Mathematical Society,* while at Duke, Leonard Carlitz edits the *Duke Mathematical Journal.* The *Transactions of the American Mathematical Society* are edited by Antoni Zygmund and S. Lefschetz edits the *Annals of Mathematics.* W. Prager is managing editor of the *Quarterly of Applied Mathematics* and J. Ginsburg founded the quarterly *Scripta Mathematica.*

Naturally if we were to include associate editors, the list would be much longer. Thus, we see how the Jews in America have carried on the traditional activity in this branch of science. Here, at any rate, they have advanced beyond the mark of their British brethren. Certainly the list is far from exhaustive, but we must proceed to other fields.

Considering the mathematical strength of the Jews, it is small wonder that the *Scripta Mathematica et Physica* (volume I) of the Hebrew University and Library of Jerusalem (edited by Albert Einstein) shows an excellence which has probably never been paralleled; for here are brought together a galaxy of men, each of whose writings would do honor to any publication; and the fact that perhaps none of them has written his paper originally in Hebrew does not invalidate the national status of the volume, especially as each of the papers appears in Hebrew translation. The collection of *Scripta* is a unique phenomenon because of the international canopy which overspreads a group of scientists with a like national subconsciousness, dormant though it may have been for a generation.

Jews and the Internationality of Mathematics

We have come to the end of this section, and if there is still the question open to what extent modern mathematics has been influenced by Jewish investigators, the reason can only be that so many factors are apt to becloud the issue, personal, philosophical or psychological bias being not the least.

Aside from the original work of men like Jacobi, Georg Cantor, Kronecker, Cremona, Volterra, Levi-Civita and a score of others, there is to be recorded their international *élan* in welding the science, their vision, their disinclination to keep it within national or local bounds.

Cantor was particularly active in separating the German mathematicians from the general group of naturalists and physicists, and became chairman of the first convention which finally took place in 1890. But that was not sufficient. Cantor still felt that the German conclave was too narrow. He wanted mathematics to be *free* from the shackles of any foregone conclusions or clique, and had formulated plans of a far-reaching nature, but they were in advance of the time. It was only in 1897 that the first International Congress of Mathematics took place in Zürich; and it is interesting as well as instructive to note who the mathematicians were that ranged themselves with Cantor, who could perceive the value of his theories, despite the fact that little was being made of them in the "halls of the mighty". We find here the names of Hurwitz, Minkowski and Hadamard.[8] In other words, Jews in France as well as in Germany sensed the significance of the transfinite series. One might almost say that although Kronecker was the marring exception, the concept of the infinite, which Spinoza had made the foundation of his philosophy, was the guiding star or pillar of fire for Jewish mathematicians. Not only the men mentioned but others are to be included in the taking of sides. Felix Bernstein supplied an important proof which smoothed Cantor's path. Schoenflies, Haussdorff and others, too, soon took up the cudgels, and although there were many non-Jews too who ranged themselves with Cantor, while Julius König, a Jew took it upon himself to refute Cantor at one of the Congresses, which drew the latter's ire to such a pitch that he wittily exclaimed that it was not the King that he suspected so much as the Minister (i. e., Kronecker's minister) there is some indication, at least, that Jewish mathematicians were on the alert to see the originality of Cantor's work in the possibilities especially that the system opened up. Certainly they were not considering Cantor's origin, even if that were at all known to them. It was their progressiveness that drew them close to him.

Philosophy of Mathematics

A list of illustrious names may be drawn up here of Jewish philosophers who dealt with this realm—Otto Liebmann's important paper on the "Philosophical Value of Mathematical Natural Science" made some stir about 25 years ago. Hermann Cohen's little book on the *Principle of Infinitesimal Methods* was apparently avidly read by William James, to judge from his notations and underscorings, and was reviewed by G. Cantor, but it had been recognized also in general as a penetrating study. Gaston Samuel Milhaud who taught mathematics at Montpellier, in several works, considered most painstakingly the foundations of mathematics, while his countryman Léon Brunschvicg treated the étapes of mathematical philosophy in his masterly way. It is scarcely known that Edmund Husserl, the founder of the most important philosophical school of the past generation—phenomenalism—made his debut as a lecturer in Halle with a dissertation "on the concept of Number", and one of his early works was entitled *Die Philosophie der Arithmetik*.

Among the leading symbolic logicians in America are Ernest Nagel, Professor at Columbia, Alfred Tarski, formerly of the University of Warsaw, and now at the University of California, and Henry Sheffer, Professor at Harvard.

Probably the chief mathematical philosopher today is Hans Reichenbach (1891-   ) who was Professor at the University of Berlin, but with the accession of Hitler in 1933, left for Turkey where he taught at Istanbul until 1938, when he received a call from the University of California at Los Angeles. He has written extensively in German on topics such as probability, natural philosophy, the space-time relationship, and relativity. In English there appeared several volumes, among which *Experience and Prediction* is the best known.

III

ASTRONOMY AND METEOROLOGY

Astronomy is associated with mathematics on the one hand, and with mechanics or dynamics, on the other. It is not quite as abstract as the former and not as concrete as the latter. For mathematical research, only paper and pencil are required. To observe the stellar bodies more than a bright night is needed. Astronomy was relatively late in developing for lack of telescopes and other paraphernalia. Perhaps that is one reason why Jews could not have been among the pioneers of the science, but it does not fully explain why the number of celebrated mathematicians by far exceeds the number of distinguished astronomers among the Jews.

Astronomy, as a matter of fact, because of the very remoteness of its objects and their romantic associations attracted scores of rabbis and Jewish scholars, so that a few hundred might be listed of those who dabbled in astronomy, but in the first place, they were too deeply rooted in Talmudical studies to specialize even to the extent of acquiring the propaedeutics of methodology; and then, too, their training along mathematico-physical lines was limited, with the result that at most they could turn out popular presentations in Hebrew or scattered speculations which showed an interest in the subject. Of these, Davis Gans and Joseph Delmedigo were the most outstanding, largely because of their friendship and correspondence with the pioneers.

In general, however, it is small wonder that Jewish astronomers were sooner recognized than Jewish mathematicians. Astronomy was bound up with the needs of Jewish religion, inasmuch as problems of the calendar, as Neugebauer, the foremost historian of ancient mathematics and astronomy contends, directed the first steps in astronomy. It was not only the calendar as such; such matters as the start and close of the Sabbath and festivals or the blessing of the new moon prodded some of the learned Jews centuries ago to become preoccupied with the stars and the moon.

At the present time, Millas Vallicrosa, of the University of Barcelona (a non-Jew) is preparing an edition of Abraham Ibn Ezra's astronomical treatise which he believes was originally written in Latin, in 1154. Prof. Millas Vallicrosa has already written two articles on this remarkable work by a man who was a great poet, a philosopher, a Biblical commentator of acute powers, and a globe trotter who even visited England, at a time when travel was beset by all sorts of hazards; and wherever he set foot, he seemed to be at home, making his influence felt, in learned circles.

In the current issue of *Isis* (February 1949) the eminent mediaevalist, Lynn Thorndike, in an article entitled "More Abrahamismus" writes, "It seems strange that an author whose astrological treatises later so popular in Latin translation, who travelled in Christian Europe and was in close relation with Christian scholars, and himself put forth astronomical works in Latin should have had to wait for over a century for the Latin translation of his numerous astrological tracts".

The distinguished writer apparently does not know of Ibn Ezra's epigram in Hebrew, about his fate, to the effect that if he were to begin selling candles, the sun would shine forever, and if he were to deal in shrouds no one would die. Ibn Ezra was the vagabond genius. Had he settled somewhere and specialized in astronomy, his lot might have been different.

Of the older Jewish astronomers, men like Isaac Ibn Said and Abraham Zacuto became well-known, the latter even teaching at the University of Salamanca. His part in the discovery of America has already been dwelt on in the Introduction, where such names as Joseph Vecinho and Pedro Nuñes, "the glory of Portugal", have also been mentioned.

It cannot be said that the Jews have produced a Copernicus, a Kepler, a Newton, or a Tycho Brahe; and although some apologists, in their zeal, will seize on the fact that both Tycho Brahe and Kepler corresponded with David Gans, or that Galileo knew a Marrano poet, it is not till the advent of William Herschel that the Jewish contribution takes on a gigantic proportion. But how could it be otherwise? The Jews were secluded in their ghetto. The Talmud was their mental fare. The universities were closed to them. Observatories, even the most primitive, were non-existent for them. They could indeed be star-gazers, but it required more to become an astronomer.

William Herschel (1738-1822), the young musician who came from Hanover, Germany, and settled in England as a part-time organist, while studying astronomy, achieved the impossible except for a genius such as he was, and became the greatest astronomer of his century. Together with his sister he charted the sky, discovered planets, constructed his own telescope on a large scale, and in a practical way, it may be said that no astronomer, not even the great pioneers who gave a new turn to science, compared with him.

Of him, Brodetsky writes "There can be no doubt that William Herschel was of Jewish origin. Whether we have any right to claim him as in any way belonging to us is a different matter. His connection with the Jewish people or anything that can be called Jewish was absolutely zero."[9]

The truth of the matter is that we do not consult the words or the acts of the scientists, in this regard, but take cognizance of their origin. Once we are aware that Herschel's parents were both Jewish, we have every right to claim him as our own, for without his heredity, all the telescopes in the world and all the royal favors which were lavished on him would not have made of him an acceptable astronomer.

If we were to drop every Jewish scientist who left his people, or who took no interest in their weal and woe, then we should make a sorry showing in the intellectual sphere. That scientists, devoting their life in quest of truth, should deny their heritage, when faced with the dilemma of pursuing an academic career or turning their back on their ancestors, is a telling commentary. In some cases, even when it was not necessary to forswear their antecedents, the snobbish attitude still prevailed. The *reductio ad absurdum* of this perverseness was evinced in the lawsuit of Karl Landsteiner, a Nobel Prize man, against the publishers of a Jewish *Who's Who,* wherein a great scientist revealed himself a small man, and unbelievably naïve; for the *cause célèbre* only served to advertise the very fact which he was anxious to conceal.

In general, scientists claim to be international, but their achievement redounds to the credit of their native or adopted country, but why should their racial origin be totally ignored?

If a Herschel ("a young deer") ruled in modern astronomy, a "bear" played a prominent part, on a smaller scale; for Wilhelm Beer (1797-1850), brother of the famous composer Meyerbeer, after service in the army and success in commercial pursuits, devoted himself entirely to observing the course of the stars in a privately built and equipped observatory. Together with another astronomer he charted the moon so carefully that the joint work received the Lalland prize from the French Academy. He may be regarded as the selenograph, *par excellence,* but his observations of Mars were also well received. For a businessman and banker to have become an astronomer of note and to have ended his days as a member of the Upper House in Prussia was an achievement which academic astronomers cannot boast of.

Another Jew made a thorough study of the moon. This time it was the Viennese, Maurice Loewy (1833-1907) who arrived in Paris while quite a young man and succeeded in becoming the Director of the Paris Observatory as well as a member of the *Académie des Sciences*. If Loewy had done nothing else than to invent the bi-partite telescope, which has been such a boon to astronomers, because while one half is fixed, the other rotates and can be so adjusted as to catch a beam of light from the stellar body, he would have deserved great recognition, but the instrument called the equatorial conde, which he devised in collaboration with Puiseux, aside from his observations and cataloguing of numerous asteroids, brought him in the forefront of nineteenth-century astronomers.

Painting and astronomy are scarcely related, yet H. Goldschmidt (1802-1866) like Beer, gave up his previous vocation and turned astronomer, discovering many of the minor asteroids and planets. Goldschmidt was awarded the Lalland prize of the Académie des Sciences in Paris and also the Gold Medal of the Astronomical Society in London.

In Russia, Ilia S. Abelman (1866-1898) might have shed lustre upon Russian astronomy, if he were given the opportunity such as his confrères had had in Engand or France. He was not quite 32 when he died, yet his texts and articles have become well known.

We know little about the Jewish astronomers in U.S.S.R., but occasionally a news item in connection with awards reveals a Jewish name. Thus in March, 1950, Grigory Sheyn was the recipient of 200,000 rubles for discovering the heavy isotopes of carbon in the atmosphere of a number of stars. Sheyn is the Director of the Crimean Astro-Physical Observatory.

In Poland, the versatile Khayim Zelik Slonimsky, famous as the editor of *Hatsefirah* (Hebrew Weekly) was, in addition, a mathematician and amateur astronomer, who nevertheless was highly regarded by scientists of his day.

In England, in addition to the renowned Herschel, mention must be made of Sir Arthur Schuster, who, although primarily a physicist, as we shall see later, directed several solar expeditions, particularly the Eclipse expedition to Siam in 1875, and Lord Burnham *i.e.*, *Edward Lawson* (*né* Levy) who, outside of his newspaper ventures, devoted much time in observatories.

France has had its native Jewish astronomers like Armand Lambert, who has distinguished himself through numerous researches.

Italy, with its Azeglio Bemporad in Catania, and Vittorio Boccara, who was the director of the meteorological observatory at Leghorn, and others, reminds us only faintly of its Jewish stronghold in mathematics.

As usual, however, it is in Germany that Jewish names appear most frequently in connection with astronomy, even though in order to reach their goal, they have severed their ties with their people. Karl Schwarzschild (1873-1916) stands out as one of the foremost mathematicians and astronomers of the past generation, and one whose researches on space and gravitation helped greatly to intrench Einstein's theory of relativity. Fritz Cohn (1866-1922), who was director of the Astronomical Institute in Berlin, Berthold Cohn (1870-1930) who taught many years at Strassburg, Eugen Goldstein of the Babelsberg Observatory and Friedrich S. Archenhold, whose devices in photographing celestial bodies brought him considerable attention, as well as Adolf Marcuse, who had undertaken expeditions for the purpose of astronomical observations in various countries, are among the leading names, although they by no means exhaust the list of able astronomers in Germany.

We can scarcely omit, e. g. a man like E. W. Freundlich (1885-   ) who was Director of the Potsdam Einstein Institute until 1933, when he took up a similar post in Istanbul,

Turkey. In 1937, he returned to Europe and settled in Prague. We have yet to discover what has become of him since. His chief work was an examination of the law of gravitation and a thoroughgoing survey of the relativity theory.

Geodesy and meteorology, which are closely related to astronomy, claim such men as Robert Rubensen, the chief meteorologist at the University of Upsala, in Sweden; V. Boccara at Leghorn, and perhaps the foremost of them all, Georg Lachmann of the Meteorological Institute in Berlin. A geodetist of a high order was Moritz Low (1841-1900) of the Prussian Geodetic Institute in Berlin.

The great contribution of Albert A. Michelson to astrophysics both by the construction of the giant interferometer and his measurement of the velocity of light should not be omitted from a survey like this, although his work will be taken up in its proper sphere, viz., experimental physics.

We have not nearly so many Jewish astronomers in the United States as mathematicians, which is understandable because there are comparatively few astronomers altogether, but even proportionately the Jews have not measured up to their usual stature.

Frank Schlesinger (1871-1943), who served, in turn, as director of the Allegheny and Yale University Observatories, is the most distinguished name we can find in the United States among Jewish astronomers. Not only was he President of the American Astronomical Society but headed, at one time, the International Astronomical Union. Among his awards were the Valz prize of the French Académie des Sciences and the Gold Medal of the Royal Astronomical Society. He was also an officer of the French Legion of Honor. Paul S. Epstein, born in Poland and trained in Russia, where he taught for some time, is professor of physics at the California Institute of Technology but his study of the composition of the moon entitles him to a place with the astronomers. One of the very few women astronomers is Sophia H. Levy of the University of California, where she is professor of theoretical astronomy.

Finally mention must be made of Louis Berman's discovery at the Lick Observatory of new types of stars.

IV

PHYSICS

The farther we get from the abstract and semi-abstract, the fewer Jews we find in the scientific realm prior to about a century ago. Not only the Jew-baiter but the sympathetic observer would conclude that the Jews in physics "are far to seek"; and naturally we would expect the usual apologetic tone of Jewish publicists in explaining the deficiency. But time has shown that there was no deficiency. Like the human child who takes longer to develop than the animal, the Jew needed centuries to mature along these lines, and once he was emancipated and could take part in the general growth of experimental procedure, he could more than hold his own, and, as we shall see later, the two greatest epics in modern physics, the establishment of the theory of relativity and the rise of nuclear physics, including the construction of the atom bomb were largely the work of Jewish physicists.

Development of Electricity

Prior to relativity, the most fruitful field was electricity; and it is here that we find a demi-Jewish pioneer in the person of Heinrich Hertz[10], whose genius was cut short at the age of 37, but in that space of life he succeeded in supplying the experimental proof of Maxwell's electro-magnetic theory, which was the first step toward the development of wireless telegraphy as well as radio, establishing once and for all the identity of light and electro-magnetic waves, a feat which won for him the admiration of men like Helmholtz, who wrote a preface to his collected works (published posthumously) and Lord Kelvin, who wrote the *Foreword* to the English translation of Hertz's chief work, while Sir Oliver Lodge delivered the Memorial Lecture in honor of the man who, in an unwitting contest, if that is not just a tale, had scored first in a series of experiments which Lodge was conducting, unbeknown to Hertz. Hertz's production and measurement of the electromagnetic waves has led to the development of radar, and had far-reaching consequences in various directions. Thus the Englishman, Faraday, the Scotsman, Maxwell, and the German half-Jew, Hertz, the Italians Galvani and Volta, the Swede Oersted, the Frenchman, Ampère, each had his share in the progress of electrical science during the early days of its history.

Hertz in his youth was also a student of languages. He could recite Homer in Greek, and had even taken up Arabic and Sanskrit, but his side-stepping Hebrew is symptomatic for a man who may have owed his mental gifts to the people which was identified with Hebrew.

A man who is not so well known as Hertz, but who also gave great impetus to the then nascent field of electricity, even before Hertz took to it, was Peter Theophil Riess (1805-1883) who was primarily an experimentalist, and his work on induction and friction became classical. To his great credit it must be said that he steadfastly refused to change his religion in order to be elected to the Prussian Academy of Science. Eventually, on his induction into this august and learned society, the great Alexander von Humboldt remarked on this occasion that the "event was the first step of atonement for the twenty-five-year-old injustice which the Prussian Jews had to endure".

Just as Hertz was the father of the radio through his electrical discoveries, so another Jew could be called the father of the telephone, for it was Phillip Reis who also contributed significantly to the advance of electricity by managing, in 1863, to translate melodies into electrical waves which afterwards were given out in tones again. Had he then been able to use the direct instead of only the alternating current, the human voice, which was reproduced too nasally for the purpose, would have had that quality required for transmission at a distance. Nevertheless it was Reis's principle which later became the basis of the telephone.

Eugen Goldstein (1850-1930), who looked like a good-humored rabbi, was also a pioneer in the field, principally in connection with the deflection and reflection of cathode rays, but his prologue part in the atom drama will be adverted to in the section on the atom. The fact that the celebrated Helmholtz was his sponsor and that Goldstein was the physicist at the Berlin Observatory should place him at once as a major scientist.

Emil Warburg (1846-1931), the father of the Nobel Prize laureate Otto Warburg, as head of the Charlottenburg Physico-Technical Institute, which was a Department of the University of Berlin, engaged in miscellaneous researches, such as the kinetic theory of gases and galvanic polarization; but electricity, again, was the nucleus—which led him to examine electric currents in gases and the process of electrolysis. His textbook in experimental physics passed into more than 25 editions, and his monograph on the thermal unit is still considered a standard work.

Leo Graetz (1856-1942), the son of the famous historian, Heinrich Graetz, is known for his many contributions in various fields, but particularly for having devised the bridge connection of rectifiers (*Graetz-Schaltung*) and his method of converting alternating into direct currents. On a lower level, his incandescent *Grätzin* light has kept his name before the public. Of his German work on electricity and its applications, about 25 editions have appeared in various languages, and his textbook on physics is highly regarded throughout the world.

Speaking of Graetz, our mind turns to another son of a famous Jew, Daniel Khvolson, the orientalist in St. Petersburg, who despite his conversion was a warm friend of his people. His son, Orest D. Khvolson, was one of the leading physicists in Russia, and it is strange that none of the half-dozen Jewish encyclopedias mention him.

Of about the same period was the Italian physicist, Moise Ascoli (1857-1921) professor at Rome. Magnetism in relation to electricity occupied his chief attention, in addition to the problems of elasticity of certain metals, especially iron.

Electrical charge through gases was the study of Arthur Schuster (1851-1934), although spectroscopy, terrestrial magnetism, and meteorology were his stamping grounds also. In general, Sir Arthur was an organizer of extraordinary ability, as was his father, a Frankfort banker, and his brothers. The name Arthur Schuster has already come up in our section on astronomy; and in England, he was held in great esteem because of his educational promotion.

One of the foremost authorities on electricity was Max Abraham (1875-1922) Professor of physics at the University of Munich. His book on the subject became a standard work having been translated into English, French, and other languages. Radiation was a specialty of his too and even the foundations of geometry were grist to his mill, probably at the time he taught at Milan.

In discussing electricity, one could also find a niche for the Nobel Prize man, Henri Moissan, if only for his spectacular electric furnace and his more theoretical inquiries into the nature of electricity, but his real place is in chemistry. Moissan is not generally known to have been Jewish or half-Jewish, but we have this information on the authority of Sir Arthur Schuster, who should be a reliable source in this connection.

But if Moissan was not a full-blooded Jew, his compatriot, Gabriel Lippmann (1842-1919) equally famous and also a Nobel Prize man, may be added to our galaxy. Lippmann was professor of mathematical physics at the Sorbonne, and later became a member of the Académie des Sciences. He was a pioneer in the then new field of electrocapillarity, although the Nobel Prize was awarded him in 1908 for his devising the process of color photography, which would imply, of course, that he was an authority on optics. His courses at the Sorbonne were among the most popular in that Institution, and his textbooks on thermodynamics and light were standard works in France for a long time.

Among electrical engineers (although engineering in all its departments will have to be treated in a separate chapter) there was probably none greater than Charles Proteus Steinmetz (1865-1923) who for all his denials, on the assumption that the Jews were a religious sect, must be added to the minority which has given so much to the majority. Steinmetz, who, in addition to his tasks as chief consulting engineer of the General Electric Company, where he found himself nicknamed the "Electrical Wizard", served as professor of electrophysics at Union University in Schenectady was just about to be deported when he arrived in the United States, in 1889, on the ground of his deformity.

An engineer and specialist along the same lines or, rather, high voltage electricity, is Reinhold Ruedenberg (1883-   ) who until the Nazi regime had been Professor at the Technological Institute in Berlin—Charlottenburg, and at present is head of the Department of Electrical Engineering at Harvard University. Ruedenberg, who is the son-in-law of the famous mathematician, Minkowski, has invented the electronic microscope and has written a number of works on applied electricity.

Felix Ehrenhaft (1879-   ) also belongs to the inventive physicists, although many of his projects seemed altogether too fantastic to his colleagues. In fact I was persuaded to delete the paragraph or two on him in this survey; and only after reflecting on the fact that he could not have risen to a professorship in the University of Vienna if he were not a physicist of high merit, did I decide to give him his place here.

Ehrenhaft was an experimentalist primarily, and his researches on the Brownian movements in the molecules of gases, as well as on the transportation of micro-particles through light, were carried on in the University of Vienna years ago. After the annexation of Austria, Ehrenhaft came to the United States, where he began to elaborate some spectacular projects which caused many of his colleagues to suspect that he was exaggerating his potentialities, but there is no denying that he did devise some very useful laboratory apparatus. It is probably due to the scornful attitude of his colleagues here that he returned to Vienna in 1947.

James Franck (1882-   ) will receive his proper place in the section on atomic physics, but he could well be discussed under several different rubrics. One of the foremost experimentalists of our time, he was the youngest Nobel Prize Laureate in the sciences, at any rate, and became Professor at the University of Berlin at the age of 36.

His chief work was done at the University of Goettingen, where he worked with Gustav Hertz on phenomena caused by collisions between the electron and the atom. For a time he was guest professor at the University of Copenhagen, then accepted a call to Johns Hopkins and finally joining the department of chemistry.

In Italy, Alessandro Artom (1867-1927) made a great contribution toward the development of telegraphy by using circular or elliptically polarized waves, thus preventing the possibility of interception—a matter of tremendous military importance. He also was the inventor of various electrical devices, among them an instrument to locate direction in the air. His investigation of the electrical properties of the diamond and other substances added to his fame in the early part of the present century.

Quantum and Mathematical Physics

In Max Bernhard Weinstein (born 1852) the modern theory of thermodynamics had an exponent of great scope. In his four large volumes (1901-1908) on the subject, he treated kinetics of gases and thermodynamics, as well as electrolysis and magnetism, electrochemistry and thermo-electricity on a comprehensive scale, but his writings on relativity and mathematical physics give him high rank in this field too. Mathematical physics always slants toward philosophical problems, and Weinstein concerned himself with such too, when he taught at the University of Berlin.

Paul Ehrenfest (1880-1933) though born in Vienna settled in Holland where he succeeded H. A. Lorentz, one of the founders of quantum physics at the University of Leyden, to which he and his wife contributed their modest part. Because of his special interests, he might be placed in the circle of Planck, Debye, and Einstein, for whom theoretical physics was the all-absorbing study.

Philipp Franck (1884-   ) who succeeded Albert Einstein at the German University in Prague has been mentioned casually in the section on mathematics, but as a theoretical physicist, verging on philosophy, he has published several works, dealing principally with the question of mechanism and idealism in modern physics. He is at present on the Faculty of Harvard University.

The most important name in theoretical physics today is probably that of Max Born (1882-   ) who, after his dismissal from the faculty of Goettingen in 1933 for the crime of being Jewish, lectured at Cambridge University and is now Professor of Natural Philosophy at the University of Edinburgh.

The dynamics of matter, in particular crystals, the atom, the quantum theory, as well as optics have all received his attention; and he is one of the most brilliant exponents of the relativity theory, so that we shall be obliged to revert to him presently. A productive writer, his many books and articles have received world-wide recognition, passing through several editions.

L. S. Ornstein (1880-1941) Professor of physics and Rektor at one time of the University of Groningen, was a productive author in several departments of physics, including ray measurement, opalescence, crystal magnetism, barometric variations, probability, optics, heat, and entropy. The Institute of Physics of the Hebrew University of Jerusalem owes much to his assistance, and the esteem in which he was held in Holland may be gathered from the virtual demonstration which his funeral in German-occupied Holland during the Nazi War was turned into.

RUSSIA

In Russia there are quite a number of Jewish physicists who have distinguished themselves, but owing to space restrictions, only three of the score or more will be dealt with. The German-trained Leonid I. Mandelshtam (1879-   ) who after teaching at various Russian institutions became Professor of physics at the University of Moscow, is one of the trio. Optics, the dissemination of light, and the radio were his territory. Abraham F. Joffe (1880-   ) is probably the most outstanding applied physicist in USSR and one who organized the scientific institutes in Russia, becoming President of the All-Russian Association of Physicists shortly after the Revolution. An assistant of Roentgen in Munich, he made radiology his central subject of research, but he did not limit himself to any one field. Of a lesser calibre than his American namesake was Vladimir A. Michelson, professor of physics and meteorology at the Agricultural Institute in Moscow about half a century ago.

Relativity

It is very seldom that the world turns a corner in scientific progress, but when it does happen, there is a sequel of events which comes about, stupendous in scope. The Jews were not, for reasons already set forth, privileged to take a hand in such turns until recent years, but the last two turns which came almost on the heels of one another might have had to wait decades, if not a whole century, were those scientists, or their parents, to have been "selected" by the Nazi Stormtrooper Commanders as material for their new crematories.

[119]

Of all the great revolutions in thought that have been thrust upon an unwilling world in the last few centuries, that of relativity seems to have had the most far-reaching effect in intellectual circles. Whatever might be thought of the special theories of relativity, the general doctrine is here to stay. The literature on the subject constitutes a library of many thousands of volumes and articles. There is scarcely a branch of science which has not been affected to some extent by this remarkable innovation, and yet its importance does not lie in its being an innovation but in being proven a fact. Its truth has been demonstrated more than once, and all its traducers put together have not been able to dislodge it from its scientific throne.

It is common knowledge that the man whose name is most intimately associated with the theory of relativity is a Jew of unmistakable Semitic origin and avowedly nationalistic tendencies. Albert Einstein has already taken his place with Galileo, Kepler, Copernicus, and Newton in the forefront of scientific achievement. But it is not generally known that the doctrine of relativity has been reared, so to speak, on a Jewish foundation. It was not Einstein alone who evolved this cosmic theory. He had his predecessors in physics and mathematics, as well as his collaborators, and it may be of significance that the most prominent among them are Jews.

Einstein was only 26 at the time his original paper on the photo-electric effect was published in 1905, but already the hint of Planck's quantum theory had become a gigantic idea with Einstein.

Perhaps the starting-point in the development of the relativity theory was the result of an experiment made possible through the ingenuity, if not genius, of another Jew, also an Albert. It was Albert Abraham Michelson, a German-born Jew, making his domicile in America, who constructed the giant interferometer which was the essential medium in the famous Michelson-Morley experiment. There were, to be sure, other experiments undertaken to ascertain whether there was an ether drift with the earth's motion or not, and possibly Michelson's rather negative result was one of several bits of evidence which were instrumental in overturning the Newtonian system; but it seems as if Einstein was more impressed by the amazing technique of the Michelson-Morley experiment, in 1887, which, by the way, was the earliest, as well as the most accurate, of all these tests.

"Discussion provoked by the negative result of the Michelson-Morley experiment was to result in the theory of relativity. It was typical of Einstein that he regarded this failure to detect motion of the ether past the earth as evidence that no such motion existed. It is also true that the world had to wait for an Einstein to hit on such a simple explanation. The ether had too firm a hold on scientific minds."[11]

Let us not, however, lose sight of Michelson's stature, when viewing a Titan like Einstein. The following evaluation by a former professor of physics at New York University is of significance here.

"Albert A. Michelson stands preëminent among American physicists. No man in any field has worked longer or more conscientiously for the attainment of his ideal. No scientist has ever left his lifework in more complete form. No physicist has ever made more exact measurements, or shown more skill in the design and manipulation of scientific apparatus. No man has been a greater inspiration to younger men. He was the first American recipient of the Nobel Prize in physics, and for a number of years the only other physicists to receive this award in America have been associates or students of his. Those who have known him best have been loudest in his praise."[12]

It is not my purpose to enter into the intricacies of the relativity theory, even were I to flatter myself in supposing that I belong to the proverbial few who are thoroughly conversant with it. It is only as an historian, approaching his subject from a certain angle, namely, the socio-psychological angle, that I am eager to bring up the matter in this brief survey.

It will be sufficient here to quote, from one of the leading physicists in England, Arthur Schuster, also a Jew, a passage written in 1908, and printed in 1911, to show how skeptical the scientific world was about Einstein's theory, until Eddington, in a spectacular expedition (1913) confirmed Einstein's assertion in regard to the curvature of space (1913); and Millikan had completed experiments in 1916 which favored the acceptance of Einstein's equation as to the light quantum, or photon.

Schuster, alluding to Einstein's "imagined law" 'the principle of relativity' has the following to say of it, in 1911.

"The theory appears to have an extraordinary power of fascinating mathematicians, and it will certainly take its place in any critical examination of our scientific beliefs; but we must not let the simplicity of the assumption underlying the principle hide the very slender experimental basis on which it rests at present, and more especially not lose sight of the fact, that it goes much beyond what is proved by Michelson's experiment. In that experiment, the source of light and the mirrors which reflected the light were all connected together by rigid bodies, and their distances depended therefore on the intensity of molecular forces. Einstein's generalisation assumes that the result of the experiment would still be the same, if performed in a free space with the source of light and mirrors discontinued from each other but endowed with a common velocity. This is a considerable and, perhaps, not quite justifiable generalisation."[13]

If Einstein has taken his cue from a Jew on the physical side, he has turned to another Jew on the mathematical side. The name of the distinguished mathematician in Italy, Levi-Civita, is, for obvious reasons, less well-known than that of Michelson, but it was this Italian Jew who practically created the branch of mathematics called tensor calculus, which enables us to analyze manifolds of any number of dimensions. The doctrine of relativity contains so many aspects that threads must be seen connecting it with a variety of scientific branches.

It is a pity that those who consider Lorentz a Jew are mistaken about his origin, for it was this Leyden mathematical physicist who served as the forerunner of Einstein, in that he supplied the famous "transformation" formula for turning one set of co-ordinates (say, at rest in a vacuum) into another set (in motion with a given velocity).

Lorentz has so often been represented to me as Jewish by his students, and looks so much like his great compatriot, Jozef Israëls, that at one time there was no doubt in my mind that he belonged to Einstein's people. Even Weyl, the chief exponent of relativity after Einstein, supposed that Lorentz was a Jew, but to make sure, I took the liberty of addressing the question, which at times is rather delicate, to the man himself, and his reply was an explicit denial that he was of Jewish descent. Lorentz's "foreignness", in this regard, somewhat lessens the solidarity of the Semitic builders of the relativity conception, but Lorentz, I understand, from some of his students, was so modest as to give Einstein all the credit for the discovery, and he even referred to the transformation formula as the Einstein equation.

If, however, Lorentz could not be added to the list of Jewish scientists who might be regarded as the midwives of the relativity principle, at least one other brilliant Jewish name can be added to our record—that of Minkowski. It was he who supplied the notation for the great symphony which Einstein conceived. According to Hermann Weyl (*Space-Time-Matter*, English translation of the fourth German edition, page 173), "The adequate mathematical foundation of Einstein's discovery was first given by Minkowski. . . . To him we are indebted for the idea of a four-dimensional world geometry, on which we based our arguments from the outset."

As Yourgrau tells us,

"The fusion of time and space in one unitary concept was already suggested by Einstein's former teacher, Minkowski, who made the following statement: 'Henceforth, space by itself and time by itself are doomed to fade away into mere shadows and only a kind of union of the two will preserve an independent reality.'"[14]

In America, the chief exponent of the relativity theory, until recent years, has been L. Silberstein, (1872-1948) formerly of the University of Rome. His *Theory of Relativity* was published in several editions. Many years ago, Silberstein, who has been with the Eastman Kodak Company in Rochester, was invited to give a series of lectures on relativity by the University of Toronto, which at the time undertook the publication of the course. He gave similar courses at the University of Chicago and Cornell University, when the subject was still in the controversial stage. In L. Infeld, the University of Toronto has now another noted specialist in the field of relativity, who has worked for a time, together with Einstein at the Institute for Advanced Study, in Princeton.

Max Born's felicitous exposition, which has passed through several editions in German, appeared in an English translation, as early as 1922, under the title of *Einstein's Theory of Relativity*. The author, a leading Jewish physicist, taught at the University of Goettingen, until Hitler came to power, but has found a haven in England since, lecturing at Oxford.

We must not forget that the theory of relativity also provoked a great deal of discussion in the academic philosophical world, and here, again, we find that those who showed a mastery of the subject and made a deep impression on workers in that field by their penetrating analysis of the concepts are Bergson and Cassirer. There have been, of course, many other writers who dealt with the philosophical phase of this universal doctrine, but the works of the French Jew and the German Jew tower above the rest. More recently, another Franco-Jewish philosopher, Emile Meyerson, has published a vigorous discussion of the relativity theory that created a good deal of comment. At the present time, Hans Reichenbach, of the University of California, who has already been discussed as a mathematical philosopher (page 230), may be regarded as one of the leading philosophers of physics, especially the theory of relativity.

Weyl himself, who ranks as the leading authority on relativity next to Einstein, and whose original investigations on the subject have been universally recognized, has also been taken for a Jew in many quarters, perhaps because his name sounds Jewish. Again I thought it best to have the fact on record, and Professor Weyl[15] was kind enough to advise me in writing that he was not of Jewish origin.

No wonder the late Alfred Korzybski, known perhaps better as a leader in the general semantics movement, but also a deep student of the implications of relativity, has written me years ago that whenever he finds it necessary to peruse a book in connection with his investigations, he almost always finds it to be the product of a Jewish author, which fact, he goes on to say, discloses not only Polish but also Jewish elements in his results.*

The best biography of Albert Einstein, before Philipp Frank's appeared, was written by Alexander Moszkowski, and

*This is what the late Alfred Korzybski (a titled newcomer to this country, at the time, but one who soon made his name count rather than vice versa) wrote me in 1926: "Many thanks for . . . the reprints. I enjoy them greatly. For Buddha's sake, is Cassirer also a Jew? If this is the case, I begin to worry rather seriously. It is not even difficult to explain. In my whole work, of course, I select my favorite authors not by noses but by the intrinsic character of the work. It happens this way that in my whole work whenever I pick a writer as very fundamental for my purposes he happens to be a Jew. This coincidence is rather more than a coincidence, but at present, of course, I do

even if it bears the earmarks of a Boswellian attitude, it is none the less fascinating. Apropos of our fundamental point of view, there is a striking sentence in this biography, which goes to show that, even in his early youth, Einstein was influenced by a Jewish work. "A new world was opened for him," Moszkowski tells us, "when he made the acquaintance of A. Bernstein's comprehensive popular books on scientific subjects."[16] This same Aaron Bernstein, who wrote *Vogele der Maggid* and other Jewish novels, also apparently wrote the first letter of relativity in Einstein's plastic mind.

CONCLUSIONS AND REFLECTIONS

I fear that some readers who are altogether sold on the slogan that "science knows of no nationality"—until, naturally, their own country's scientists are under discussion—will frown upon the idea of casting the principle of relativity in a Jewish mould. They will explain the Jewish associations in the development of this conception as due to sheer chance, or they will, after the fashion of a Jewish professor of philosophy, dismiss the matter impatiently with the remark: "What have the Jews to do with relativity? If they are interested in the theory, it is because they are always active in every new movement." This is an attitude which reminds us somewhat of the profound declaration that "not Homer wrote the *Iliad* but another man by the name of Homer."

If Michelson, Minkowski, Levi-Civita, and other Jews all had a hand with Einstein in the establishment of the great principle, only as a result of chance or coincidence, then the line between a coincidence and a miracle almost vanishes. In self-defense for broaching this delicate subject, I may call at-

not understand what, and how, and why. Your articles throw some light on the question. What worries me (rather seriously) is the fact that my whole work carries not only Polish marks but also definitely Jewish marks, *both* of which will not make my work popular." In another letter, Korzybski tells me that my enlightening him on Weyl's non-Jewish origin affords him a cue as to why he found Weyl so disturbing as a proponent of relativity. He can see now that at heart Weyl was an absolutist who finds it not easy to break away from his old moorings.

tention to the fact that the issue between the House of Israel and the principle of relativity has already been picturesquely and good-humoredly brought up by a non-Jew. Perhaps this revelation will relieve my burden.

In *The Scientific Monthly* of July, 1926, Dr. Paul R. Heyl, of the National Bureau of Standards of the United States, vividly describes a number of experiments that were conducted to disprove the Einstein theory. He himself, in fact, confesses that his own crystal weighing experiments were "indeed undertaken by the experimenter in a spirit of definite skepticism regarding Einstein's theory, which appeared (to one who had learned his physics before the discovery of the X-rays) rather too bizarre and fantastic." But the negative result of the work places the experimenter very much in the same position as that in which Balak, the king of the Moabites, found himself on a certain occasion. It requires a little self-effacement for the author to liken himself in this connection to Balak, although the analogy, to be complete, should have contained the name of Balaam instead of that of Balak.

Here, Dr. Heyl reproduces effectively the well-known story of Balak and Balaam ben Peor (which, after thousands of years, still finds its way into the average Jew's daily idiom), and therewith ends this stimulating article.

> The land of Moab had been invaded by the host of Israel, as the sands of the sea in number. A battle was impending and Balak was none too certain of the outcome. He felt that he needed moral support and ghostly counsel, and he sent messengers to Balaam, the soothsayer, saying: 'Come, curse me Jacob; come, defy me Israel!'
>
> It was a professional call, and Balaam came. Balak was glad to see him. He gave him presents; he showed him much honor; he took him up to a high place where he might see the host of Israel en-

camped on the plain below, and he waited impatiently for the soothsayer to speak.

And Balaam spoke the words which the Lord put into his mouth; but Balak looked at him aghast, and said: 'What is this? I called thee to curse mine enemies, and lo! thou hast blessed them altogether!'

This biblical allusion makes an excellent peroration, but that is not where the matter rests for us. We must go on further in our search. As psychologists, have we not a right to ask whether or not the gap between Newton and Einstein bespeaks the gulf between the gentile and the Jew? Our search may be fruitless, but the question nevertheless suggests itself. Newton's mind could not conceive a space that was not absolute. Einstein was ready to deny even to time an absolute character, so that when Lorentz suggested that the only way to reconcile the negative results of the Michelson-Morley experiment was to posit an artificial time side by side with a real time, Einstein was quick to perceive that *both times were real but relative to the observer.* Both he and Minkowski gave the most emphatic expression to the principle that space and time together go to make up a single continuum.

What, then, characterizes Einstein's type of thought? We know it was a bold step to take in the first place. While others were seeking to explain the experimental results with as little damage as possible to the existing conception of physics, Einstein dared to change the whole point of view, and on the basis of his speculation, built up a new system. It was no less an illustrious mathematician than the late Henri Poincaré who spoke enthusiastically about the originality of Einstein's mind and the thoroughgoingness with which he followed his trend of thought to its ultimate conclusion.

I do not wish to claim that none but a Jew could have formulated the principle of relativity in its definite form. That were perilously near committing the fallacy of *post hoc ergo propter hoc,* or in a broader view, it would simply be a case of faulty generalization. But it is, I think, justifiable to hold that Einstein, being a Jew, might have found it easier to cut himself loose from the absolutistic moorings of physical concepts than his Gentile colleagues.

The Jewish mind, it would seem from a survey of Jewish thought, is less susceptible to dogma, to rigid conventional discipline than, let us say, was the Greek mind. The latter always aimed at definition; and what is definition but setting a limit to a concept, laying down laws? In Jewish philosophy, from Philo to Spinoza, we find the dictum, *Omnis determinatio est negatio*—"Every determination is a negation," playing a prominent part. The Jews were not scholastic in the real sense of the term. Some of the mediaeval Jewish philosophers were, of course, influenced in their method by their non-Jewish contemporaries, but where in Maimonides, Ibn-Gabirol, Crescas and Gersonides do we find the absolutistic method pursued by St. Thomas Aquinas, the prince of Roman Catholic philosophers?

The Jews, possibly because of their constitutional make-up, steered clear of the Scylla of absolutism and the Charybdis of nihilism (Gorgias in Greece and the Hindus in general). Even the most pessimistic of Jewish thinkers, Ecclesiastes, is, as the Semitic scholar, Morris Jastrow, called him, a "gentle cynic," probably comparable in this respect with the great half-Jew, Montaigne. Out of such soil, relativity can very well be expected as a product.

It is my belief that a theory, principle, or even law, *must be in us first before we can discover it in nature.* Millions of people may have the same facts before them without seeing the unity to which they point. Is it not possible, then, that certain cultural groups are prone to make certain discoveries rather than others? Evolution as a theory may have been cultivated by German and French biologists and naturalists, but it was through Englishmen (Darwin, Wallace, Spencer, Huxley) that the evidence reached its crystallized form.

Similarly, the principle of conservation of energy was rather a German discovery (Robert Mayer), although in England and in France, scientists worked along these lines.

We are all trained to see and interpret natural phenomena in much the same way, but there is always a *personal equation*; and it is my contention that the personal equation contains an unknown *national* quantity, which sets the world athinking.

In the development of the relativity theory, it is perhaps significant that the Jewish stamp is found at almost every turn. Were Einstein, alone of all Jewry, responsible for the vast physical transformation, the connection between relativity and the Jews could be regarded as wholly fortuitous, but where the names of Michelson, Levi-Civita, Minkowski, Born, Schwarzschild,[17] and Silberstein are all associated, in a more or less intimate way, with Einstein's achievement, one begins to feel that the "Elders of Zion" have unwittingly conspired to explain the world's most baffling phenomena, and apparently have met with success.

On the eve of 1950, the world's press reported a pronouncement which, coming from Albert Einstein, in his 71st year, has interested the many millions of people who even have no notion of relativity. Einstein's new "generalized theory of gravitation", as he calls it, is an overall conception that would dovetail the relativity theory and the quantum theory, which hitherto led a sort of independent existence, even though both have been accepted by physicists the world over. To verify this theory experimentally will be far more difficult than was the proof of the relativity theory by astronomers, nearly forty years ago, but it is more than likely that the four equations which constitute the core of Einstein's new world-view, an expansion of his earlier one, will lead to something epoch-making, just as his transformation equation has figured in nuclear fission and its either beatific or catastrophic sequels, as history in the shape of political leaders' motives will decide.

V

THE ATOM AND RELEASE OF ENERGY

If the principle of relativity has developed into a cosmic drama, then its dénouement became fraught with something of a terrible nature, although it also contains, aside from adding to the store of knowledge and wisdom, potentially the greatest blessing for mankind. We thus are reminded of the Biblical injunction "And I have given you both life and death; and ye shall choose life."

The most remarkable thing about this possible universal boon or global calamity is that the tiniest thing imaginable could be the source of such a tragedy. Common sense would regard as absurd beyond words a view that a particle of matter invisible even through the most powerful microscope could wreak such destruction; and that such force could inhere in an intangible, imponderable, and invisible particle is a theoretical marvel. What would Democritus and Leucippus have said if told that their atom would, two thousand years hence, be in a position of filling a whole world with dread anxiety, and the scientists who explored it, even with anguish, if not bitter remorse?

We are, however, in this quasi-prologue anticipating too much. The experimental study of the atom began quietly enough in the English laboratories, although excitement grew as the phenomena showed up perplexities, and then pointed to solutions which, in their turn, brought forth new problems.

How far back might we go to examine the history of the atom as fashioned by apparatus and the inception of the new sub-science of electronics? Shall we start with William Crookes whose experiment with electricity passing through a vacuum gave us the first hint of the later spectra, which he called the cathode? Or should we accord the first honor to the great

Cambridge physicist J. J. Thomson, who actually discovered the electron, which meant that the atom must have dropped it. The atom indivisible really consisted of much more minute particles, but the nucleus was still a perfect mystery.

It was, however, an Australian, who taught at McGill (my alma mater) in Montreal, and eventually settling in England —Ernest Rutherford—who succeeded, not without the help of a colleague's device in another connection, in making the greatest metamorphosis in nature—something that went farther than the dream of the mediaeval alchemist to transmute ordinary metals into gold, viz., breaking up the nucleus of an atom, something which was by its very nature, as the name implied, supposed to be indivisible.

In 1919, Rutherford made it plain that not only can the atom change its constitution, which was indeed happening often, even accidentally, but that the very core of the atom could be smashed. Rutherford, too, was the first to give us an insight into the nucleus of the atom; and within the last two decades or so, nuclear physics i. e., the department of physics which deals with the tiny nucleus of that invisible atom has become the most important study, it would seem, in all science, and something upon which rests the fate of the world.[18] A lay person who for the first time hears the name "nuclear physics" is prone to associate it with vast areas, whereas in reality so far as space goes, it deals with a millionth of a pinpoint, really next to nothing. Such is the great lesson which present-day results have brought to the world. Adapting a New Testament dictum, one might say in this regard, "For the great will become tiny and the tiny will become great." The atom, with its nucleus and electrons, neutrons and protons, positrons and deuterons has become a sun for us. The atom now has the status of a large world populated with billions of particles of several different kinds.

In the interim, between Rutherford's exposition of the atomic nucleus, through a model he devised, and the next big advance, activity in the many laboratories throughout Europe and America was not lagging, and one discovery would lead to another, would become another brick in the great edifice of science, even if *via* such an infinitesimal what-not as an atom, or even its nucleus. But it was Niels Bohr's publication, in 1913, of an article explaining the structure of the atom which soon disclosed a new luminary in physics. Bohr is now considered the foremost authority on the atom, and it was in his laboratory at Copenhagen where most of the work had been done that eventuated in the perfecting of the atom bomb in the United States. Several of the most important nuclear physicists took their apprenticeship in the Bohr laboratory, and his presence in the United States during the War on special invitation would go to show his prowess in this particular branch of physics.

Niels Bohr was born in Copenhagen, Denmark in 1885, the son of a Christian father (named also Christian) and a Jewish mother (Ellen Adler). When only 35, he became Director of the Institute for Theoretical Physics at the University of Copenhagen. Later he lectured in many foreign universities, principally in England. In 1922, he was awarded the Nobel Prize for his pioneer work on the atom in relation to the release of energy. It was well that he succeeded in escaping from Nazi-occupied Denmark in a small boat in 1943; for had the Nazis laid hands on him, the atom bomb might have been *their* weapon.

> It often happens that a scientific hypothesis seems completely absurd and yet leads to significant conclusions. Such was the case with Bohr's assumptions regarding electronic orbits. He assumed that an electron might move around in an orbit of fixed size for a considerable time without radiating energy or falling in toward the nucleus. Luckily he did not have to explain this departure from current belief, but merely wondered what would happen if such were the case.[19]

It is characteristic of Bohr, as it was of his peer, Einstein, that he was not afraid to frame theories of a radical nature, theories which were soon to be validated, and indeed it was Einstein's photoelectric equation, formulated in 1905, but not verified until Millikan, in 1916, by actually making use of it, made exact measurements of Planck's elementary quantum of energy, which assisted Bohr in his inferences and experiments. While theoretical physics has often been belittled and, in Germany, the Nazis would refer to it as *Judenphysik*, in contrast to experimental physics, it is remarkable how the intuitions of such men as Einstein, Bohr, and others transcended the received conclusions based on the then researches. Einstein, in particular, turned out to be a sort of prophet-scientist, whose deductions and computations unerringly forecasted results obtained after years of laborious experimentation. Actually the first adumbration of the atomic bomb is to be found in Einstein's special theory of relativity.

If Enrico Fermi, who had to make a speedy exit from Italy, not so much because of his own Semitic antecedents as for the reason that his wife is of Jewish origin, made urgent representations when in this country to survey the military exploitation of the atomic nucleus, it was because of what he had seen going on at the Bohr laboratory; and the reason for the feverish activity in Copenhagen was the arrival there of Lise Meitner and her nephew, O. R. Frisch. Dr. Meitner was working in the Kaiser Wilhelm Institute in Berlin, together with O. Hahn and Strassmann on the neutron bombardment of the uranium atom, which, when broken up, disclosed some mysterious barium.

At this moment, the Gestapo stuck its long nose into the work, having itself discovered that Dr. Meitner was a racially diluted person. Suddenly cut loose from all that was near and dear to her, she found herself on a train Copenhagen-bound. The mystery of the barium persisted in her tortured mind, and to ease her mental pain, she wove a masterful piece of mathematics around the experiment. She already knew the exact amount of energy released by the few uranium atoms that *did* explode and she wanted a mathematical justification for the result. . . .

Dr. Meitner's pencil flew through abstruse mathematical formulae. Yes, the energy that would be released by such disunion, or splitting, was the exact equivalent of that measured by the uranium explosion in Berlin, when barium was discovered in the bombardment chamber.[20]

In the Smyth Report on the Development of Methods of Using Atomic Energy for Military Purposes, which the United States Government issued, there is the following significant paragraph "The announcement of the hypothesis of fission and its experimental confirmation took place in January 1939. . . . There was immediate interest in the possible military use of the large amounts of energy released in fission. At that time American-born nuclear physicists were so unaccustomed to the idea of using their science for military purposes that they hardly realized what needed to be done. Consequently the early efforts both at restricting publication and at getting government support were stimulated largely by a small group of foreign-born physicists centering on L. Szilard and including E. Wigner, E. Teller, V. F. Weisskopf and E. Fermi."[21]

It was G. Breit who proposed the formation of a censorship committee to control publication in all American publications, and it was he who served as the chairman of the subcommittee which dealt with uranium fission—the first of the many subcommittees that were to take up the gigantic task.

To what extent Jewish ingenuity and zeal shaped the atomic bomb, just after O. Hahn and F. Strassmann in Berlin discovered the isotope of barium on bombardment of uranium by neutrons, may be gathered from another passage in the same report.

On January 16, 1939, Niels Bohr of Copenhagen, Denmark, arrived in this country to spend several months in Princeton, N. J., and was particularly anxious to discuss some abstract problems with A. Einstein. (Four years later, Bohr was to escape from Nazi-occupied Denmark in a small boat.) Just before Bohr left Denmark two of his colleagues, O. R. Frisch and L. Meitner (both refugees from Germany), had told him their guess that the absorption of a neutron by a uranium nucleus sometimes caused that nucleus to split into approximately equal parts with the release of enormous quantities of energy, a process that soon began to be called nuclear 'fission'.[22]

Refugees they were all four, and what kind of refugees? Jews who were candidates for the Maidanek or Auschwitz crematories.

The conference between Fermi and the Navy Department which Pegram of Columbia University arranged was the first attempt made to contact the Government, but it was not until Einstein, in conference with Szilard and Wigner (all three Jews), sent a personal letter, through A. Sachs, a non-scientist, to the late President that the War Department began to take this matter seriously, although there apparently was not a great deal of faith evinced in the project. Meeting after meeting was held, committee after committee was organized, and only the fear that the Germans would appear on the scene first with their diabolical weapons led to the grants which enabled the carrying on of collective research and made possible the coördination of results which culminated in the construction of the Los Alamos Laboratory in New Mexico, with its seven distinct divisions. Among the heads here we find G. B. Kistiakowsky of the Explosive Division, R. F. Bacher of the Bomb Physics Division, while J. Robert Oppenheimer was the Director to whom all the chiefs were to report their findings. Niels Bohr, arriving from Denmark, served in the capacity of an adviser. According to the official War Department report "He is to be credited with achieving the implementation of atomic energy for military purposes." The man who was charged with the actual assembly core was R. F. Bacher, Professor of physics at Cornell. When the assembly of an important section was delayed because of the tight wedging of an insertion, Dr. Bacher assured the anxious group of scientists watching over each process that this would work itself out in minutes, and so it did. It was P. H. Abelson who submitted, in September of 1940, a 17-page memorandum on the possibility of separating the isotopes of uranium by thermal diffusion. The suggestion was accepted, and under Abelson's direction at the Naval Research Laboratory, work was begun on thermal diffusion.

It is not necessary to go into further details on the atom bomb. The awesome event in Los Alamos is now common knowledge to all who read the newspapers of that period. In the Laboratory there worked many young Jewish scientists in addition to those already mentioned, e. g., Frank Oppenheimer, brother of Robert, K. Cohen, M. Benedict Weinberg, and Finkelstein, while the British group arrived here during the winter of 1941-1942. "At that time the British were planning a diffusion separation plant themselves so that the discussion with F. Simon, R. Peierls and others were particularly valuable." (From the Smyth report). H. Halban had visited this country in 1942, to tell about his 165 liters of heavy water. It would appear that the three names mentioned are Jewish, but this is in the form of a conjecture.

It was principally K. Cohen, of Columbia, who had developed the theory for the single units and for the series of cascade units that would be necessary.

It is certainly not fortuitous that of the chief workers on the atom smashing, and particularly in the military applications, over a score were Jews, that Einstein was probably the first to recognize the tremendous import of the release of

energy, and that his simple equation in connection with the
Planck constant, which was questioned by the majority of
physicists until Millikan supplied the experimental evidence,
was the first step toward the ushering in of a new era, that
Bohr, Meitner, Frisch, Oppenheimer, Rabi, Goudsmith, Breit,
Wigner, Cohen, and a dozen others engaged in this stupendous task were Jews. Robert Oppenheimer is chairman of the
Atomic Energy Commission's Advisory Council, and at the
same time Director of the Institute for Advanced Study, an
institution, incidentally established with the funds of the late
philanthropist, Louis Bamberger, and his sister Mrs. Fuld.
It is at this Institute in Princeton that Albert Einstein found
a haven, when he shook the German dust off his shoes.

Of the 26 sponsors of the *Bulletin of the Atomic Scientists*
11 are Jews, and these include four Nobel Prize laureates. One
may, as is often done, refer to some as refugees or immigrants.
The fact remains that they are Jews, whether immigrants or
not. Nor does it mean that the Jewish physicists are bent on
fashioning destructive implements. It must be borne in mind
that the release of energy from the smashing of the atomic
nucleus is not necessarily in itself lethal and need not serve
a deleterious purpose. The forces may be harnessed in such a
way as to bring about the greatest comforts at the least possible expense. Medicine, too, has already profited by the result of the scientists whom we call nuclear physicists.

It is true, however, that in 1941, when Hitler and his hordes
were about to strangle Europe and America, there was nothing
so imperious in the world as a weapon to stem their advance,
particularly as the rockets which the Germans were working
on, and the atom bomb too, were becoming real dangers. Had
the Nazis not banished the Jewish scientists, then even if they
were not engaged on the atom projects, it is very doubtful
whether the United States could have forestalled the havoc
created by the German scientists' diabolic inventions. Whether
it was destiny or a quip of fate, or just the folly of madmen
who planned their own destruction, it was thanks to the Jews

that the antidote against the dreadful pest was found, even if the Nazis did not get the medicine after all. Its value, however, is unmitigated, and "forearmed is forewarned" just as much as "forewarned is forearmed", and *"foreatomed"* is the best security in a topsy-turvy world, at least until an iron-clad pact is possible.

Dramatis Personae *of the atom performance*

Before this section is concluded, it would be in order to become acquainted, so to speak, with the Jewish heroes of the atomic drama, which, for the first time has convinced the war chiefs that science can accomplish in a minute what all the combined forces cannot achieve in years—a drama which has no parallel in all history.

The following names are mostly of those scientists who have played an important role in the preparation of the material and the devising of the processes, but some of the Jewish sponsors and members of the Advisory Council on Atomic Energy have already been referred to in other connections. Only a few lines have to suffice for each of the men, although pages have been devoted in some of the national publications to several of them.

The order of the names is not significant, nor is there any attempt made to evaluate the work of each. Their status as professors in the best American universities, their awards, including the Nobel Prize, should be sufficient for us to perceive their merit, whether we have ever had a course in physics or not.

Isidore Isaac Rabi, who was one of the youngest Nobel Prize laureates (1944) at the age of 46, is head of the Department of Physics at Columbia University, and Chairman of the National Research Council. A member and fellow of many learned societies and recipient of numerous awards, he has devoted most of his time to the study of the spin and electrical, as well as magnetic, properties of the atom. The director of one of the most important laboratories at Harvard told me that Rabi's achievement is so complicated, so ramified, that even in his seminars with advanced students, he finds it difficult to give an adequate exposition of it.

Samuel Abraham Goudsmith (1902-   ) now at the Brookhaven National Laboratory (a Gompers on his mother's side) received his intensive training at Leyden, Holland, and arrived in this country in 1927, joining the Faculty of the University of Michigan. In 1941, he was visiting professor at Harvard. In 1944-1945 he was chief of the Scientific Intelligence Mission to Europe, receiving the Medal of Freedom in recognition of his services. Together with G. E. Uhlenbeck, he discovered the so-called "spin" of the electron in 1925. His collaborations on the structure of line spectra and on atomic energy states were fundamental in building up the practical possibilities of the atom.

Edward Teller, of the University of Chicago, born in Hungary, and trained in the best laboratories in Germany, leaving soon after the Nazis got into the saddle during the second World War, has been engaged in nuclear physics research, and took part in the collective experimentation on the atom bomb.

Another Hungarian-born physicist who had a part in the fission super-drama and the consequent release of energy, culminating in the preparation of the atom bomb, was Eugene Paul Wigner, whose mother was Elizabeth Einhorn. Coming to the United States in 1930, he taught mathematical physics at various universities, and though theoretical rather than experimental physics has been his domain, he was among the first to confer with Albert Einstein on the momentous question of using the information at hand for military purposes.

Still another Hungarian Jewish physicist who has been of the greatest service at the time when the civilized world was fighting for a chance to live is Leo Szilard. Together with Enrico Fermi, Bohr's brilliant student, he devised the chain reaction system composed of uranium and graphite without which the atom bomb could not have been effective. Gaining his specialized experience in Berlin, London, and Oxford, he is now Professor at the University of Chicago.

The organization of the uranium fission project was practically in the hands of Gregory Breit, who was born in Russia in 1899, and after studying at Harvard and Leyden, he specialized in terrestrial magnetism. During the War, he acted as either chairman, adviser, or coördinator of various committees connected with the development of atomic energy. His name is mentioned frequently in the Smyth report.

Julian S. Schwinger, one of the youngest of the atom scientists, who took his doctorate at Columbia and, scarcely 30, is full professor of physics at Harvard University, has made the scattering of neutrons his chief study.

Victor F. Weisskopf, who is professor at the Massachusetts Institute of Technology, had received his doctorate at Goettingen, and soon began to engage in investigations along the line of spectroscopy, radiation, and nuclear physics.

Another Professor at the same institute, probably the greatest of its kind in the world, Jerrold Reinach Zacharias, is on the Board of Sponsors of the Atomic Scientists. His researches on molecular rays happen to tie up closely with the development of the most formidable weapon known to man.

A Laboratory Hero and Martyr

Nor was the work on the atom without its martyrs. We do not know how many of the nuclear scientists will have in subsequent years shown the effects of their proximity to the dangerous material in the laboratory, but the death of Dr. Louis Slotin, of Winnipeg, Canada, is decidedly and directly the result of a heroic attempt made to save the lives of seven or more scientists engaged in preparing the piles for the chain reaction, in the Los Alamos Laboratory, which in this case was precipitated violently. Let us quote from *Time* part of the story: "Perhaps Dr. Slotin was watching the warning instruments more carefully than his fellows; perhaps he saw the bluish glow. At any rate, he realized that the chain reaction had spurted to high intensity. The room was being swept with deadly radiation. He leaped forward, put his body between his colleagues and the radiating mass, scattered its materials. The chain reaction halted immediately.

"Then Dr. Slotin was taken to the hospital where, nine days later, he died of the peculiar and imperfectly understood burns produced by radiation. Seven co-workers, less seriously injured, hoped to recover."

The letter to his parents from Major General Groves, praising Dr. Slotin's "Keen mind, technical skill, and heroic action" and telling of the high esteem and admiration he was held in by all of his colleagues and associates is an adequate characterization. Furthermore The Newspaper Guild of New York dedicated a Page One Award to "the memory of the late Dr. Louis Slotin, who willingly laid down his life to save fellow workers from certain death during experiments at the Los Alamos atomic research project.

"Louis Slotin knew that he had only about a week to live but decided to make the best possible use of this short time. He called his secretary and began dictating, handing over to humanity the heritage of his short but fruitful life.

"More and more he felt the approach of death and the gradual weakening of his body. His hands which were most directly exposed to the influence of the dreadful rays had to be packed in ice to soothe the terrible pain. His hair turned brittle. But relentlessly he continued to dictate. His body finally gave way to the impact of the force which his brain had helped to create.

"His parents who spent the last few days of his life at his bedside reported that even in the dreams of his agony he was thinking of his duty only. 'Why couldn't I finish my work?' was the cry that he repeated again and again between the moans of his last few painful hours. Until his death he kept his wartime activities secret from his parents.

"In honor of the late scientist, his friends and fellow workers in the Los Alamos laboratory, established a memorial fund to care for two refugee children in special rest centres under the Foster Parents Plan."[23]

I understand that the top nuclear physicist in Russia is Capittsa, who on a visit to the USSR after he had made his residence in England was not permitted to leave. His name occurs frequently as the hydrogen bomb is looming larger and larger in our turbulent discussions.

Custodians of Atomic Energy

If J. Robert Oppenheimer is Chairman of the Advisory Council of the Atomic Energy Commission, then another Jew, David Lilienthal is practically the custodian, the man who is responsible to the Government for the scientists. His appointment and the incidents revolving around it, the opposition by reactionary senators, have constituted an interesting episode in American history, disclosing the parallelogram of forces in American political life. To the credit of the United States, it must be said that all the red herrings brought in by the prejudiced and narrow-minded gentlemen, even to the extent of wishing to make capital out of the fact that Lilienthal's parents were born in Czechoslovakia, which *today* is a satellite of the USSR, although at the time of their birth it was under the heels of Austria—all this puerile sophistry was of no avail, and Lilienthal, in an inspired apologia, which was really the vigorous expression of an American credo worthy of Jefferson or Lincoln, carried the day and his appointment as Chairman of the Atomic Energy Commission was a triumph for the principle of democracy.

Later, in consequence of the spying cases which came before the courts, another attempt was made to force the resignation of Lilienthal, or his dismissal. Promises and threats were made by politicians who had some power in the Investigating Committee. It transpired that a fraction of an ounce of uranium was not accounted for, and that a student with Communist leanings had been awarded a fellowship in nuclear physics. Lilienthal, in spite of his more difficult position under the circumstances, managed to pull through. When toward the end of 1949, he ultimately resigned his post, President Truman prevailed upon him to stay in office until February 1950, because, as it transpired, there is no one in the United States who could replace this extraordinarily efficient and conscientious public servant especially at a time when the hydrogen bomb is under way.[24]

If Lilienthal may be called the custodian of atomic energy in the United States, then Bernard Baruch, the "elder statesman" as he has been admiringly known in government circles for decades, may be considered to be the chief executive, in this connection, in dealing with the world at large, for he represents the United States in the United Nations Commission; and his policy has heretofore been the deciding factor as to what extent the information should be released or kept a secret.

Thus we have in Lilienthal and Baruch the controls of atomic energy; and that is perhaps as it should be; for their judiciousness, efficiency, and experience have long been established by enlightened public opinion and more than one President of the United States. The responsibility with which they are invested is perhaps greater than has devolved upon the shoulders of anyone else since the War, but it is possibly another symbol of destiny that atomic energy, the most salutary and at the same time the most dangerous instrument known, the *very core of nature,* should be, in large part, the handiwork of Jews and also in charge of Jewish guardians; for we cannot imagine any ethnic group which would approach the colossal problems—virtually the question of being or not being, not in relation to a single individual, but as it affects *mankind as a whole*—with the prophetic vision peculiar to this ethnic group.

THE HEBREW IMPACT ON WESTERN CIVILIZATION

The man who evinced most concern about the outcome, as
we know from his fervent appeals in national monthlies and
the press, was no other than Albert Einstein himself, who
had more to do with evolving the weapon than anyone else;
and if there is a concerted effort made by the atomic scientists
to take the control out of the hands of the military authorities,
and set up an international policy banning the use of such
an infernal weapon especially in its infernal hydrogen shape,
we may be certain that the Jewish members of the group have
exerted considerable influence in this direction. Both Oppenheimer and Rabi have discussed the seriousness of the situation in a frank tone.

One of the number, Norbert Wiener, whose field is mathematics, has even gone so far as to state in print that he would
not lend his assistance to bolster up the war machine. Had
German scientists abided by such a principle, there might
not have broken out even the First World War, and certainly
the murderous experiments on innocent victims would not
have been carried out. Certainly the Maidanek and Auschwitz
gigantic furnaces would not have smoked from the burning
of human flesh, after the scientific asphyxiation of human
beings, whose only crime was to have been born in a Jewish
family.

In fine, the closing reflection is that there is a line of
continuity from Isaiah to Einstein, and that the ominous atom,
with its global catastrophe in store, can be turned to benign
uses, if justice and righteousness be our guide. This prophetic
strain appears to inhere in most of the Jewish scientists engaged in eliciting the secrets out of nature. Scientists under
the aegis of Nazidom would experience no compunction in
making out of the world a shambles, so long as their own
party or group or *Herrenvolk* survives and rules with super-
brute force.

VI

THE JEW IN CHEMISTRY

Chemistry is a comparatively young science, not even two hundred years old, and it is only within the last 125 years that the remarkable discoveries began in the rather primitive laboratories in France, Germany, England and Italy. Since then, largely because of its practical and industrial possibilities, it has advanced by leaps and bounds.

Prior to about 1850, we do not find Jews prominent in this branch of science, although occasionally a Jewish convert, like N. W. Fischer, born in 1782, manages to become a professor in a German university (Breslau). Fischer was one of the first experimenters to have established the laws of sublimation and vapor-tension.

The first Jew who distinguished himself in chemistry, to the point of winning the Nobel Prize was Adolph von Baeyer (1835-1917). True, only his mother was Jewish, scion of the wealthy and cultured Itzig (Hitzig) family, but the cross-inheritance theory (son after mother and daughter after father) would allow us to include him in our survey without the decided reserve shown in the Heinrich Hertz case. Von Baeyer was one of the pioneers of organic chemistry having discovered eosin, a boon in medicine, and many aniline dyes, including artificial indigo. His seminars and laboratory in Munich became a sort of Mecca for ambitious students throughout Germany, and even other countries.

About the same time, industrial chemistry received its great impetus, and largely through Jews. Adolf Frank (1834-1916) made a careful study of the nature of potash, and established the potash industry in Germany through his own large factory. The manufacture of bromide, ammonia, and the chlorides owes much to him too.

The notorious I. G. Farben Company, which played such a sorry part in Hitler's day, would never have been so powerful were it not for the efforts of Jews like Heinrich Caro (1834-1910) who practically started the dye industry in Germany, and much later Richard Willstätter (1872-1943), Nobel Prize winner, who, for all his extraordinary labors on behalf of his country in raising the German dye industry to an enviable position, for all his invaluable discoveries in the field of biochemistry, resigned his post at the University of Munich in protest against the Nazi dismissals of Jewish professors. Prior to that, when told that he would be retained because of his unusual services, his characteristic reply was "Of genius there is no dearth; but character is a rare article", and he clung to his decision.

Another Nobel Prize laureate who came to grief during the same dreadful period in history was Fritz Haber, the very man who, by ingeniously deriving the very much needed ammonia from the nitrogen in the atmosphere and hydrogen, made it possible for Germany to carry on during the first World War. Haber, a convert to Christianity, was only a lieutenant, although famous already as a chemist, and when he wished to make his discovery known to the desperate German general staff, in 1917, the problem presented itself how that Jewish bedraggled lieutenant could enter the presence of the august high command without contaminating it. During the early part of the Hitler regime, Haber, who had also made some studies on poisonous gases, which the Germans were about to use, went into voluntary exile, and died of a broken heart. It took the courage and high standing of Max Planck, who was the venerable head of the Prussian Academy of Science, to pronounce the eulogy on a mental giant who abandoned his own people, working for the Germans, with all his might and zeal, only to be cast aside as so much refuse.

Victor Meyer (1848-1897) at the age of 19 became Bunsen's assistant, and at 23 became Professor at the Stuttgart

Polytechnicum. After advancing to other institutions, he settled at Heidelberg as the successor of his famous master, Bunsen. In 1897, in a fit of despondency, he died by his own hand. Meyer was one of the pillars of organic chemistry. His investigations of vapor densities, which were carried out by means of an apparatus he himself invented, his extension of our knowledge in regard to iodine; more especially, his establishment of the new field, stereochemistry, were all of vast importance in the young science. Indeed his work was so fruitful whether he dealt with derivatives of benzene, or the principle of isomerism, or the aromatic maines, or the constitution of camphor, that he was a sort of Midas, whose very touch turned out derivatives and substitutes. His imagination and intuition were such as were found in scientists of the highest order. His discovery of theophene compound in impure benzene belonged to such original flashes, and had he lived his natural years, he doubtless would have joined the illustrious array of Jewish Nobel Prize men.

Matthias E. O. Liebreich (1839-1908) Director of the Pharmacological Institute in Berlin, served as a seaman before taking up the study of chemistry, and eventually medicine, rising to the privy councillorship in medicine, which, in Germany, meant a great deal. His discoveries ranged from anaesthetic drugs to lanolin, a paste from sheep's wool, and the mercury treatment of syphilis. His contributions to chemical therapy were immense. Medicine is obligated to him for the phaneroscopic method in treating lupus, the effect of cantharides on pathological capillaries and many other studies. Between 1895 and 1900, he published three volumes of an encyclopedia of therapy, and his book on boracic acid (1903) is still regarded as valuable. Among the many researches he had tackled successfully are the use of strychnine as an antidote to chloral hydrate cresol, formaldehyde and methyl violet. Furthermore, he established the presence of protagon in the brain. He was also the first to differentiate between neurin and cholin.

It is interesting to note that the Jews made such rapid strides in chemistry that C. Liebermann (1842-1914), who was professor at the Berlin Technical Institute, served, for a time, as President of the German Chemical Society. He was best known for his investigations of naphthalene alkaloids and the synthesis of alizarin from anthracene.

Of the various fields of chemistry, organic, inorganic, analytical, industrial, and physiological chemistry, there is no doubt that the Jews have contributed most to organic and industrial chemistry, with biochemistry a close third. At the present time, biochemistry is taking the lead.

We have seen that Victor Meyer was one of the founders of organic chemistry, but another Meyer, Lothar, was a bold explorer in the field of biochemistry. According to P. Blackman, himself a chemist, "Lothar Meyer was one of the originators and founders of biological chemistry, and by his wonderful investigations and marvellous presentation of the results on the absorption by defibrinated blood of oxygen, nitrogen, and carbon dioxide, and of the action of carbon monoxide on blood, together with other work in biochemistry, was the first to place the chemistry of the gases of the blood upon a firm and sound experimental basis; and not only did he carry out a vast amount of work independently, but he also advised, directed and collaborated with others in kindred researches, all of which produced results of the utmost value and importance in this branch of chemistry."[25]

It is surprising that the Meyers and Mayers, not a common Jewish surname, had at least a dozen representatives in chemistry, not to mention the philosopher, Emile Meyerson, who was an industrial chemist before devoting himself to philosophy. R. J. Meyer specialized in inorganic chemistry, at the University of Berlin, while K. F. Meyer, a biochemist, who has significantly added to our knowledge about anaerobic bacteria, is another distingushed namesake.

Eduard Lippmann (1842-1919) an organic chemist of distinction, occupied the chair of chemistry at the University of Vienna, and the preparation of quinine homologues is associated with his name.

As regards physical chemistry, James Franck, the Nobel Prize man, who has been mentioned in the section on physics, O. W. Sackur one of the former deans at the Dahlem Kaiser Wilhelm Institute (Berlin University), Kazimir Fajans (1887-   ) sometime head of the Physio-Chemical Institute at Munich, whose discovery of the element brevium has been hailed at the time, F. Paneth noted for his work on radio-activity, Alfred Byk, who was professor of physical chemistry in Berlin, and Lassar Cohn (1858-1922) who was professor at the University of Koenigsberg, and a popular writer (*Chemistry in Everyday Life*) as well as a researcher—are sufficient proof that this phase has not been neglected.

It would be possible to compile a book about the contributions of Jewish chemists in Germany alone, but only a few of the shining lights can be presented in the space at our disposal; and certainly one of these is Otto Wallach (1847-1931) a former Director of the Clinical Institute at Goettingen and Nobel Prize laureate, in 1910, for his work on alicyclic compounds, which was an innovation in organic chemistry. He, too, advanced the dye industry in Germany by dint of his aniline investigations.

The recent development of colloid chemistry, which is a phase of organic chemistry, is due, in a large measure to Jews like Jacques Loeb, who later, as we shall see in another section, became a towering physiologist, and Herbert Freundlich, who, partly Jewish, was compelled to leave the German laboratory for an English one.

Perhaps even more than in mathematics and physics, chemistry has been lagging behind in France; so that the French Jews, too, favored the humanistic and the social sciences, and yet the half-Jew, Henri Moissan (1852-1907) who was awarded the Nobel Prize, in 1906, for his great contributions to mineral chemistry was one of the leading figures at the Sorbonne. His artificial reproduction of diamonds and other minerals caused a sensation. He also devised processes which made the manufacture of acetylene simple and thus inexpensive.

England, while not equal to Germany in the sciences, could at least offer some competition in industrial chemistry; and again the Jews have come forward to strengthen, nay to build up, this branch.

One of the most esteemed chemists of his time, in England, was the cultured Raphael Meldola (1840-1915) scion of a distinguished Portuguese Jewish family, who was President of the British Chemical Society, a naturalist too, and on intimate terms with Charles Darwin. Meldola's sphere of activity was chiefly photochemistry and the dye industry, and coal-tar; and here he has a number of valuable compounds to his credit.

There were, of course, a few organic and physiological chemists, like Philip Hartog, I. M. Heilbron, who taught organic chemistry at the University of Liverpool, J. B. Cohen (1859-1935) Professor of organic chemistry at the University of Leeds and several others; but it was Ludwig Mond who founded the greatest chemical plant England had known. Discoverer of the Mond gas and nickel carbonyl, he was able, together with his son, Alfred, the later Lord Melchett, to set England on a high industrial footing. The reclamation of sulphur from alkalies (waste) is his achievement. Herbert Levinstein did something similar on a smaller scale for the dye industry in England, while Julius Lewkowitsch was the leading stereochemist in England, and director of the London Research Institute, in which capacity he was the most sought authority on oils and fats; but we cannot afford to overlook the indebtedness of England to Chaim Weizmann, who, prior to his election as President of the new State of Israel, was regarded as one of the most eminent chemists in the British Empire, and one of great service to the army and navy in both of the World Wars.

His discovery of various derivatives, his research on fluorescence, on the glycerides of amino-acids, his work on butyl-alcohol, which was put to use in the preparation of synthetic rubber, his more recent work on plastics, are all evidence of his highly ingenious brain; and when we take into consideration the fact that unlike most academic men, his mind was weighed down with the knotty problems of Zionism, that he was a statesman during all the years that these researches were carried on, that his continual travels on behalf of the cause had not only consumed much of his time but naturally must have interfered with his concentration and lastly that his eyesight was seriously impaired for years, we can only give him all the more credit for his achievements.

As to Russia, even during the Czarist rule, a few Jews succeeded, after conversion, in obtaining university posts in chemistry, but their number now both in educational institutions and government service is tenfold, although there are now fewer Jews in that country. It is difficult, as is well-known, to obtain statistical information of such a character, especially as many Jewish scientists bear Slavic names, and to all intents and purposes are Russian, change of faith being unnecessary. Among the leading chemists known to be Jews are Michael Altshul and Michael Goldstein of the past generation while Aron Frumkin belongs to our own time. In Warsaw, under Russian domination Jakob Natanson held the post of professor at the local university.

Among the noted Italian chemists are I. Giulio Ascoli at the Milan Technical Institute, G. Errera of Messina and Padua Universities, B. N. Pincherle of the Polytechnic Institute at Milan, and F. Jarach, who was President of the Italian Metallurgical Association.

We finally come to the United States which now harbors the greatest contingent of Jewish chemists. Many of them, of course, are research workers or teachers who have thus far not made a dent in the world, but of the score or more who have made international reputations, the following may be singled out—C. L. Alsberg, a biochemist, for many years Dean of the Graduate School at Leland Stanford University, E. J. Cohn, one of the most distinguished biochemists in the country, chairman of the Division of the Medical Sciences at Harvard Medical School, Moses Gomberg, a former President of the American Chemical Society, Michael Heidelberger of Columbia University, J. S. Jaffe, an expert on soils and agricultural chemistry, M. E. Jaffa, an authority on the chemistry of foods, W. A. Jacobs of the Rockefeller Institute, a top-ranking chemotherapist, David Klein formerly a professor at Johns Hopkins, P. A. T. Levene, of the Rockefeller Institute, a biochemist of a high order, Lafayette B. Mendel, one of the leading professors at Yale, and recognized throughout the world for his work in nutrition; G. W. Raiziss, Professor of chemotherapy at the Graduate School of Medicine, University of Pennsylvania, M. A. Rosanoff and A. Silverman, both of the University of Pittsburgh; J. O. Stieglitz, late head of the Chemistry Department at the University of Chicago (whose brother, Alfred Stieglitz was probably the foremost authority on photography in America) and L. E. Wise, one of the few specialists in forest chemistry. Nor is it generally known that Gerty Cori, who shared the Nobel Prize in medicine, with her distinguished husband, is herself Jewish (Radnitz was her maiden name). Their researches in carbohydrate metabolism and enzymes of animal tissue signallized a great advance in biochemistry. Both husband and wife are professors of pharmacology and biochemistry at Washington University in St. Louis.

One of the most important biochemists in recent years, Leonor Michaelis (1875-1949), after apprenticeship under the great Paul Ehrlich became first professor of medicine, then professor of physical chemistry at the University of Berlin. In 1922, probably anticipating the Hitler Walpurgis night in Germany, he left for Japan and in 1926, he received a call to Johns Hopkins. Later, he became head of the physicochemical department at the Rockefeller Institute for Medical Research in New York.

His best known book is called *The Dynamics of Surfaces*, but he has a standard textbook on mathematics for biologists and chemists; he has written on ion concentration, and on colloids, and was instrumental in developing research methods and techniques in physical chemistry which yielded a scientific harvest. This was referred to by one of his students who, in 1950, received a special award (gold medal) for discoveries which, he maintained, had been initiated by his teacher, Michaelis.

The above select list could easily be extended without including mediocrities. It may be added that because of the Nazi *"Gleichschaltung"*, many Jewish chemists are now serving the United States, either as research workers or university teachers; and the Cohens and Cohns in *American Men of Science* seem to have a special predilection for chemistry.

The Nobel Prize laureate, Otto Heinrich Warburg, who is dealt with under the Natural sciences may surely come under the present rubric, for primarily he is a biochemist.

Thus we see that although comparatively little space has been devoted to the Jews in chemistry, it is not because they have not "patronized" the science, but on the contrary, there are so many of them engaged in it that the chapter would be just crowded with names, if one were to make an attempt to be comprehensive.

In PETROGRAPHY and MINERALOGY, we shall find among the foremost the names of Henri Moissan (referred to under chemistry) and Auguste Michel-Lévy who revolutionized the methods in studying the minerals microscopically and gave us a standard classification for all igneous rocks, emphasizing the importance of mineralizing agents in processes of differentiation. Another Lévy (Armand) was a professor of mineralogy in France more than a century ago.

In Germany one of the most outstanding mineralogists of the past century was undoubtedly Emil Wilhelm Cohen (1842-1905) who taught at Greifswald, Germany, and wrote several extensive reports of his expeditions. Perhaps of a greater calibre was Victor M. Goldschmidt (1888-1947) who was professor at Heidelberg up to 1935, when he was forced out by the Nazis, settling in Oslo, Norway, and afterwards escaping to England where he was of service to the British war effort. His greatest work was the three-volume atlas of crystal formations in minerals.

In the United States, the death of Harold Berman at the age of 42 in an airplane crash during his stay in England, on a war mission, removed one of the most promising men in the field; for at the time of the tragedy, he held the office of assistant curator of Harvard's Natural History Museum and was in line for promotion to the curatorship.

HISTORY OF SCIENCE

Even in this relatively new department, one can point to Jewish scholars as well as promoters who have added a new story to the great structure.

Charles Singer and E. J. Cohn have extended our knowledge of the medical sciences. The philosopher, Emile Meyerson, was one of the recognized authorities on the history of science in general. As anyone who only thumbs through his last work *Du Cheminement de la Pensée* (3 vols.) will observe, the man was conversant with a dozen different disciplines, in addition to chemistry.

Federigo Enriques was the co-founder and editor of *Scientia,* the international periodical which is still looked up to by scientists, while, in our own country, *The Philosophy of Science* was founded by Boris Malisoff (1895-1947) whose premature death left a gap in the promotion of the subject in this country. Another journal *The History of Ideas* was also founded and edited by Jews, but this belongs rather to the philosophical sphere.

VII

THE JEW IN THE NATURAL SCIENCES

We have seen that the contribution of the Jews to mathematics and physical science was immense, but could the same be anticipated in the field of the natural sciences? The Jews for many centuries had been deprived of a natural life, in two senses. They were driven to concentrate in cultural matters, as their ghetto became barer and bleaker and devoid of the beauties which are associated with gardens, parks, conservatories, and even meadows, for landed estates were not within their sphere of ownership, and agriculture was outside of their domain for many centuries. How then could they expect to become naturalists in any sense of the word?

And yet, the natural sciences have been substantially advanced through Jewish effort. Indeed, more than one branch owes so much to its Jewish cultivators, as we shall presently observe, that without them, it might have been impeded in its growth for lack of stimulation and ingenious grafting. Let us not look for a Jewish Darwin, Buffon, Cuvier or Lamarck. Their ancestors—if we may indulge in an Irish tale, understandable enough—were probably killed off by the Holy Inquisition, The Crusades or mobs during the Black Plague as well as by the legal murders pursuant to the blood and other libels. Aside from that, it was not until about the eighteenth century that solitary Jews were admitted to university study; and it was not until much later that even converted Jews, let alone such as practiced their faith, could utilize the facilities of research which were afforded the promising non-Jewish scientist, as a matter of course.

Through what secret channels did Jewish scientists come into their own despite the restrictions and bans will not be discussed here. Partly, of course, it was through the baptismal font, partly through sheer persistence and a singleness of purpose which stagger the imagination; but there was one trend which had been kept alive throughout the Dark Ages, despite Christian prejudice, and thanks to this, the new vistas of natural science had opened up to the Jewish investigator who further broadened the horizon and disclosed possibilities not hitherto dreamt of. It was the long medical tradition of the Jews that wafted them into anatomy, physiology, biology, bacteriology, and even zoölogy and botany including agriculture; for the common denominator of all these is *life;* and it was the task of the physician to prolong life and save lives, hence the structure and the function of the bodily organs, as well as the study of the organisms which interfered with their well-being, were within his province, and the practical purpose of healing became the foundation of the new theoretical disciplines, which turned into experimental sciences furthering human and animal life.

What is to be encompassed in the natural sciences, and where are we to begin in our survey? A systematic account of Jewish achievement in all the fields which may be subsumed under the head of the natural sciences is out of the question. The space at our disposal already has been exceeded. Perhaps it will be necessary to confine ourselves to those sciences enumerated above. Certainly the medical sciences, although they are presumably forms of anatomy, physiology and bacteriology, will have to be eliminated in the hope that they are treated in the chapter on the Jew in medicine.

As to where to begin, it scarcely matters, since it all depends on the avenue of approach. We might begin with the soil, or the microbes, plants, or anatomy and physiology. Since it is the latter that will occupy our chief attention, we might as well start with it, especially as it is in direct line with the medical pursuit which the Jews have been associated with in every country and in every age. It will scarcely be possible, in many cases, to keep the fields apart, for not only do the sciences merge into one another, but Jewish investigators, as a rule, are versatile, and, like their race, wander from one field to another.

ANATOMY AND PHYSIOLOGY

That the great founder of modern anatomy, Andreas Vesalius (1514-1564) incorporated in his epoch-making works, *Tabulae Anatomicae Sex* (1538) and the *De Humanis Corpora Fabrica* a number of Hebrew terms will be a surprise to many readers. Vesalius himself could hardly be said to have even understood the most elementary Hebrew words, but Hebrew, in its mediaeval garb, was the vogue in medical centres then, and so Vesalius, the pioneer, was in fashion. Even Arabic terms would appear in Hebrew characters in those days. C. Rabin tells us, in his learned disquisition, that "the Jewish adviser to Vesalius did not use the printed Hebrew Avicenna but borrowed from the medical jargon of Italian Jewish doctors",[25a] so far as the *Tabulae* was concerned, but the Hebrew Avicenna version was utilized for the more important *Fabrica* (1543).

It is curious that in the *Tabulae,* one may find Hebraized forms of Latin and Italian terms, and sometimes the Latinized terms would pass through the Hebrew on their way from Arabic.

Perhaps the first of important Jewish names in the medical sciences is that of G. Jacob Henle (1809-1885) who taught in several German universities, but principally at Goettingen. He was a research man, as well as a systematizer, a rare combination in science, and his range was phenomenal. As an anatomist, he was probably without an equal toward the middle of the nineteenth century. Our knowledge about the optic nerve, the cornea, the blood vessels, the intestinal cells, and the kidneys has been advanced considerably through his investigations, and the U shaped loop in kidney (vesicular canal) is called the Henle loop. Through his *Zeitschrift für rationelle Medicin,* one of the most important medical journals in the world, he promoted the cause of anatomy, physiology, and pathology perhaps as much as his illustrious contemporaries, Wunderlich, Virchow, and his own great teacher, Johannes Müller, with whom he collaborated in the volume on plagiostomi (sharks and rays). His handbooks or atlases on pathology and anatomy were standard works for decades, and his lectures on anthropology were in reality devoted to what would now be considered the psychology of personality. In William James's psychological textbooks many a diagram bears the acknowledgment to Henle.

Benedict Stilling (1810-1879) although primarily famous for his technique in surgery, having been the first to operate on the ovary without abdominal incision, and a pioneer in urethral surgery, was an eminent authority on the nervous system, particularly the spinal cord, to the knowledge of which he has added a great deal. As an extraordinarily skillful surgeon he would be in great demand throughout Germany and even France, yet he has taken the time to turn out solid works of an experimental nature.

There are several other anatomists of renown who might be referred to such as Pio Foà in Italy (1848-1923) but they were largely pathologists, and thus should be treated under the rubric of medical sciences.

That physiology should be among the sciences to have brought out the eminence of the Jews soon after their emancipation was to have been expected; for physiology is closely related to medicine; and it is in medicine that the Jews have distinguished themselves for many centuries, even during the Dark Ages. It is in Germany that their endowments seem to have realized themselves on a systematic scale, even though their ambitions did not have the same chance in that country, unless they approached the baptismal font. Scores of them raised the prestige of German science, but often they had to go to Switzerland or other countries to earn their livelihood as university teachers.

This was the fate of Gabriel Gustav Valentin, born in Breslau in 1810, who had received the award for experimental physiology offered by the Academy of Science in Paris, as a result of his Latin essay on the history of the evolution of the muscular system. The great Alexander von Humboldt interceded so that he might receive a call in Germany, but to no avail. The 26-year-old scientist accepted a professorship at the University of Berne, in Switzerland, and it was only much later that he found his place in Bonn, where he died in 1883.

Exclusive of numerous original researches, Valentin published a number of standard textbooks on anatomy and physiology, especially the nervous system. The Purkinje flicker effect which every elementary course in psychology mentions is said to have been discovered by Valentin while working together with his teacher.

It was the nervous system, and especially the brain, which attracted most Jewish physiologists, and during the '70's and '80's of the nineteenth century, the names of Munk, Rosenthal, Heidenhain, and Schiff were persons to conjure with. Sometimes casual remarks in letters are apt to give us an insight into the merit of some of the men. Thus William James, the greatest figure in American philosophy and psychology, writing to his friend, Henry Bowditch, the Harvard physiologist, describes his studies at the University of Berlin in 1867. He speaks of the series of lectures by Du Bois-Raymond and goes on to say that "two ambitious young Jews give six more a week between them, which are almost as instructive." Who these two young Jews were he does not tell us, but from the frequent citations in his *Principles of Psychology,* I should gather that one of them was Hermann Munk, who would have been only 28 then, while the other might have been Isidor Rosenthal, born in 1836.

William James, it will be borne in mind, was not only the ranking psychologist early America has produced but ranked, toward the end of the nineteenth century, as the leading scientist in the United States, according to a vote by the members of the American Association for the Advancement of Science. In his youth he had visited Germany and came in contact, as a student and instructor, with some of the greatest scientific minds in that country. I happen to have in my library a number of the textbooks which he had marked and annotated. About a dozen or more were by Jewish physiologists who are listed in this section. He was not partial to Jews, but they happen to have been the pillars of the science in the '60's and '70's, as they were, indeed, right up to the advent of Hitler. Furthermore, they all seemed to be gravitating toward neurology; and that was the closest, in those days, to psychology, which had not yet been made an academic discipline. About a hundred years ago specialization did not preclude a knowledge of allied fields and even philosophy; and James must have been drawn to the stimulating lectures of these men who were dynamic teachers as well as ingenious experimenters, and could write in a clear and attractive style.

In his *Principles of Psychology*, and even in his *Briefer Course*, James frequently cites these physiologists, anatomists, and neurologists. In 1882, he sets down his impressions of two Jewish scientists he had met in the following words:

> Yesterday I went to the veterinary school to see H. Munk, the great brain vivisector. He was very cordial and poured out a torrent of talk for one and a-half hours, though he could show me no animals. He gave me one of his new publications and introduced me to Dr. Baginsky (Professor Samuel Porter's favorite authority on the semicircular canals, whose work I treated superciliously in my article). So we opened on the semicircular canals, and Baginsky's torrent of words was even more overwhelming than Munk's. I never felt quite so helpless and small-boyish before, and am to this hour dizzy from the onslaught.

The references here are to Hermann Munk, one of two brothers famous for their brain researches, and to Benno Baginsky, one of the foremost laryngologists and otologists of this time, a brother of Adolf Baginsky, equally renowned as a child specialist.

Hermann Munk, born in Posen, in 1839, must have ranked as one of the greatest physiologists of his generation,—a generation which, by the way, teemed with distinguished names in physiology,—to have become the head of the physiological laboratory at the Veterinary School in Berlin, where he died in 1912. Munk's experimental researches on the cerebral cortex, on nerve stimulation, etc. have been discussed to this day. Immanuel Munk, a younger brother of Hermann, was perhaps even more brilliant, but he died comparatively young at the age of 51, in 1903, but even in his forties, he had become a noted figure in his field and rose to the directorship of a department of the Physiological Institute at the University of Berlin. His textbook *Physiology of Man and Mammals* went through many editions, and his chief researches were on nutrition. He was also editor of the influential *Zentralblatt für Physiologie.*

Rudolf Peter Heinrich Heidenhain (1834-1897) who at the time of his death served as Director of the Physiological Laboratory at the University of Breslau, was an experimentalist of rare distinction. His investigations on muscular metabolism, the ductless glands, and his physiological studies in general have been rated as classical.

Although Heidenhain was a convert to Christianity and may have married a non-Jewish woman, it may be mentioned *en passant* that his son, Martin, was a noted anatomist, specializing in cellular structure. He was associated with the University of Tübingen.

Like Heidenhain, Isidor Rosenthal, born in a town in the province of Posen, in 1836, was interested largely in the physiology of nerves and muscles, but his experiments in electrotherapy were among the earliest in that field of medicine, and brought prestige to the University of Erlangen where he held the chair in physiology and hygiene.

THE HEBREW IMPACT ON WESTERN CIVILIZATION

Salomon Stricker (1834-1898), although primarily a pathologist, having founded the pathological institute of Vienna, is regarded as a pioneer in several departments of physiology. His original discoveries of the subdivided cells in living tissue, as well as of the extravasation of the blood, the transformation of substance tissue into migratory cells, and the vasomotor center of the abdominal viscera, afforded him an international reputation and brought hundreds of students to his class rooms at the University of Vienna. It was he, too, who developed the theory of motor imagery in speech which the behaviorists in psychology took to be the essence of all thought. His books stressed the psychological as well as the physiological in medicine, and he might easily rank as one of the leading neurologists of his day. Had he lived a few years longer, he doubtless would have received the Nobel Prize; for, in 1920, the Danish physiologist, A. Krogh, was awarded the Prize for virtually proving experimentally the theory of the function of the capillary vessels which Stricker formulated and elaborated almost half a century earlier.

Ludwig Edinger's (1855-1918) work in neurology and anatomy was of such a high order that many of his brilliant students are still under his spell. As a comparative anatomist he had no peer during the latter part of the nineteenth century, and his *Lectures on the Central Nervous System* enjoyed many editions in German.

A physician and pharmacologist, Rudolf Magnus (1873-1927) taught at Heidelberg in Germany and Utrecht (Holland) contributing substantially to the knowledge of the central nervous system and the reflex mechanisms of bodily posture as related to the earth's motion.

Kurt Goldstein (1878-   ) has been associated with the *Gestalt* School in psychology for over 30 years, but his field is neurology, and his work on brain lesions and the more theoretical survey of the human organism have given him a prominent position in this country, where he has been residing after leaving Frankfurt during the Nazi reign of terror.

[163]

R. W. Semon (1859-1919), a practicing physician, nevertheless made his mark as the originator of a biological theory which makes memory a universal function and acquired characteristics inheritable. He was well thought of by the British Darwinists, and his book *Die Mneme*, translated into English, was well received in medical, psychological, and biological circles.

Only to deal with the most distinguished physiologists in Germany, of Jewish extraction, would require a book in itself if one were to do them justice. Almost every university in Germany, Austria, and Switzerland could boast a Jewish ornament as the head of its physiological department or "Institute" as it would be called. Among the most noted in his day was Julius Bernstein (1839-1917) son of the autodidactic popular-science writer, Aaron Bernstein, who played an important part in the Berlin Jewish Community. Julius served, in turn, as professor at Berlin, Heidelberg, and Halle, where he was Director of its Physiological Institute. His specialty was the nervous system and the sense organs, while his textbook on animal physiology was the standard work for decades.

Siegmund Exner (1846-1926), professor at the University of Vienna, will be remembered for his microscopic researches on animal tissue, his optical investigations, but particularly for his work on brain localization. His special field was neurology.

Nor can one omit such a name as Hugo Kronecker (1839-1914), brother of the mathematician who received some space in another section. Kronecker, who gave us an insight into the physiology of the heart, taught at Berne (Switzerland) and at Leipzig and Berlin. G. Embden (1874-1933), of the famous Embden family, was professor at the University of Frankfurt, and Hans Friedenthal was professor at the University of Berlin, until the Nazi regime completed its programme of *"Gleichschaltung"*. Sigmund Mayer (1842-1910) was Director of the Physiological Institute at the German University in Prague; while at Cologne, Bruno Kisch served as professor until the advent of Hitler. The localization of brain function has been established through the felicitous experimentation of Fritsch and Hitzig. At the time I absorbed this information in my elementary textbook in psychology, it hardly occurred to me that Eduard Hitzig (1838-1907), who was a professor at Halle, was descended from Frederic II's Jewish banker, Daniel Itzig.

It may well be pondered in certain quarters whether all these celebrities could be of Jewish descent, but the reader may be assured that there are not a few who have succeeded in keeping their origin a secret, and I have refrained from mentioning those whose Jewish extraction is problematic.

Among contemporary biochemists and physiologists Otto Meyerhof (1884-   ) has made a mark for himself with his researches on the chemistry of muscles, which did much to explain the cause of fatigue, and for which he, in 1922, shared the Nobel Prize in medicine, with A. B. Hill. Meyerhof seems to have lasted under the Nazi regime as late as 1938, when he was compelled to leave his post as Director of the Institute of Physiology at Heidelberg and after a year in Paris accepted a research professorship in chemistry at the University of Pennsylvania Medical School.

Another Nobel Prize man who brought fame to Germany, and is now connected with the College of Medicine of New York University, is Otto Loewi, formerly of the University of Vienna. Loewi's contribution lay in discovering the chemical nature of nerve impulses and also in his researches on the structure of the heart, as well as in his investigations on metabolism and the kidneys, but his chief work was associated with the nervous system.

Again we see how chemists and pharmacologists become pillars of physiology or, perhaps better, guideposts, which physiologists must consult in their own studies.

One of the most honored scientists of the past generation was Karl Landsteiner, and even though he was a pathologist and immunologist, his service to physiology was of incalculable value, for it was he who discovered the four blood groups, a discovery which made blood transfusion a relatively safe and simple matter, thus saving millions of lives. Not only was he the recipient of the Nobel Prize, in 1930, but medals came to him from many organizations and lands.

Through some quirk of racial inferiority, this superior mind ridiculously took legal measures to prevent a Jewish biographical reference work from listing him as a Jew, which fact he attempted to conceal even in his own home.

In Poland, the name of Marian Eiger, scion of the great talmudical Eger family, shone in the annals of physiology for several decades. It was he who discovered the electric nerve-cell in the heart, which is now called the Eiger cell, and he had also a hand in the application of insulin in diabetic cases, independently of Banting.

Another luminary in the firmament of Polish natural science—and there were few among the Poles—was Maximilian Rose, probably the foremost neurologist in Poland. One of the ironies of our age was revealed when this ornament of science, lecturing in the University of Warsaw, in the thirties, would find his daughter standing together with other Jewish students, since there was a Jim Crow rule about Jewish students not being allowed to sit, on the same benches, with Gentile students.

Enrico Sereni (1901-1931), uncle of Enzo Sereni, who gave his life as a voluntary parachutist with the Jewish brigade in the Nazi war, was director of the Physiological Institute at Naples. At the University of Rome, the chair of physiology was held by Giulio Fano (1856-1930) who was also Dean of the Faculty of the Natural Sciences, while at Palermo, Simone Fubino (1841-1898) exercised a similar function.

In Holland, we find Hartog Jacob Hamburger invested with the professorship in the department of physiology, and in Belgium, T. G. Gottlieb (1812-1898) rose to eminence not only because he was physician to the royal family in Brussels, but because of his microscopic researches which led to his appointment as professor at the University of Brussels. Even Estonia had its Jewish Director at the Physiological Institute in Dorpat—Alexander Lipschütz. Indeed there is scarcely a country in Europe which does not have a Physiological Institute graced by a Jewish Director.

Botany and Plant Pathology

In the survey of the biological sciences as affected by Jews, we might have started with vegetable life, plants, the flora, etc., since life begins here, but the physiological record is far more impressive, and occupies our attention especially as it is nearer home. Our body is always with us, and we are ever aware of its processes. It would be a mistake, however, to suppose that botany has been neglected by the descendants of the ghetto denizens, as we shall see in the following pages. Experimental botany would have been in a backward state were it not for the endeavors of Ferdinand Cohn and Julius Sachs during the latter half of the nineteenth century.

Ferdinand Julius Cohn (1828-1898) was, without doubt, one of the greatest, if not actually the greatest of nineteenth century botanists. Aside from his original contributions to the morphology of algae and fungi, it was he who might be considered the father of modern bacteriology; for in the first place he established, about the middle of the last century, the fact that bacteria were plants and secondly he gave the *congé* to the doctrine of spontaneous generation, although it was Pasteur who gave it the *coup de grâce* through his celebrated experimental thesis, which won the prize of the French Academy. Cohn, furthermore, was fortunate in his students many of whom forged ahead on their own, perhaps the most distinguished being the non-Jew, Robert Koch, the conqueror of tuberculosis. The founder and director of the Breslau Botanical Institute, Cohn enjoyed the esteem and admiration of his colleagues throughout the world and on the occasion of his seventieth birthday in 1898, 250 botanists of many lands issued an album in his honor, in which were mounted the portraits of his collaborators and students.

One of the outstanding figures in modern botany was the Breslau-born Julius Sachs (1832-1897) son of an engraver. From his humble circumstances, thanks to his stimulating teacher, Purkinje, he rose to fame as the Director of the Plant Institute which he founded at the University of Würzburg. His researches, particularly on plant physiology, and the influence of ultra-violet rays and heat on the growth of plants were both numerous and definitive. His handbook of the experimental physiology of plants and his textbook on botany, as well as his history of botany, which, incidentally, stresses the contribution of his contemporary Ferdinand Julius Cohn, are still highly regarded by authorities.

Another important botanist, a contemporary of both Cohn and Sachs was Nathaniel Pringsheim, whose brother Alfred, was mentioned in the section on mathematics, and whose nephew, Ernest, was adverted to in the section on physics. It was Nathaniel Pringsheim who founded the Institute for Plant Physiology at the University of Jena. Pringsheim's many and fruitful investigations on chlorophyll and plant life led to the discovery of sexuality and the nature of cryptogamy among plants. Microscopic botany owes much to his ingenious technique.

Plant pathology had in Paul Sorauer, another Breslau-born scientist, one of its chief representatives. It must be borne in mind that a hundred years ago, the notion of diseases among plants was quite novel, and Sorauer had made the peasants beholden to him for his "preventive medicine". As founder of the first periodical devoted to plant pathology, he was instrumental in advancing this branch of botany, which was later to make such remarkable strides.

It is perhaps more than a coincidence that these four giants in botany were all born in Silesia, and three of them (Cohn, Sorauer, and Sachs) in Breslau, which is now a Polish city, so that they might have been regarded as Polish Jews. Breslau has been considered the most Jewish city in Germany, next to Frankfurt-a-M. But other towns have contributed their share.

There is, for instance, the Berlin-born Paul Ascherson (1834-1913) who accompanied Rohlf on his expedition to Libya and studied the flora of Ethiopia, Egypt, and Tripoli. Later he made a thorough survey of Central European flora. Ascherson became Professor at the University of Berlin while scarcely forty, and participated in the publication of several standard handbooks.

Plant cytology and that part of botany which deals with fertilization, and the histological phase, in general, were cultivated, on a large scale, by the Warsaw-born Eduard Strasburger, who made a career for himself as Professor of botany at the University of Bonn. The yearbooks of scientific botany which he published, as well as the cytological studies, which appeared periodically at the Bonn Botanical Institute, gave considerable prestige to the Department which he directed at Bonn.

Among the more prominent botanists of the past century were: Eugen Askenasi, born in Odessa (1845-1903), who taught at Heidelberg and published, besides many valuable papers on plant physiology, a critical examination of Darwin's theory which drew a flattering comment from the great naturalist himself; Leo Abraham Errera (1858-1905) Director of the Botanical Institute at the University of Brussels, but unlike his German synethnicists (I propose this term in place of co-religionists, since Jews and converts to Christianity can hardly be called co-religionists) he always took a keen interest in the life of his brethren; Siegfried Friedländer, Professor of agricultural technology at the University of Breslau; Paul Wilhelm Magnus, Professor at Freiburg, and many others.

In England, Dr. Redcliffe N. Salaman has been long known for his dealing with the potato virus. In Palestine, Aaron Aaronson who was the discoverer of wild wheat was a name to conjure with in the early pioneer days of the Jewish colonies. The progress of Palestine which led eventually to the emergence of Israel, was definitely associated with agriculturists and botanists of the stature of Otto Warburg (1859-1938) who, prior to his incumbency at the Hebrew University was professor of botany at the University of Berlin.

In India, we find Moses Ezekiel heading the department of botany in Wilson College, Bombay; and in New Zealand, E. B. Levy occupies a high position as a specialist on various grasses.

In the United States, Jewish investigators have reached a high level of achievement. One can point, for instance, to the work of Jacob J. Taubenhaus (1884-1937) who, although born in Safed, Palestine, into a family remarkable for the prominence of its members, received his principal training at the National Farm School and at Cornell University. Serving in the capacity of plant pathologist at Delaware College and at the Agricultural Experiment Station in Texas, where he also taught soil bacteriology and plant pathology, he was instrumental in saving the crops of this country time after time through his application of sprays, containing sulphur, and became a much sought consultant in connection with perishable foods, on the part of railroad authorities. Several of his books on diseases of vegetables, like the sweet pea, onions, sweet potatoes, etc., have attracted considerable attention in agricultural circles.

A ranking agriculturist was Jacob Goodale Lipman (1874-1939) who like his successor, Selman Waksman, brought fame to his alma mater, Rutgers University, where he founded the department of bacteriology and soil chemistry, later becoming the Dean of its Agricultural College.

On more than one occasion, Lipman represented the United States Government at the International Institute of Agriculture in Rome, which, by the way, was the brain-child of another Jew, the Polish-born David Lubin, whose centenary was recently observed with great solemnity, in Rome, on an international scale. Elected President of the First International Congress of Soil Science, in 1927, Lipman received several awards for his numerous studies on soil bacteriology and kindred subjects.

Equally recognized as a soil expert was his younger brother, C. B. Lipman (1883-1944) who like his brother had served on many committees, scientific, academic, and philanthropic and yet had the time to produce important papers on heat resistance of bacteria, the relation of plant physiology to colloidal chemistry, bacteria found alive in ancient rocks, bacteria in the sea, and the mineral metabolism of higher plants. Lipman was Professor of plant physiology at the University of California, and later became Dean of the Graduate Division there.

On a lesser scale, but certainly influential in his own sphere, was Joseph Rosen (1876-1949) whose rather eventful life took him as a young Moscow student very reluctantly to Siberia, whence he escaped to Germany. Graduated from the University of Heidelberg, he came to America in 1903. After the First World War, he returned to Russia not as a political fugitive from justice but in order to resettle 250,000 Jews on farms in the Crimea and the Ukraine. As director of the Agro-Joint, he was mainly the administrator and executive, but he was also the discoverer of a type of winter rye now grown in a large part of the United States, and highly esteemed for introducing American farming methods and American Indian maize into the frequently famine-stricken Volga region in Russia.

Zoölogy

Although the Jews are not to be credited with as much zeal and genius in zoölogy as they have shown in other branches of the biological sciences, it is curious that the man who may be said to have laid the foundations of ichthyology (the study of fishes) was Marcus Eliezer Bloch who was born in 1723 and died in 1799 at Carlsbad. Taking his degree in medicine, he abandoned the medical career in order to devote his energy toward studying the life of fish, first in the waters both of and surrounding Germany; and then elsewhere. No one before his time had such an ambitious project in zoölogy, and no one has given the world such a comprehensive and illustrated survey, together with an essay embodying a new system of classification, as did Bloch. As an ichthyologist, Bloch was without a rival for decades; and he was especially proud of a letter in praise of his work he had received from King Frederick's daughter.

But let us not suppose that Bloch was the only zoölogist of Jewish stock in Germany. There were quite a few, although not as many or as great as in other fields covered in this survey.

We can e.g. add names like Hermann Loew (1807-1879) who in his *horae anatomicae* presented a system of insect anatomy and joined the small band of entomologists who flourished at the time.

A more important naturalist was Emil Selenka (1842-1902) the author of a series of volumes on zoölogy and animal evolution, which he published while he was teaching at the University of Munich.

In Italy, the standard textbook in zoölogy was long held to have been that of Paolo Enriques (1878-1932) who occupied the chair of zoölogy and comparative anatomy at the University of Padua, and who was regarded as the dean of Italian zoölogists. If it were only for his experimental studies on protozoa and his conception of the cellular theory, he might have had an honored place in the annals of zoölogy, but the man was also an authority on genetics, as we shall see in the section on genetics.

In the United States, Libbie H. Hyman has written several excellent textbooks. Her volume on the *Invertebrates* is particularly well thought of. Ornithology is well represented by H. Friedmann, Curator of the Department of Birds in the United States National Museum of the Smithsonian Institution, who has been the head of several expeditions to distant lands. David E. Fink, who has spent many years as an entomologist with the United States Department of Agriculture, has revealed a number of interesting facts in relation to insects, particularly on the effect of certain poisons on the respiratory system of such organisms.

The British Jews, as in the other sciences, do not offer a galaxy of names in the biological sciences, but the few we encounter are significant. There is *e. g.,* Marcus Hartog (1851-1924). His work on the egg cell, on protozoa, and on rotifera has been widely discussed in the biological literature; and his *Problems of Life and Reproduction* contains a survey of his views. Born in London, he taught at Owens College, in Manchester and Queen's College, Cork, Ireland, until a few years before his death.

Salomon M. Herzenstein, who died at the age of 40, nevertheless was sufficiently recognized under the regime of Alexander II to be appointed custodian of the Zoölogical Museum of the Imperial Academy of Science in St. Petersburg. Published at the age of 30, his report on the fish and molluscs on the coast of the Murmansk Sea, brought him considerable praise from veteran scientists.

In the domain of ornithology and especially entomology, the names of Lionel Walter Rothschild (1868-1937) and his brother Nathaniel Charles Rothschild will be remembered because of their devotion to these branches of natural science. The elder of the two, Lionel, might have become the head of the great banking firm which his father built up in England, but he chose to cultivate the life of a naturalist. His collection of birds and butterflies was probably the rarest in the world, having taken 40 years to assemble and costing over a million dollars in periodic purchases. Of his million and a-half varieties of butterflies and moths, the larger part went to the British Museum.

Genetics

Genetics has attracted a fair number of Jewish investigators, both on the theoretical and the practical side. The best known is probably Jacques Loeb, who has to his credit many discoveries in chemistry, physiology, and biology, but his chief results were obtained in the genetic field where he has shown through an ingenious technique that in disparate crossings of certain organisms, the male parent contribution consists in initiating growth, but not in implanting characteristics. Let us see how Jennings, himself one of America's foremost biologists, describes Loeb's achievement.

> A method of inducing cross-fertilization between certain very diverse marine organisms was discovered by J. Loeb. By putting certain chemicals in the sea water, he found that the sperms from one type could be carried to enter the ova of very different types bringing about development. In this way he induced fertilization of the ova of the sea urchin by sperms of starfish, holothurians, and even mulluscs and annelids.
>
> It turned out that in such crosses between very diverse organisms the development of the egg produced offsprings that were not intermediate between two parental types but were like the mother only . . . showing no influence of the male parent.[26]

The explanation of this phenomenon lies in the fact that there is incompatibility between the two different organisms so the sperm merely initiates the development of the ovum but dies thereafter, and only the chromosomes of the mother play a part in further process. This laboratory technique on the part of Loeb has earned the name "artificial parthenogenesis".

Loeb, who studied in Strassburg (now part of France but at that time belonging to Germany) seemed to have been influenced by the French physiologists of the nineteenth century, breaking away from the German trend which then predominated over the scientific world. Later, his views comported with the experimental results in Russia. Both Loeb and Pavlov were intent on reducing instincts to elemental mechanisms, tropisms in the case of the former and reflexes in the case of the latter.

"Loeb," writes Emanuel Rádl, a Czech authority on the history of the natural sciences, "was the real founder of the modern school". According to Rádl, Loeb was influenced not only by his teacher, Goltz, who, as every psychology student knows, showed us that the decerebrate dog can still not only live but perform a good many functions, but by Julius Sachs's views on plant physiology.

> In his early experiments, he treated the animals purely as chemical aggregates, neglecting all the facts relating to structural differentiation or to systematic position. . . . Loeb afterwards settled in America and the result of his marvellous industry was the new science of comparative physiology. In its broad outlines, this new subject followed his teaching. No attention was paid to the facts of anatomy, but the organism was treated as a "chemical machine consisting essentially of colloidal substance".[27]

It is interesting to note that Henle and Edinger were the founders of comparative anatomy, while Loeb was the founder of a new school in comparative physiology. Loeb had given the world the doctrine of tropisms, showing that insects had no other motives in their activities than turning toward or away from light, water, earth, etc., as *e. g.,* in the case of the cockroach. It looked as if Loeb might convince a too eager scientific world that man, too, was simply a tropic animal, but Loeb's extreme materialistic system did not last. As a trained chemist, he wanted to reduce everything to chemistry or physical properties.

It may be related casually that at one time, his close friend, the Columbia psychologist, J. McKeen Cattell, proposed his election to the exclusive Century Club in New York, but Loeb was blackballed, whereupon Cattell, one of the most influential figures among men of science, resigned from the Club, attributing the rejection on the part of the majority of the members to anti-Semitism. The Club denied that this was the motive and pointed to Loeb's erratic doctrines and methods.

Few living geneticists are on a par with Hermann Joseph Muller (1890), who began his career as a zoölogist, teaching at various universities, including Columbia, and the University of Edinburgh, and now settled at the University of Indiana. Muller's chief work has been in genetics, much of which he carried on at the Institute of Genetics in Moscow, USSR. His breeding experiments on the fruit fly, drosophila, his analysis or arrangements and methods of recombining hereditary units, particularly his studies on mutation, and artificial transmutation of the gene through X-rays, changes that heralded a new era in genetics and shed a flood of light on chromosome activity earned for him the Nobel prize in medicine, in 1946. Although he has not written many books, his scientific papers, which are numerous, are marked by significant results.

RUSSIA

Our knowledge about the rôle of Jewish scientists in Russia is scant, but it must not be supposed that there were no Jewish professors of physiology in Russia during the Czarist regime. Naturally most, if not all, had to make the supreme national or religious sacrifice. Thus one may list Friedrich Arnheim (1845-1893) who taught at St. Petersburg, Natan Bernstein (1836-1891), who was a lecturer at the University of Odessa, and of course there were quite a few others, but none were of international repute, as Lina Shtern is today. Naturally since Germany or Switzerland offered a greater arena for their activities, many budding scientists in the natural sciences would leave for better opportunities. We do know that in the laboratories of Pavlov and Bekhterev, there were always a few promising Jewish assistants.

It is characteristic of the present age that perhaps the foremost physiologist in USSR at the present time is a woman of

Jewish birth, Lina Shtern (born in 1892), who is the recipient of many awards and honors both in her own country and abroad for her work on the chemistry of nerve action, endocrinology, and other related fields. A prolific and ingenious researcher, she is also an organizer of unusual ability, having been appointed by the USSR Government to take charge of research projects in several of the most important Institutes in the country. Not only has she been officially recognized as an "honored scientist" but she is the first woman to have been elected to full membership in the Academy of Science, founded by a woman (Catherine "The Great"). Her service in preparing young scientists to engage in important war activities, as well as in rehabilitation work, is outstanding; and many of her students have themselves become distinguished physiologists.

Of almost equal prominence is the Director of the Physiological Laboratories at the Institute of Experimental Medicine in Leningrad, Joseph Rozental.

As a result of the upsurge of Mitchurinism in USSR, with the stress on environmental influence in growth, we have come to learn that at least a few of those who have brought on their head the ire of Lysenko and his political biologists, or rather agriculturists, are Jews, e.g., Rapoport and Shmalhausen. Whether they have lost all means of earning a livelihood because of their adherence to Western views, which means a belief in the processes of heredity as promulgated by Mendel, Weismann, and Morgan, we do not know at this writing, but it is safe to say that their scientific career is at an end, unless the party line changes in this matter; and it is very doubtful whether any other theory will suit dialectical materialists who must never compromise as to whether Marx and Darwin were infallible on the point of extra-organismic circumstances playing an overwhelming part in the shaping of an individual physically, mentally, or morally.

In genetics, Norway has scarcely a greater authority than Otto L. Mohn (1886-   ) while in Denmark, Harald Goldschmidt exercises a similar influence in the practical phase of cattle breeding.

Although genetics has not had the same following in Germany as other branches of biology, several Jews in pre-Nazi Germany have made a reputation for themselves along these lines, e. g., Richard B. Goldschmidt (1878-   ) who is at present Professor of Zoölogy at the University of California. Goldschmidt, who began with an experimental investigation of the cell, later became one of the foremost exponents of the theory of heredity. His book on the determination of sex was translated into English in 1923. Goldschmidt published the Silliman lectures, which he was asked to deliver at Yale, under the title of *The Material Basis of Evolution.* He was also the founder of the *Archiv für Zellforschung.*

Eugenio Rignano (1870-1930) who, in Italy, took over the editing of *Scientia* after the death of Enriques, was influential as a philosophical biologist, aligning himself with the school of Driesch, in Germany, and the group, in England, who believed in the transmission of acquired tendencies. He wrote on international affairs, socialism, the psychology of reasoning, biological memory; and his system or view of life may be called biological synthesis. He was strongly averse to materialistic doctrines and leaned toward vitalism. Many of his books appeared in English translation; some in French. It is scarcely surprising to find no reference to him in the *Universal Jewish Encyclopedia,* with its many omissions, but the absence of his sketch in the great *Enciclopedia Italiana* is truly puzzling.

UNITED STATES

With the decline of German science, after the Nazi purge, this country is fast becoming the world's scientific centre; and although we have had several distinguished Jewish physiologists years ago, the influx of scientists from abroad had strengthened that branch of the natural or medical sciences considerably. The name of Samuel J. Meltzer (1851-1920) who was the head of the department of physiology at the

Rockefeller Institute is one to be met with quite frequently in physiological periodicals, and Moses Kunitz, who once assisted Jacques Loeb, has now turned to biochemical problems. Selig Hecht (1892-1947) who was on the staff of Columbia University for years was regarded as one of the chief authorities in vision, and was a good physicist, too, while Harold E. Himwich, now chief of the Clinical Research Branch of the Army Chemical centre has brought out some important papers on brain and carbohydrate metabolism as well as on respiration. There is a full score, at least, of Jewish physiologists in the professoriate of leading universities, but I fear that the list would hardly be appreciated in an altogether too long section.

Although primarily a biochemist, and probably the foremost at the present time, Otto Heinrich Warburg (1883-   ) Director of the Kaiser Wilhelm Institute für Zellphysiologie (until his Semitic origin could no longer be countenanced despite his conversion) and winner of the Nobel Prize in 1931, has been regarded highly by physiologists because of his fundamental discoveries about the metabolism of tumors (which constitutes a ray of hope toward the conquest of the dreaded cancer) and the catalytic effects of living tissue.

Latterly, however, he had been directing research on vegetation, and the discovery of his group that the soil could yield a great deal more in the form of food products at a fraction of the energy which is required from the sun is on the way to revolutionize the accepted order in that regard; for it points to methods of supplying the world's needs without the recurrent fears of famine. The report read at the 1949 meeting of the American Association for the Advancement of Science was one of the most encouraging heard for a long time in these days of atom bombs.

Warburg has only returned to his old preoccupation, for as early as 1932, he had been engaged in studying the yellow enzyme and was able to separate from the crystallized protein the vitamin we now know as riboflavin. "In 1935, Warburg showed that nicotinic acid in conjunction with phosphates, certain sugars and a specific protein, was an essential catalyst in the oxidative process occurring in the living organism and indeed that a particular point in the nicotinic acid molecule was the specific locus of the oxidation reaction".[28]

Thus we see that the most recent development along nutritional lines was only the result of his earlier hypotheses and experimentation.

Of all the German scientists who were forced out of their fatherland, Otto H. Warburg is the only one who returned to rehabilitate the sadly declining sciences in that country. What is more, he is attracting some American experimentalists to his Institute.

VIII

THE JEW IN BACTERIOLOGY

At first blush, it would not be difficult to surmise Jewish interest in bacteriology, or what is now called microbiology; for that is closely associated with medicine; and since Jewish physicians have been the banner bearers of the medical sciences, such contacts might readily be anticipated.

There is, however, another angle to the story; and a story it is of rare human interest; nay, of blood and fire; and, of course, it was the Jews who were subjected to both ordeals with ne'er a chance of eluding them.

Many a reader may have never heard the phrase "desecrating the host". The present writer has known the phrase before he reached his teens, but it took another decade or more to discover what that crime really meant. I had thought till then that it was supposedly looking at the gilded cross in a Corpus Christi procession with a smile of scorn. That it had something to do with the Last Supper and the symbolic rite of Holy Communion, when the blessing pronounced over the wine and the wafer is supposed to turn the drink and food into the blood and flesh of Jesus was not even dreamed of in my student days. And yet because of the assumed desecration of this wafer which has via the blessing become the Host, hundreds of thousands of Jews were tortured, burned, hacked to death, the ghettos pillaged, and, indeed, on one occasion alone, when a German ruffian named *Rindfleisch*, in 1298, led a mob from one town to another, covering Franconia, Bavaria, and Austria no less than a hundred thousand Jews were slaughtered—possibly one third of the Jewish people—and nearly 150 communities were wiped out.

This was only the repetition, on a larger scale, of what had happened in Berlin a few decades earlier; and these brutal attacks on the strength of a "desecrated" wafer recurred almost periodically until the late Renaissance. All that some fanatical priest or bigoted demagogue had to do was to demonstrate a red-stained wafer with the splenetic outburst that the Jews had pounded the wafer into a mortar, knowing that it was the body of the Lord—and the inflamed fury of the rabble knew no bounds. Had there been a grain of reason functioning in the minds of the masses, it would have been at once perceived how monstrously absurd the charge was *prima facie*; for if the Jews had believed that the wafer could be transformed into the body of Jesus, they would have become Christians themselves. But those were not reasoning days, and centuries hence, the same will be said about our hydrogen bomb era.

What concerns us here is the connection between the particular charge and bacteria. That connection was discovered only during the last century, and appropriately enough, it was the Jewish botanist, Ferdinand Cohn, who made a thorough investigation of the phenomenon after it transpired that the polenta—a sort of maize gruel which is a favorite dish with the Italian peasant—was apparently blood-stained. The ignorant peasants naturally looked upon this as an ill omen, but the Italian scientists found that the red color was due to the multiplication of a bacillus which settled on the food in specially hot and damp weather and ingested parts of the food, so that even the bread would become moist and gummy. Now it can be understood that the wafers kept in the damp cellars of churches would precipitate a growth of these bacteria on humid days, and often overnight, the yellowish color of the wafer would turn crimson. Here was a case of a bacterium, which is no more harmful than most of the microbes we find in milk, water, or other edibles becoming the unwitting cause of a frightful extermination of a people through witless "macrobes". The particular microbe, incidentally, was named "bacillus prodigiosus" i. e. the "wonder microbe". This was no more wonderful than the moulds which have given us penicillin, streptomycin, and other antibiotics, but, I suppose the blood association made it look awesome.

This was not the only account which the Jews had to square with the microbe. While in the case of the *monas prodigiosus,* the Jews were blamed for *killing* a wafer that was supposed to be divine flesh, in another instance, where microbes were active, the Jews were charged with causing the dread scourge known as the Black Death, which took a heavy toll of both Jew and Gentile, but because of their hygienic and dietary laws, the Jews were favored by fate. Did I say favored by fate? They were favored by the germs only to be more brutally dealt with by their inhuman human neighbors.

It was reasoned that since the Jews were spared in many cases while the Gentile population was ravaged, the Jews must have had something to do with it; and since the wells were more or less accessible, it occurred to the unreasoning minds of the prejudiced that the Jews had been poisoning the water. It was in Germany that this belief was especially current, and naturally the Jews in Germany suffered the most; and those who survived the plague were slaughtered by the incited mobs. In Spain, although the Black Death carried off members of the royal family, even the king himself, there was no mass hysteria welling up against the Jews, but elsewhere they were mowed down by the frenzied hordes who were only looking for an excuse to vent their wrath and plunder their victims of their possessions.

Thus the microbes played a large part in Jewish history, and it was perhaps poetic justice that the Jews should play an equal part in the history of microbes, but curiously enough it was not from the medical side that they were first approached but from the botanical. We all know the pioneer labors of the great Pasteur, who incidentally was no medical man but a chemist, but during the same time that Pasteur was investigating these unseen devils, there was a young man in Breslau probing their life and behavior and using somewhat different methods. That scientist was Ferdinand Julius Cohn, who was the first to call that organism a *bacillus*, and to classify it under the head of vegetative life. As we have seen in an earlier section, Cohn was primarily a botanist, perhaps the greatest experimental botanist of the century, but he was also the founder of plant pathology, and thus his connection with bacteriology. One of his numerous brilliant pupils, by the way, was Robert Koch, thanks to whom tuberculosis has become a relatively infrequent cause of death.

In Pasteur's own institute, the Jewish tradition seems to have been unbroken for nearly a century; for, shortly after the famous Pasteur Institute began to function, we find Elie Metchnikoff intrenched therein as director of research; and after Pasteur's death, it was he who carried on as the chief.

Elie Metchnikoff, although his father was not Jewish, deserves an honored place in our account of Jewish endeavor because he resembled his mother, and unlike virtually all the Jewish Nobel laureates, made special mention of his Jewish mother, and probably he was named for his maternal grandfather.

Metchnikoff's colorful and hard life, in spite of his eventual triumphs was described by his devoted wife, Olga, whom he married after losing his first wife under the most trying circumstances. Born in Russia, in 1845, we find him a professor of zoölogy at the University of Odessa before he had passed the quarter-century mark. Soon he came into conflict with the authorities and left for Sicily, where he began the series of microscopic observations that were to make him famous.

We must remember that the nascent science of bacteriology was hardly in its swaddling clothes. Pasteur, its founder, was still a comparatively young man when Metchnikoff made his epoch-making discovery that there were wandering cells in the blood, the phagocytes, which wage battle on the incoming bacilli in case of disease; and thus the body is really a theatre of war, and not merely a theatrical stage.

Metchnikoff's theory was not taken kindly to in all medical circles. The Germans particularly were opposed to his con-clusions. It was thought generally that the chemical action of the blood was sufficient to rise to the occasion and immunize the body, but Pasteur, genial genius that he was, recognized the man's scientific prowess and invited him to work in his Institute directing the laboratory research, which, thanks to him, yielded some of the most fruitful results in immunology. In 1908 Metchnikoff was awarded the Nobel Prize, and his co-winner was Paul Ehrlich of Salvarsan fame.

Metchnikoff's name is often popularly associated with the buttermilk fad which came into vogue as a result of the doc-trine that the bacteria in this substance, a favorite food among the Bulgarians, who were particularly known for their longevity, alkalized the putrefying bacteria in the large intes-tine, but surely his discovery of the curative properties of calomel ointment when applied in the early stages of syphilis was of vastly greater importance.

Metchnikoff died in Paris, in 1916, a celebrated scientist, and his *Immunity in Infectious Diseases* was translated into several languages. The microbe known as *spiralis Metchni-kovii,* which will be found in the dictionary, was named in his honor by an admiring disciple.

While Metchnikoff was startling the scientific world with his epoch-making theories, a young Jew from Odessa was engaged in experiments in the Pasteur Institute. That young man was destined to be regarded as a savior by millions of Asiatics. But let the Dean of medical biographers tell the story in his crisp but dramatic style.

> The Russian-Jewish physician, Waldemar Morde-cai Wolff Haffkine (1860-1930), was destined to be one of the foremost explorers of the disease-map of India. He made his mark (1891) when Pasteur, importuned by the kingdom of Siam for a remedy against cholera, placed the problem in the hands of the bacteriologist from Odessa, who discovered the method of inoculation with attenuated virus against cholera. Upon the request of the British Government that he investigate cholera in its homeland (1893), Haffkine surveyed extensive regions in India, includ-ing all of Bengal and the Punjab. Next the Indian Government (1896) asked him to study the plague in its ancient habitat, and Haffkine, in India, devised the prophylactic inoculation which robbed the Asiatic plague of its world-terrorizing power.[29]

What the article on medical explorers did not state nat-urally was that Haffkine, who looked, for all the world, like a high-minded French church dignitary, and was brought up without a religious training, nevertheless toward the end of his life became attached to Jewish orthodoxy and spent a large part of his time and fortune aiding its cause, not only in organization work but by writing and monetary contribu-tions. His will left close to a quarter of a million dollars for the establishment of yeshivahs and religious schools for the Jewish youth. He was pious himself and often his prayer shawl (*talith*) or phylacteries were seen on him by visitors, who expected the world famous scientist to have shed long since the religious rites and customs of his people.

Another conquest was to be made by the Pasteur Institute and again it was a Jewish scientist who carried on the tradition. This time it was Alexander Besredka, who prepared a serum which was to kill off the dread typhus microbe.

Alexander Besredka (1870-1940) also hailed from Odessa, although he afterwards not only became a naturalized Frenchman but fought in the French army against the Germans. Besredka's theories on immunization represented a revolt against accepted doctrine in medical circles, and his results bore out his theory. The Besredka method in administering serums has saved thousands against the frequent accidents consequent upon anaphylactic injections. Most of his works have been translated into English and other languages.

And to complete the cycle, the Pasteur Institute has recently electrified the world by announcing the preparation of an elixir which rejuvenates the tissues. The man who was responsible for this elixir is the young Jewish physician, Bardach.

But let it not be supposed that all the while, the Jewish medical men in Germany were resting on their oars. Perhaps no name in modern medicine has been more signally honored than that of Paul Ehrlich, who is known to millions as the man who had given to the world an effective cure for syphilis, under the name of Salvarsan, more popularly labelled "606", because of the 605 previous attempts at such preparation which failed; but this great scientist thanks to whose efforts, the sins of the fathers are no longer visited on the innocent children and who has inspired the "Magic Bullet", a film seen by many millions, is the pioneer of a new field in medicine—chemotherapy, based on the theory that each bit of tissue is chemically constituted so as to react specifically to various changes. In proving this theory through ingenious dye methods, he had in Karl Weigert, an able partner.

If Ehrlich found the cure for syphilis, it was August Wassermann (1866-1925) who discovered the blood test which is now clinical routine with everyone undergoing a thorough hospital examination. The difference between a "positive" and a "negative Wassermann" is of far-reaching significance to the examiner as well as to the patient. An equally great name in bacteriology and immunology is that of Albert Neisser, the man who discovered the microbe responsible for the development of gonorrhea.

One might be tempted to recount the exploits of the galaxy of Jews who toiled to relieve suffering or, better still, to *prevent* it—men like Joseph Goldberger, who gave us the key to the pellagra scourge, or Belá Schick, who has devised the test for diphtheria, which bears his name, and many others, but again the space restriction looms up, and it is quite likely that many of the purely medical achievements will be treated in chapters on the medical sciences. We are here confining our attention to the part Jews have played in exploring the inroads of the bacteria. When we consider that a microbe is about 1/25000 of an inch in length, in other words that it takes 25000 of them to make an inch, we can only marvel at the superhuman patience of these men who have devoted their lives in the interest of science; and let us also bear in mind that bacteria have been investigated largely by other than medical men. Those microscopic organisms are not all harmful; indeed some are very useful, and from various fields of research men converged to study them.

Even Weizmann had worked with bacteria. That was at the time of the first World War. Acetone was needed badly by the British for their shells, and Weizmann was sought out by a high officer of the navy to set his mind on the problem. First he had to find a supply of butyl alcohol. He was not interested in the ethyl alcohol which is produced through fermentation by the action of yeast bacteria. It was not long before he discovered a bacterium which gave him both butyl alcohol and acetone—and in large quantities. The manufacture of acetone became a war industry on a gigantic scale, and distilleries were set up not only in England, but in the United States and Canada as well. Just as Fritz Haber was able to produce synthetic ammonia out of the nitrogen in the air, thus making it possible for the Germans to protract the war, when they appeared to be at the end of their rope, so Weizmann solved the British problem.

It was said that when the then Premier, Lloyd George, asked Weizmann what premium he might choose for the incalculable assistance, either in the form of a royal honor or a pension, he declined to accept anything for himself but asked that his only reward be the establishment of Palestine as a homeland for the Jews, a plea which resulted in the Balfour declaration. This was particularly appropriate, since A. James Balfour was at the time First Lord of the Admiralty.

Boris Chain (originally the name was *Kheyn*, which is the Hebrew for *charm*) has written another illustrious page in the annals of science, when he, H. W. Florey and Alexander Fleming were jointly awarded the Nobel Prize.

Like Metchnikoff, Haffkine, and Besredka, Chain, too, hailed from Russia, but settled in Berlin, where he was a member at large of the Jewish bohemian colony, which had its headquarters in the Romanisches Café near the zoölogical gardens. He even belonged to the *Sholem Aleichem Club*, which would indicate that he is familiar with Yiddish. When Berlin became more of a hazard than a nuisance for Jews, he settled at Oxford, England, working in Florey's laboratory. At the time, Fleming's discovery of penicillin was known but not fully recognized even in medical circles. Florey and Chain then turned their attention to the next possibilities of penicillin, and it was through their efforts that the mould became so efficacious in therapy. Although Florey was Chain's superior, it was no doubt that the Jewish scientist had the special task of working out the specific technique of the experiments.

Chain received many honors in addition to the Nobel Prize, such as the Berzelius Medal of the Swedish Medical Society and the Pasteur Medal, and he is also a commander of the French Legion of Honor.

If this section concludes with the exploits of Selman Abraham Waksman (1888-   ) it is not because there are no other bacteriologists who deserve a place here, but because his life work represents a typical story of the Jewish immigrant boy who brought fame to his adopted country and comfort to the world's sufferers without profiting materially from his intense and arduous labors.

Like his great predecessors in the field which he has so thoroughly cultivated, he originally came from Russia, in fact close to the birthplace of Metchnikoff, Haffkine, Besredka and Chain's family, and after studying at Rutgers University, under the eminent soil chemist and bacteriologist Jacob G. Lipman, also Russian born, he took his Ph.D. at the University of California, under the latter's younger brother, and then settled down to teaching at his alma mater, where he is the most important man on the campus, for aside from the prestige which has accrued to him because of his discoveries— discoveries that should have afforded him the Nobel Prize, he may be regarded as one of the greatest benefactors to Rutgers University, in that the royalties accumulating on the drugs which Merck's has been putting on the market, are going toward the establishment of an Institute of Microbiology which promises to be the greatest in the world. But let us quote *Time*, which has had occasion to issue news stories on Waksman on more than one occasion.

> When Rutgers University needed to save some money during the war winter of 1941-42, a budget official had a bright idea: Why not fire Selman Waksman, an obscure Ukrainian-born microbiologist who was getting $4,620 a year for "playing around with microbes in the soil"? That sort of fun and games, the moneyman pointed out, had never really paid off.
>
> Fortunately for Rutgers—and for mankind—Dean William H. Martin of the College of Agriculture saved Dr. Waksman from the ax. Within two years Selman Waksman's "playing around with microbes" had paid off with one of the biggest jackpots that

has ever gushed from a scientist's laboratory. Dr. Waksman (rhymes with boxman) had become the discoverer of streptomycin, which ranks next to penicillin among the antibiotics and is the first of these "wonder drugs" to show hopeful results in the treatment of tuberculosis.

Today, the department of microbiology is the brightest spot on the Rutgers campus at New Brunswick, N. J., and its chairman, Dr. Selman Waksman, is one of the world's top microbiologists. He has won for his university not only fame but fortune. Streptomycin for a 60-day course of treatment costs $60 to $80. A dozen chemical companies are turning out the new wonder drug, and for every gram (1/28 of an ounce) sold, Rutgers gets 2¢. By last week, the university's harvest of pennies had reached more than $2,000,000.

With this money (and more still to come), Rutgers and Waksman are planning to build an Institute of Microbiology. Quiet, modest Dr. Waksman will enjoy the new equipment and the more spacious laboratories. For himself he asks little. By taking advantage of the unusually liberal Rutgers policy in such financial matters, he might have claimed all the proceeds of his discovery and become a millionaire. But he turned over his royalty rights to the Rutgers Research and Endowment Foundation with the mild observation: "Rutgers won't let me starve."[30]

And thus we see that the bacteria which have been the nemesis of the Jews because they more or less passed them by during the Black Plague became the object of intensive study on the part of their indirect victims.

There are a few other reflections which occur to one. First, the general belief in scientific circles that Jews are only good theoreticians but shy away from experimentation is not true.

In the natural sciences, particularly, the Jewish botanists and microbiologists have been second to none; and furthermore. it was the East European Jew who excelled in the fight against the microbes. Even the botanists largely came from that part of Germany which now is part of Poland; and a third reflection is that although agriculture has been thought to have been repugnant to the Jew (what had been accomplished in Palestine is sufficient disproof of the notion) the science of the soil and its products has been materially deepened thanks to Jewish efforts; and, as will be realized, the soil cannot be studied at an office desk.

Yes, the story of Jewish scientific endeavor is a long one, both instructive and revealing. Knowing the facts will go a long way toward exploding some of the myths about Jewish one-sided proclivities.

FOOTNOTES

1 Harvey Cushing: *The Life of Sir William Osler,* vol. I, page 215.

2 A. A. Roback: "National Traditions in Philosophy and Science." Paper read before the American Philosophical Association, 1946.

3 Cantor's Jewish origin has been questioned by some, but A. Fraenkel, who may be regarded as a disciple of the great mathematician, tells us in his well documented monograph that Cantor's father was a Jew.

4 G. Cantor: *Contributions to the Founding of the Theory of Transfinite Numbers* (Jourdain's translation) page 74.

5 A. Fraenkel: *Georg Cantor,* page 61.

5a S. Gandz: *Isis,* Vol. 39, No. 79 (1938) p. 419.

6 F. Cajori: *A History of Mathematics,* page 327. Cajori is, of course, not Jewish, and probably did not know that most of those mentioned in the passage were Jews.

7 Sylvester is here referring to the Jew, Jacobi.

8 A. Fraenkel: *Georg Cantor,* page 25.

9 S. Brodetsky, in *The Real Jew* (edited by H. Newman) page 167.

10 Heinrich Hertz's mother was supposed to have been a non-Jewess. Under ordinary circumstances, the son of a non-Jewish mother would, according to my own cross-inheritance theory, be regarded as a Gentile. But whether Hertz belongs to the exceptions who take after their father is something which should be examined genetically (family records). Roth makes Gustav Hertz, the Nobel Prize winner in physics, out to be a cousin of Heinrich on the father's side, but actually he was his nephew, so that Gustav Hertz was only a quarter-Jew, which

fact constitutes no good reason for the inclusion of his more famous uncle in our survey. But this omission might be considered a gap by some of the Judaeologists.

11 C. T. Chase: *The Evolution of Modern Physics*, page 142.

12 *Ibid.*, page 151.

13 E. Schuster: *The Progress of Physics, 1875-1908*, pages 110-111.

14 W. Yourgrau: *Jewish Affairs*, March 1949, page 12.

15 It is a pity that the solid essay ("Jewish Thought in the Modern World") by Leon Roth in *The Legacy of Israel* (1927), planned by the late Israel Abrahams and edited by E. R. Bevan and Charles Singer, both of whom are reputed scholars, should have been marred by such an error as thrusting upon Professor Weyl a Jewish ancestry. Once more we must realize that we cannot be too careful in investigating a man's racial origin.

16 A. Moszkowski: *Einstein The Searcher*, page 225. (English translation)

17 His investigation into the principle of gravitation has been mentioned in the chapter on Astronomy.

18 When Rutherford was asked at the time of the First World War why he did not abandon the tiny atom and turn to something more impressive, his reply was that the outcome of the work on this bagatelle would prove more important than the War itself. His prediction came true, though he did not live to see it verified.

19 Chase, C. T.: *The Evolution of Modern Physics*, page 131.

20 R. F. Yates: *Atom Smashers*, pages 153-154. (Didier)

21 H. D. Smyth: A General Account of the Development of Methods of Using Atomic Energy for Military Purposes under the Auspices of the United States Government.

22 *Ibid.*, page 17.

23 *Canadian Jews in World War II*, page 2. (Issued by Canadian Jewish Congress)

24 Another member of the Atomic Energy Commission who has resigned in February, 1950, is Rear Admiral Louis L. Strauss.

25 *The Real Jew* (edited by L. Newman) page 195.

25a C. Singer and C. Rabin: *A Prelude to Modern Science*, p. LXXVII (Oxford University Press).

26 H. S. Jennings: *Genetics*, pages 266-267.

27 E. Radl: *History of Biological Theories* (English translation) page 379.

28 E. J. Cohn: "Research in the Medical Sciences". *Amer. Scientist*, 1949, vol. 37. page 252.

29 V. Robinson: "The Physician as Explorer in Asia". *Ciba Symposia.* Nov. 1940, vol. 2, page 630.

30 *Time*, Nov. 7, 1949, vol. 54, page 70.

BIBLIOGRAPHY

BEVAN, E. R. and C. SINGER, *The Legacy of Israel*, 1927.

GERSHENFELD, L., *The Jew in Science*, 1934.

Jewish Encyclopedia (12 vols.) 1901-1906.

Jüdisches Lexikon (5 vols.) 1927-1930.

NEWMAN, CH. (Ed.) *The Real Jew*, 1925.

ROBACK, A. A., *Jewish Influence in Modern Thought*, 1929.

———, *Our Reply to Hitler.* (A series of essays on Jewish contributions in philosophy, science, art, law, medicine and music). Special edition of *Forward*, 1933.

ROTH, C., *The Jewish Contribution to Civilization*, 1937.

Universal Jewish Encyclopedia (10 vols.) 1939-1943.

WININGER, S., *Grosse Jüdische National-Biographie* (7 vols.) 1926-1932.

The Influence of the Jew on Modern Medicine

By Solomon R. Kagan, M. D.

MODERN medicine begins with the 19th century, and is characterized mainly by the introduction of systematic methods and facilities for scientific research in medicine. The new teaching of medicine as a science, experimental research in adequate laboratories, and organized studies of preventive medicine are the development of the 19th and 20th centuries. Among the factors that revolutionized modern medicine was the effect of the emancipation of Jews early in the 19th century. The admission of Jews to universities, to teaching positions, and to institutions for scientific research brought forth a great number of brilliant Jewish collaborators who have contributed substantially to the advancement of their traditional field of medicine in all its branches. The Jews have participated in the gigantic work of building a new medicine as clinicians, teachers, investigators, authors, translators, editors, organizers, educators, pioneers and leaders in the profession. They took an ever-increasing part in the progress of medicine over the world, but particularly it was marked in the German-speaking region which became in modern times for a century the center of Jewish intellectual life. In pre-Nazi Germany Jews were the best scientific exponents and creators of new ideas in medicine. They provided distinguished mathematicians, physicists and physicians in about thirty times their due proportion. Of the outstanding German mathematicians and medical researchers about twenty-five per cent were Jews. In Italy, Jewish intellectual supremacy was even higher in certain departments of science. Since 1908 eleven Jewish doctors were awarded the Nobel Prize for medicine in recognition of their outstanding contribution to medical science, which constitutes about twenty-five per cent of all Nobel Prize winners in medicine.

The Jewish doctors have contributed important work to all branches of medical science and its allied subjects, and their research work was mostly centered on the study of the minute structures and composition of normal and diseased tissues of the body and their correlation with function; on prophylactic measures against infectious diseases; on otology, ophthalmology, neurology and psychiatry. By means of their epoch-making discoveries in medicine, the German Jewish doctors were the main factor in making German medicine the most authoritative during the second half of the 19th and first quarter of the 20th centuries.

Sir William Osler, one of the greatest physicians of his time, wrote in 1884: "Should another Moses arise and preach a Semitic exodus from Germany, and should he prevail, they would leave the land impoverished far more than was ancient Egypt by the loss of the 'Jewels of gold and jewels of silver', of which the people were 'spoiled'. To say nothing of the material wealth, enough to buy Palestine over and over again, there is not a profession which would not suffer the serious loss of many of its most brilliant ornaments, and in none more so than our own." Osler's prophecy was realized. Since 1933 the German people have lost their main source of intellectual and creative work; they have lost their former claim to respect from the world of intellect. So far as the products of the intellect and science are concerned, German occupies a second place; henceforth German will be a language of secondary importance in the field of learning.

From the beginning of the 20th century American medicine started to grow rapidly. In 1930 Professor William H. Welch declared: "America has taken a position of leadership in the application of the new knowledge to the prevention of disease and to personal and public hygiene." The high development of American medicine was due partly to the genius of the American people and partly to private benefaction in the

United States of America which enabled the organization of research facilities on a large scale. The American Jewish physicians also collaborated in this great work to their full share, and directly and indirectly helped the progress of American medicine.

Among the many Jewish educators who helped the raising of the standard of medical education in the United States, the following deserve particular mention. Isaac Hays (1796-1879) of Philadelphia was the first to present a resolution at the New York Medical Convention in 1846 proposing a National Medical Association for the better management of standards of ethics and education. He was a founder of the American Medical Association in 1847, for which he composed a code of medical ethics. His code was approved, and is still accepted by every state and county medical society in the Union. By these medical ethics Hays placed our medical profession on the highest plane. He was among the earliest practitioners in this country to make eye diseases a specialty. He edited the *American Journal of the Medical Science*, called "Hays' Journal," which influenced medical thought in this country for more than a half century. He paved the way for American medical journalism, attracted the best medical writers to his journal, and inspired young gifted men to medico-literary work. He introduced some important ophthalmic instruments and wrote many scientific books on medicine. Another outstanding Jewish physician, Jacob M. DaCosta (1833-1900), also of Philadelphia, was professor of medicine at Jefferson Medical College, did pioneer work in cardiology, described a syndrome of irritable heart in soldiers. He was the ablest teacher of his time in the country, and wrote the best treatise on medical diagnosis (1859). His ideas on respiratory percussion were accepted in Europe by Friedrich. He and Dr. S. D. Gross founded the Philadelphia Pathological Society in 1857. Significant was also the accomplishments of Dr. Aaron Friedenwald (1836-1902) who was professor of eye disease at the College of Physicians and Surgeons in Baltimore. He helped to organize the Maryland Ophthalmological Society in 1898, and was elected its first president. Friedenwald's greatest service to the American medical profession was his activities with the formation of the Association of American Medical Colleges. In 1890 there was called a meeting of representatives of the Baltimore Medical Faculty to discuss the possibility of introducing a reform in medical education in Baltimore. Friedenwald, who was the president of the Faculty, suggested calling a national conference for the consideration of reforms throughout the country, and his view prevailed. As a result of his convictions, circulars signed by Friedenwald as chairman and Cordell as secretary were sent out by the Baltimore Medical Schools. The meeting for the organization was held at Nashville in 1890, and Friedenwald presided at the opening. At this meeting a permanent organization was established, of which N. S. Davis was president and A. Friedenwald the first vice-president. The newly organized Association of American Medical Colleges resulted in higher standards of instruction in medical schools throughout the United States. A great influence on American medical education was later exerted by Abraham Flexner (1866-   ) of Louisville, Ky., who, at the instance of the Carnegie Foundation for the Advancement of Teaching, made comprehensive studies of the status of medical education at home and abroad. His book, *Medical Education in the United States and Canada* (1910) served as an impetus to raise medical education in all medical colleges and hospitals throughout the country. Morris Fishbein (1889-   ), of St. Louis, was editor of the *Journal of the American Medical Association* from 1924 to 1949, and author (with G. H. Simmons) of *The Art and Practice of Medical Writing* (1925), and editor of many medical books dealing with various medical problems. As editor and author Fishbein made substantial contributions to the uniformity and advancement of scientific medical literature.

[197]

THE INFLUENCE OF THE JEW ON MODERN MEDICINE

It is not the object of the author to list in this monograph the names of all great Jewish physicians who left a landmark in modern medicine. The following will present a limited number of names of outstanding Jewish physicians who exerted a decisive influence upon modern medicine. One of medical fields in which the Jewish doctors were particularly noteworthy was internal medicine. They discovered new diseases and elucidated their nature, outlook and treatment; they described new signs, syndromes and tests for the diagnosis of many diseases; they also introduced new concepts, principles and theories relating to certain diseases. The earliest Jewish clinician of modern times was Ludwig Traube (1818-1876) of Silesia, who was one of the first Jewish doctors to become a professor at the University of Berlin in 1857. He made his mark in medicine as a founder of experimental pathology and of scientific researches of the action of drugs. He was one of the greatest teachers and clinicians of his time. Many structures of the human body are identified with his name such as Traube's space, Traube's curves, Traube's corpuscles, Traube's membrane, Traube's murmur, and Traube-Hering's waves. He was the first to introduce the thermometer in his clinic. Garrison tells that his clinics in Berlin became very popular on account of his brilliant methods of teaching and his sincere attitude toward the patient. Another outstanding German Jewish physician was Ottomar Rosenbach (1851-1907), also of Silesia, who distinguished himself by introducing revolutionary concepts in medicine. A great deal of his original ideas are accepted universally, such as his statements on functional diseases, the power of suggestion, the value of psycho-therapy, his theories on energetics in biophysics and biochemistry. His name is associated with the so-called Rosenbach bile test, Rosenbach's digestive reflex, Rosenbach's law, Rosenbach's disease and Rosenbach's sign for hemoplegia. Outstanding, too, was William Ebstein (1836-1912) of Goettingen who introduced tactile percussion for physical diagnosis and who ad-

vocated treatment of obesity by a diet from which all carbohydrates are excluded. Prominent was a French Jewish physician, George Hayem (1841-1933) of Paris who contributed
fundamental work to medicine. He is most memorable for his
discovery of the blood platelets. He invented the so-called
Hayem's solution for preserving the red blood corpuscles in
microscopical examination of the blood. He described Hayem's
ventricle, Hayem's disease, Hayem-Widal disease, and a new
type of acute nonsuppurative inflammation of the brain. He
discovered a serum for injection in cases of infectious diseases.
Simon Baruch (1840-1921) of New York described a sign for
typhus fever, a sign for perforated appendicitis, was the first
in the country to operate upon a patient with appendicitis successfully, established free bath houses in Chicago and New
York, and was a pioneer of hydrotherapy in the country. Solomon Solis-Cohen (1857-1948) of Philadelphia was a pioneer
in the field of organotherapy. He was among the first to advocate gland treatment, introduced the use of adrenal and pitui-
tary products in hay fever, asthma and hives. Ismar Boas
(1855-1938), a native of Posen, established gastro-enterology
as a specialty. He founded the first polyclinic for gastro-intestinal diseases in Berlin. He is best known for the Boas-Eswald
breakfast test and the Boas-Oppler bacillus. Max Einhorn
(1862-   ) of New York has been the leader in the field of
gastro-intestinal diseases. He invented gastrodiaphany which
is the best means for mapping out the stomach, as he succeeded
in introducing an electrical light into the stomach, so that it
became transparent through the anterior abdominal wall. He
made possible the duodenal intubation, which affords the possibility of obtaining specimens of bile and pancreatic juice for
examination. He is the inventor of many important instruments and apparatus in relation to stomach and intestinal
maladies, some of which were accepted throughout the medical world. Among his inventions are the fermentation sac-
charometer (1887), the stomach bucket and gastrograph
(1890), the stomach spray (1892), the stomach powder

blower (1899), a new esophagoscope (1901), the duodenal bucket (1908) and an intestinal tube (1919). David Riesman (1867-1940) was professor of clinical medicine at the University of Pennsylvania. He made many valuable contributions to internal medicine, pathology and medical history. He described a sign of diabetic coma and a sign of ophthalmic goiter. Emanuel Libman (1872-1946) was a professor of clinical medicine at Columbia University. He did pioneer work in cardiology and bacteriology and made many contributions to internal medicine. He and B. Sacks described a new disease—a form of valvular and mural endocarditis—known as Libman-Sacks disease (1924). He was the first to describe subacute bacterial endocarditis (1906). The dean of American medicine W. H. Welch pointed out the significance of Libman's conclusions relating to the conditions favoring or opposing the entrance of bacteria into the blood stream, the possibilities of bacterial multiplication in the circulating blood, bacterial emboli, and the clinical and pathological significance of blood cultures.

Of particular importance are the achievements of Jews in the field of metabolism. Gustav Valentin (1810-1883), professor of physiology at Berne, Switzerland, was a pioneer in histology and experimental physiology. He discovered the diastatic role of the pancreating juice in the digestion of carbohydrates (1844). He also discovered the so-called Valentin's corpuscles and Valentin's ganglion. He introduced polarized light in microscopy. Oscar Minkowski (1858-1931), professor of medicine at Breslau, proved that the removal of the pancreas in a dog causes diabetes; thus he discovered the relation between the pancreas gland and diabetes. This discovery makes him one of the originators of modern treatment of diabetes with insulin. He was the first to describe hemolytic jaundice, suggested a new method of palpation of the kidney, first described the relation between dextrose and nitrogen in the urine, and discovered the etiology of acromegaly. Hermann S. Senator

(1834-1911) of Gnesen investigated the treatment of diabetes
(1879). Moritz Schiff (1823-1896) succeeded in 1856 in
producing artificial diabetes by his experiments on the nervous
system. S. J. Plaschkes (1886-   ) of Tel Aviv, Israel, was
the first to advocate the use of bean bread for diabetic patients (1932). Max Kahn (1887-1928) of New York introduced intarvin for the treatment of diabetes. Hermann Strauss
of Berlin studied diabetes, and was one of the first physicians
who administered insulin to diabetics in Germany. Moses Barron (1893-   ), professor of medicine at Minnesota Medical
School, published a paper in 1920 in which he emphasized the
role of the islands of Langerhans of the pancreas in the control
of carbohydrate metabolism and thus of diabetes mellitus.
This important article served as a basis of Banting's revolutionary discovery of insulin. Banting gave due credit to Dr.
Barron, stating that the latter's article stimulated him to start
laboratory research for securing pancreatic degeneration, and
this work resulted in the discovery of insulin in 1921.

Of importance are also the accomplishments of Jews in the
field of nutrition and vitaminology. Casimir Funk was born
in Poland in 1884, received his degree of Ph.D. from Berne
in 1904, made scientific studies in Pasteur Institute (1904-
1906) and Lister Institute (1911-1913). In 1915 he emigrated
to New York City, where he was connected with Cornell Medical College and Columbia University. He has done pioneer
work in the field of vitamins, and has contributed original
work to synthetic organic chemistry, nutrition and internal secretion. He was the first to discover certain substances of unknown composition which exist in minute quantity in natural
foods and are necessary to normal nutrition, and he coined the
term "vitamin" in 1912. In 1913 he advocated the application
of his discovery of vitamins to practical dietetics and to certain
medical problems. In 1914 he emphasized the necessity of the
antineuritic vitamin for utilization of carbohydrates, and he
was the first to describe some anatomic changes in polyneuritic

pigeons as typical of the result of vitamin B deficiency. Lafayette B. Mendel (1872-1935) was Sterling professor of physiological chemistry at Yale University and was a recognized
leader in the field of nutrition. He and T. B. Osborne were
the first to describe eye changes as a sign of a deficiency of
vitamins in the diet. They discovered calculi and calcarous de-
posits in the kidney passages in rats long deprived of vitamin
A. They also found that vitamin B protects against polyneuritis.
In 1918 Mendel and B. Cohen produced experimental scurvy
in a guinea pig by means of certain diets. They demonstrated
the existence of the antiscorbutic vitamin C and made studies
of its properties. Professor Mendel exerted an influence on
medicine by training his pupils and co-workers in medical research, and a number of his pupils became outstanding teachers
and leaders in medical research in the country. Joseph Goldberger (1874-1929), of Washington, D. C., accomplished
much in the field of public health. He is most memorable for
his pioneer work in his discovery of the cause of pellagra in
1913. This is a fatal skin and spinal disease of Southern
Europe, and also in the southern and central parts of the
United States. Goldberger proved that the disease is caused by
a deficiency of certain substances (Vitamin B^2 or G) which
are contained in lean meat, milk and yeast. He demonstrated
that it is not caused by infection, and he first placed it in the
same group of diseases with scurvy and beriberi. With this
discovery he became a benefactor of mankind. Alfred H. Hess
(1875-1933) was professor of children's diseases at the University and Bellevue Hospital Medical College in New York.
He was among the first to report the curative properties of
vitamin D in rickets. In 1919 he and L. Unger discovered
vitamin C. Hess (with Weinstock) discovered a method of
radiation of food for producing a vitamin factor in it. In 1927
Hess received the John Scott Medal awarded by the Franklin
Society for his discovery of a method of producing a vitamin
factor in food by the influence of ultraviolet rays. Prof.
Ludwig F. Meyer of Tel Aviv, Israel, found vitamin C in

milk and fresh vegetables. Barnett Sure (1891-   ), professor of agricultural chemistry at Arkansas, discovered vitamin
E. He is the author of *Vitamins in Health and Disease* (1933),
investigated the value of vitamin E in reproduction and lacta-
tion, vitamin B requirements of nursing the young, and changes
in the minute structures of the body due to a deficiency of
vitamins in the diet. He received a grant of the Committee on
Scientific Research of the American Medical Association in
1938. Simon B. Wolbach (1880-1945) of Boston (with P. R.
Howe) made studies concerning the pathologic changes in
cases of vitamin A deficiency. Israel S. Wechsler (1884-   ),
professor of neurology at Columbia, advocated the treatment
of amyotrophic lateral sclerosis with vitamin E (1940). Alfred
T. Shol (1889-   ) made scientific contributions to diseases
of children and chemical hygiene. He investigated the physiology of vitamin D (1938). He and Barnett Sure discovered
that under the influence of vitamin D a readjustment of the
calcium-phosphorus ratio is produced which requires a new
supply of these ingredients.

Among the outstanding Jewish medical teachers was Hermann Strauss (1868-1944) of Berlin, who for forty-two years
was teaching and lecturing not only in Berlin University, but
also in many countries, including the United States and Palestine, everywhere stimulating medical research work. He developed original technical methods for clinical studies, constructed new medical devices, such as the Strauss' chloridom-
eter, the Strauss' canula and an apparatus for procto-sygmos-
copy. He devised a lactic acid test and introduced a levulose
tolerance test for liver function. He was the first to describe
proctostasis, investigated the metabolic role in diabetes, and
described a salt-free diet for the treatment of kidney disorders.
He trained many German students for scientific research work,
and attracted pupils from everywhere to Berlin. But the German people mistreated their great teacher and educator Professor Strauss. They humiliated and tortured him in a concentra-

tion camp in Theresienstadt. When he learned that it was ordered to take him to the gas chambers of Oswiecim, he committed suicide in October 1944. We do not know the day of his tragic end and the place of his grave. Among the eminent Jewish hematologists is William Dameshek (1900-   ), professor of clinical medicine at Tufts College, Boston. He has made many important contributions to the study of blood, particularly in the study of the bone-marrow, chronic iron deficiency, hemolytic anemia, disorders of the spleen and the chemotherapy of leukemia and agranulocytosis. He discovered the abnormal hemolytic antibody in acquired hemolytic anemia. He trained many young men in the study of blood who later became hematologists throughout the world.

In the field of children diseases the Jews were pre-eminent not only by their scientific achievements but also by their organizational activities. Edward H. Henoch (1820-1910), professor of pediatrics in Berlin, was the first to establish a clinic for children's diseases in Berlin. He discovered the so-called Henoch's purpura. Max Kassowitz (1842-1913) of Vienna introduced the phosphorus cod liver oil in the treatment of rickets. Heinrich Finkelstein (1865-1942) of Berlin described many pediatric symptoms-complexes, and introduced a new concept in the alimentary disorders of infancy. Finkelstein's "albumin milk" was a great advance in the treatment of severe diarrhea in children. Abraham Jacobi (1830-1919) was professor of diseases of children at Columbia and is known as "the father of pediatrics in America". He was the first to establish a clinic for children diseases in New York City. Henry Koplik (1858-1927) of New York was the first to establish milk stations in the United States. He discovered the diagnostic spots of measles, known as Koplik's sign. Isaac A. Abt (1867-   ), professor emeritus in pediatrics of Northwestern University Medical School, Chicago, made valuable contributions to pediatrics. As clinician, teacher, writer and editor he was a leader of pediatrics for more than a half century. He was one of the foremost exponents of modern pediatrics, was the first to introduce in this country the Czerny-Finkelstein philosophy of nutritional disorders, and was also the first American pediatrician to use protein milk in the treatment of diarrhea in infants. Bela Schick (1877-   ) of Columbia University originated the so-called Schick test for determining susceptibility of a person to diphtheria (1913). Abraham Levinson of Chicago made original studies in spinal fluid.

Karl A. Meninger stated that although the fact is well known that Jewish physicians are distinguished for their scientific accomplishments in all fields of medicine, however, they have demonstrated a special gift for psychiatry. Records show that the Jews not only discovered new diseases and methods of treatment in neuro-psychiatry and discovered various anatomic parts of the nervous system, but also have changed the current medical thought, practice and education. They have changed the outlook of modern psychiatry and psychology in its medical application. The following may serve as an illustration. Moritz Heinrich Romberg (1795-1873) of Meningen became professor in Berlin in 1838. He was the author of a classical book on nervous diseases, which was the first formal text on the subject, and it made an epoch by its careful collation of hitherto scattered data, its clear, precise clinical picture and its attempt to systematize treatment (Garrison). He described a sign for locomotor ataxia (Romberg's sign), discovered a disease of facial hemiatrophy, known as Romberg's disease. After him is also named Romberg-Paessler syndrome and Romberg-Howship sign. He is considered the founder of modern neuropathology. Robert Remak (1815-1865) of Posen became professor at Berlin in 1859, and made outstanding contributions to medicine. He discovered the non-medullated fibers (fibers of Remak) and the ganglionic cells in the sinus venosus of the frog's heart (Remak's ganglion). He was among the first to state that the proliferation of cells to build tissue is accomplished by cell division (1852). In 1842, long before Pasteur and Koch, he separated the fungus from the genus Oidium, and using himself as a guinea pig, he produced the skin disease favus on himself experimentally, proving that this disease is caused by a specific microscopic organism. He simplified von Baer's classification of the germ-layers (1851), and was the first to describe ascending neuritis (1861). He was the founder of microscopic anatomy of the nerves, a pioneer in electrotherapy, and substituted the galvanic for the induced current (1856). Ludwig Lichtheim (1845-1928) of Breslau published original work on tumors of the brain and spinal cord, paralysis of eye muscles, progressive muscular atrophy, and meningitis. He described a disease and a syndrome, both named after him. He was among the first to perform a puncture in the brain for diagnostic purpose. Ludwig M. Hirschfeld (1816-1876) published a classical textbook on neurology, and discovered the so-called Hirschfeld's nerve. Hermann Oppenheim (1852-1919) described congenital myatonia (Oppenheim's disease), Oppenheim's cerebral infantile paralysis, Oppenheim's mouth reflex, Oppenheim's sign in spastic conditions of the lower extremities, and Oppenheim's course of multiple sclerosis. He did pioneer work in the study of traumatic neuroses. Nathan Weiss (1851-1883) of Vienna was the first to investigate the spinal cord, medulla and basal ganglia in tetany (Weiss sign for tetany). Ludwig Edinger (1855-1918), professor of neurology at Frankfurt a. M., made substantial contributions to brain anatomy. After him is called Edinger's nucleus, Edinger's fibers and Edinger's law. Joseph A. Hirschl (1885-1914) of Vienna made the discovery that syphilis is the cause of general paralysis (1896). After him it is called Hirschl's phenomenon. Emanuel Mendel (1839-1907) of Germany was the most popular psychiatrist of his time. He described the clinical picture of paranoia, epilepsy and mania, and advanced the method of treatment of mental and nervous diseases. In 1868 he founded a hospital for mental patients in Pankow, near Berlin, which won world recognition. Joseph Breuer (1842-1925) of Vienna originated the theory of equilibrium, and it has been universally accepted. He contributed much through his scientific investigations of the relation of the vagus to breathing and through his studies of the function of the semicircular. He originated the method of catharsis in the treatment of psycho-neuroses, and Freud gave him due credit for this discovery. Sigmund Freud (1856-1939) of Vienna made fundamental contributions to the study of neuropsychiatry. In 1884 Dr. Joseph Breuer related to Freud that he was able to penetrate deeply into the causation and significance of hysterical symptoms, and that he cured them by getting the patient to recollect in a state of hypnosis the circumstances of their origin, and spoke of this method as catharsis. Freud concluded that there can be mental processes which remain hidden from the consciousness of man. On the basis of his observations, he stated that many mental processes never attain consciousness and can be exposed only through psychoanalysis. He discovered a method of free association and was able by assurances and encouragements to force the forgotten things and connections into the consciousness of his neurotic patient. He replaced the treatment of hypnosis by free association and coined the term "psychoanalysis" as a therapeutic method. Freud was a great teacher of human nature. He was a genius, a man of originality, depth of thought and vision, and influenced greatly the human conception of his time. He revolutionized psychiatry and altered the content and direction of human thought. His teachings closed a chain in the philosophy concerning the meaning of man. Alfred Adler of Vienna founded the school of individual psychology. Otto Marburg (1874-1948) first showed the association of trophic skin changes with lesions in the spinal ganglions. He and Frankl Hochward introduced neuro-surgery in Vienna.

Jewish doctors left a mark in dermatology. Moritz Kaposi (1837-1902) of Hungary described pigmented sarcoma of the skin, diabetic dermatitis, and various forms of lichen ruber. Oskar Lassar (1849-1907), of Hamburg, was the first to transmit syphilis to anthropoid apes, introduced electro-physical treatment in skin diseases, and described the so-called Lassar's paste which is still used in the practice of dermatology. He established disinfectant stations and public baths in Berlin. Paul G. Unna (1850-1929), of Hamburg, described seborrheic eczema (Unna's disease), discovered a paste for eczematous patches (Unna's paste), introduced ichthyol and resorcinol, and various staining methods in dermatology. He also described the pathology of leprosy, the plasma cells, the different foci of favus, and the so-called bacillus Unna-Ducray. Jay F. Schamberg (1870-1934) of Philadelphia was the first to describe the progressive pigmentary skin eruption (Schamberg's disease). He and Joseph Goldberger described the straw itch. He founded the Research Institute of Cutaneous Medicine in Philadelphia. A. Dostrovsky, of the Hebrew University in Jerusalem, first described the nature of endemica urticaria (1925). He and F. Sagher discovered the treatment of oriental sore of the skin by Grenz-rays (1940).

In surgery, gynecology and urology Jews also accomplished much. Samuel Kristeller (1820-1900) of Berlin introduced a method of grafting mucous membrane and described a method of manipulation in obstetrics. James Israel (1848-1926) of Berlin was a pioneer in the field of surgery and urology. Anton Woelfler (1850-1917) of Berlin contributed to surgery of the tongue, kidney, thyroid gland and gastrointestinal tract. He performed the first operation of gastro-enterostomy. Max Saenger (1853-1903) of Prague devised sutures for closure of the uterine wound in cesarean section, and modified the technic of this operation. Howard Lilienthal (1861-1946) of New York made fundamental contributions to abdominal, genito-urinary and thoracic surgery. He was the first to resect the thoracic esophagus for carcinoma without gastrostomy, and was the first in America to apply the diagnostic aid of X-ray in diseases of the jaws and teeth. He was the inventor of the two-stage operation of the prostate. He advocated a new and simple method of intestinal resection, and invented a number of surgical instruments and appliances. He invented a new portable operating table which is especially useful in operations upon the kidney and gall-bladder. This was accepted and slightly changed by the United States Army, and was employed as the regular field operating table during World War I. Dr. Lilienthal's name, however, was omitted. Dr. Lilienthal contributed to the high standard of the surgical department of the Mount Sinai Hospital. His many faceted contributions place him among the American leaders of surgery. Leopold Freund (1868-   ), professor of radiology at Vienna, advanced the knowledge of Roentgen-rays. Among other important things, he was the first to introduce X-ray treatment in certain diseases, such as skin diseases, bone tuberculosis, ischias, and in some surgical cases. He discovered the cumulative effect of the X-rays, found the effect of ultraviolet rays and the absorptive ability through the skin. Robert Lenk (1885-   ), of Tel Aviv, Israel, was the first to apply bronchoscopy for the diagnosis of tumors in the bronchi. Ernst Wertheim (1864-1920) of Vienna introduced the so-called Wertheim's operation for cancer of the uterus, modified Watkins' operation for uterine prolapse, and improved the technic in other vaginal surgical operations. Joseph B. De Lee (1869-1942), professor of obstetrics and gynecology at the University of Chicago, was the author of three standard textbooks: *Notes on Obstetrics*; *Obstetrics for Nurses* (11 editions) and *Principles and Practice of Obstetrics* (9 editions). He was the inventor of twenty-two obstetric instruments, and a pioneer in the production of educational motion pictures in obstetrics and gynecology. He raised the standard of obstetric teaching and practice, and increased the dignity of obstetric art in the United States by his contacts, lectures, writings, and visual education. Bernhard Zondek (1891-   ), professor of gynecology at the Hebrew University in Israel, is the leader of modern endocrinology. He and Selmar Aschheim originated the so-called Aschheim-Zondek test for pregnancy (1927).

Zondek described methods of preparation of the estrogenic and the gonadotropic hormones. Felix Mandl of Jerusalem, Israel, suggested a radical method of sacral operation for carcinoma of the uterus (1941). Ludwig Halberstaedter (1870-1949), professor of radiology at the Hebrew University in Jerusalem, made many contributions to the study of roentgenology. He demonstrated the destruction of ovaries in a dog under the effect of Roentgen rays (1905). In 1941 he recommended the use of artificial menopause in the treatment of cancer of the breast. Max Cutler (1899-   ) of Chicago first described transillumination as a diagnostic aid for tumors of the breast. He developed a new method of X-ray and radium treatment for cancer of the mouth and larynx. Max Thorek (1880-   ) of Chicago made fundamental contributions to the science and technic of surgery. He distinguished himself as surgeon, teacher, author and editor.

The founder of modern scientific otology was Adam Politzer (1835-1920) of Vienna who was the leading otologist of his time. He originated a method of opening up the blocked Eustachian tube and a method of illuminating the ear drum. He introduced the so-called Politzer's cone, a bag for inflating the middle ear, an ear speculum and a test for deafness of one ear. He was the founder of *Archives of Otology*, a clinic for ear diseases at the University of Vienna, and the Austrian Otological Society. Marcus Hajeck (1861-1941) of Vienna was a leader in laryngology. He improved the treatment of empyema of the sinuses, invented many practical nasal instruments and several devices for the resection of the septum. His approach to the treatment of diseases of the nose and sinuses was based on anatomical and pathological studies. Sidney Yankauer (1872-1922) of New York originated many surgical instruments, now in common use in the practice of laryngology. Robert Barany (1876-1936) of Upsala invented a caloric test for the labyrinth, Barany's pointing test of the cerebellum, and Barany's symptom-complex. In 1914 he was awarded the

Nobel prize for his work on the vestibular apparatus. Jacob Solis-Cohen (1838-1927) of Philadelphia performed the first successful operation of opening up the larynx to remove a cancer (1867). He was among the first to make otolaryngology a specialty in the United States. Gustav Alexander (1873-1932) of Vienna introduced an operation for thrombosis of the lateral sinus. He was a pioneer in organizing kindergarten classes for the early training of deaf-born children. He was tragically killed in Vienna by a syphilitic insane patient in 1932.

Among the great Jewish leaders in eye diseases was Louis Emile Javal (1839-1907) of Paris. He made many important contributions to ophthalmology. He introduced a method for the diagnosis of astigmatism, invented an ophthalmometer, and originated eye exercises in the treatment of strabismus. Louis Hirschberg (1843-1925) of Berlin introduced the electromagnet for removing particles of iron from the eye, discovered deep blood vessels in keratosis, described a method of measurement of the deviation of a strabismic eye, and demonstrated the changes in the eyes due to syphilis. He wrote the best history of eye disease. Carl Koller (1857-1944) of New York introduced cocaine as an anesthetic in eye surgery, which inaugurated a new era of local anesthesia in various branches of medicine and surgery. Stephan Bernheimer (1861-1918), professor of ophthalmology at Innsbruck, discovered the partial crossing of the fibers of the optic nerve in the chiasma (Bernheimer's fibers). Jonas S. Friedenwald of Johns Hopkins University made substantial contributions to the field of eye pathology. He suggested a new astigmatic chart and a new ophthalmoscope.

The most important achievement in modern medicine is the understanding of the complexity of the functions and the cells of the body and to learn their relations to the microorganisms that produce disease. After extensive researches the scientists discovered means of producing immunity against a number of infectious diseases and saved many millions from death. They succeeded in increasing the power of a living organism to resist and overcome infection by using certain serums for producing passive immunization and vaccines for producing active immunization. In this field Jewish discoveries are overwhelming. Waldemar Haffkine (1860-1930), a native of Russia, discovered a prophylactic vaccine against Asiatic cholera (1893) and an antiplague vaccine (1896). He became a benefactor of mankind, and in recognition of his effective work many honors came to him, including the naming of the Haffkine Institute in Bombay after him. Fernand Widal (1862-1929) of Paris discovered bacterial agglutination (1895) and its application in the diagnosis of typhoid fever (Widal test). His polyvaccine against typhoid was introduced in all armies during World War I. He introduced clinical sero-diagnosis and cytodiagnosis, and described anaphylactic hemoclastic crisis. Simon Flexner (1863-1946) of New York discovered the dysentery bacillus (Flexner's bacillus). In 1908 he originated an antimeningococcus serum used in the treatment of cerebral meningitis (Flexner's serum). Alexander Marmorek (1865-1923) of Paris discovered a serum antitoxic to streptococcus pyogenes (1896) and a serum antitoxic to the tubercle bacillus (1903). Max Neisser (1869-   ) studied immunity against staphylococci, diphtheria, typhus fever, and Friedlander's group of bacteria. His name is identified with Neisser-Wechsberg phenomenon, Neisser-Sachs complement fixation reaction for albumins, and Neisser's stain for the polar nuclei of diphtheria bacillus. Hans Aronson (1865-1919) of Koenigsberg prepared diphtheria antitoxin according to his own method. He discovered an antistreptococcus serum (Aronson's serum). Alexander Besredka (1870-1940), professor at the Pasteur Institute in Paris, discovered a method of producing local immunity, and introduced a method of anaphylactic desensitization. He originated the method of anaphylactic vaccination with small doses. This discovery is of great importance, as it prevents anaphylactic shock. After him is named the so-called Besredka's reaction and Besredka's vaccine. Israel J. Kligler (1889-1944), professor of bacteriology and hygiene at the Hebrew University, Jerusalem, developed scientific methods for combating malaria. He made extensive researches on the production of vaccines for prophylactic purposes against certain infectious diseases. Selman A. Waksman (1888-   ) of New Brunswick, N. J., discovered a new antibiotic agent called streptomycin, which proved to be a great boon in the treatment of heretofore incurable bacterial diseases such as tuberculosis, dysentery, influenza, meningitis and whooping cough. In 1948 he discovered neomycin which is of benefit in cases where streptomycin and other therapeutic agents are helpless. His purpose was to originate an antibiotic factor capable of inhibiting or destroying certain bacteria and yet non-toxic in its effect, and after isolating more than 10,000 cultures of actimycetes, he succeeded in isolating the streptomycin-producing organism which is a potent agent for destroying certain bacteria.

The following Jewish doctors are among the greatest pathologists and bacteriologists. Julius Cohnheim (1839-1884), professor of pathology at Breslau, was a pioneer in pathology. He revealed the nature of inflammation and suppuration by proving that the white corpuscles of the blood form the pus. His name is identified with Cohnheim's fields, Cohnheim's areas and Cohnheim's frog. Carl Weigert (1845-1904), of Silesia, was one of the greatest microscopic anatomists of the 19th century. He was the first to stain bacteria (1875). He introduced various methods of staining tissues for microscopic examination. By his improved technic for staining bacteria and tissues he rendered great service to modern scientific medicine. He advanced the knowledge of the structure and function of the nervous system. His name is associated with the so-called Weigert's mixture, Weigert's myelin sheath, Weigert's picrocarmine, and Weigert's stain for fibrin. Ludwig Briger (1849-1919) of Berlin described a test for strychnin, coined the term of "toxins", described bacillus cavicidus (Briger's bacillus), and discovered cachexia reaction in malignant disease (Briger's reaction). He also did pioneer work in hydrotherapy. Paul Ehrlich (1854-1915) of Silesia opened a new domain in experimental pharmacology and therapeutics, and is considered the founder of chemotherapy. He also did pioneer work in the morphology of the blood, in tissue staining, and immunology. He is most known for his discovery of Salvarsan. In 1908 he with Elie Metchnikoff (half Jew) shared the Nobel prize for his work on immunity. August Wassermann (1866-1925) of Berlin discovered the sero-diagnostic test for syphilis (1906). Karl Sternberg (1872-   ) of Vienna discovered the so-called Sternberg disease, Sternberg's giant cell, and Sternberg leukosarcomatosis. Karl Landsteiner (1868-1948) of Rockefeller Institute in New York discovered the four blood type differentiating characteristics and designated them as A, B, AB, and O. The discovery made blood transfusion a safe procedure, and saved thousands of lives. In 1930 he was awarded the Nobel prize for this discovery. Alexander S. Wiener (1907-   ) of Brooklyn, N. Y., with K. Landsteiner discovered the Rh factor. He discovered new methods of grouping dried stains of blood and secretions. Philip Levine (1900-   ), a native of Russia, with K. Landsteiner discovered the blood factors M, N, and P. In 1941 he discovered the cause of erythroblastosis fatalis, a disease of the newborn. Reuben L. Kahn (1887-   ) of Ann Arbor, Mich., originated the Kahn test for syphilis (1921). The League of Nations Health Commission recognized the significance of the Kahn test and helped to popularize it among the nations. Kahn introduced a new concept of immunity. In 1933 he received the award of the American Association for the Advancement of Science for his work on immunity.

Of great importance was the work of Jews in the field of hygiene and preventive medicine. A distinguished leader of Jewish hygienists was Milton J. Rosenau (1869-1948) who was a prime mover in the field of public health and sanitation. His textbook, *Preventive Medicine and Hygiene*, was called the bible of preventive medicine and passed six editions. Prof. W. G. Similie stated that Rosenau's book on preventive medicine has had more influence upon the advancement of public health throughout the world than any other single factor. The book was translated in many languages, including Chinese. Among his achievements was his method of standardizing diphtheria antitoxin and tetanus antitoxin. He and his co-workers confirmed and amplified the epoch making discoveries of the U. S. Army medical officers on the prevention and control of yellow fever. He popularized Schick's test, thereby saving many lives. Rosenau's organizing ability was manifested by his work at the U. S. Public Health Service in Washington, D. C., and in Boston, where he was professor of hygiene and preventive medicine at Harvard. He devised the unit for diphtheria, fought for protection of the community against smallpox by vaccination, led a battle for the pasteurization of milk, and succeeded through his effective work in lowering the death rate of infants and children. In the words of Eliot Joslin: "Rosenau has saved his native land from epidemics of cholera, the plague, and has fought smallpox, and freed Washington from typhoid."

At one time Palestine was great with scientific knowledge but had fallen into decay during four centuries of neglect under Turkish rule. During the past quarter of a century, Jewish scientists of the Hebrew University and the Jewish medical leaders have inaugurated a national public health program where none had been before. Prof. S. Ralph Harlow of Smith College has said of the country: "In 1914 when I first visited Palestine, it had been a dreaded waste of malaria-infested swamps, rocky barren hillsides, and sandy acres of unfertile soil. My second visit, in 1929, revealed a transformation that was hardly believable. Since the Balfour Declaration, the Jewish colonists had introduced modern agricultural methods, extensive sanitation projects, hydro-electric power, bringing light where all had been darkness. Most impressive of all was their courageous and constant battle with disease and the fastest lowering of the infant-mortality rate throughout the Near East." The following will serve as an illustration of the achievements of the Jews at Palestine in the field of hygiene and public health. Saul Adler (1895-   ), professor of parasitology at the Hebrew University in Jerusalem, is a world-famous authority on tropical medicine. He made comprehensive studies on the transmission of leishmaniasis which has relation to the control of kalaazar and oriental sore. This oriental sore has a marked virulence in the Far East, and the officials of the United Nations suggested to Prof. Adler to go to China to study on the spot an outbreak of oriental sore which is threatening the lives of millions of people. Prof. Ludwig Halberstaedter of Jerusalem, Israel, accomplished much in the treatment of cancer. Prof. Israel J. Kligler made fundamental contributions to the study of immunology and bacteriology. The fact that Palestine is the only country in the Middle East whose malaria is now of minor importance is due mainly to his practical methods of combating malaria. Dr. Kligler's pioneer work has been continued by Prof. Gideon Mer. During World War II, Prof. Mer was placed in charge of a malarial control unit which served in highly malarial areas in Iraq, Persia and Burma. For his meritorious contribution to the war effort, he was decorated by the British Empire.

Jews have been productive in biology and organic chemistry. Ferdinand Cohn (1828-1898), professor of botany at Breslau, was the author of the first monograph on bacteria, and is considered the father of bacteriology. At that time bacteriology was a department of botany. Cohn stated that organisms which were morphologically similar could be physiologically different. He made extensive studies in the minute fungi, and established the identity of bacteria with plants. He rendered to science a great service by his aid to a young and unknown district physician, Robert Koch. At that time many doctors entered Cohn's institute with claims of important discoveries in bacteriology, but Cohn proved that their theories were wrong. When Koch applied to him for a demonstration of his discovery that anthrax is caused by a specific bacteria, Cohn encouraged him, and he first publicized Koch's discovery in 1876. Julius Sachs (1832-1897), professor of botany at Würzburg, did pioneer work in the study of chlorophyl, and showed that sunlight plays a decisive role in determining their action in reference to the absorption. Jacques Loeb (1859-1925), head of the department of experimental biology at the Rockefeller Institute in New York, investigated the effect of electrolytic, thermal, and radiant energy upon living matter. In 1899 he demonstrated that the unfertilized eggs of the sea-urchin can develop into the swimming larvae by treating them with hypertonic sea water. Richard Willstaetter (1872-1942), professor of organic chemistry at Berlin, discovered several forms of chlorophyl in plants. He demonstrated relationship between this green coloring matter and the red coloring matter in the blood of animals. He also produced the anesthetic avertin. In 1915 the Nobel prize was awarded to him for his researches in the chemistry of chlorophyl. Otto Meyerhof (1884-   ), formerly professor of physiological chemistry at Cologne, investigated the mechanism of oxidation of the cells and the respiration of the muscles, enzyme chemistry, and fermentation. In 1922 he shared with A. V. Hill the Nobel prize for his scientific work on the physiology of the cell. Otto H. Warburg (1883-   ), professor of biology in Berlin, contributed to the chemistry of the cell. He demonstrated the peculiar fermentative type of metabolism of cancer cells. In 1931 he received the Nobel prize for his work on respiratory ferments and their mode of action. Otto Loewi (1873-   ), professor of pharmacology at Graz, Austria, made studies of metabolism, the vegetative nervous system, kidney function, digitalis, diabetes, and described a test for pancreatic insufficiency. In 1936 he received the Nobel prize in medicine and physiology for his fundamental discovery of the chemical transmission of nerve-impulses. Joseph Erlanger (1873-   ), professor of physiology at Washington University, made studies on metabolism in dogs, traumatic shock and other important problems in physiology. In 1944 he shared with H. Spencer the Nobel prize for their studies on the function of individual nerves and influence of pulse pressure on kidney secretion. Dr. Ernst B. Chain (1906-   ), a native of Russia, Professor at Oxford, England, shared with Sir Howard W. Florey and Sir Alexander Fleming the Nobel prize award for their discovery of the wonder drug penicillin. H. J. Muller, Professor at Indiana University, Bloomington, Indiana, was awarded the Nobel prize for his work in genetics. Moritz Schiff (1823-1896), professor of physiology at Geneva, was a man of great originality, displaying an almost prophetic insight into many medical problems. He anticipated Claude Bernard in pointing out the existence of the vasodilator nerves. He also anticipated Pavlov's pupils in the conception of conditioned reflex. He was the first to notice the effect of excitation of the cerebral cortex upon the circulation. He was a pioneer in the field of brain physiology. His classical experiments on excision of the thyroid made him a pioneer of the doctrine of internal secretion and thyroid treatment. He described the biliary cycle, which is named after him. Hugo Kronecker (1839-1914), formerly professor of physiology at Berne, made contributions on his specialty of a permanent nature. He investigated the problem of fatigue and recovery of muscle. He demonstrated that the heart's activity is "all or none", that means that it will either contract to its fullest extent or not at all. He invented the phrenograph, the frog-heart manometer, the perfusion canula, and the graduated induction coil. Samuel J. Meltzer (1851-1924), head of the department of physiology and pharmacology at the Rockefeller Institute in New York, was a leader in the profession. He is known as the discoverer of the so-called Kronecker-Meltzer's theory of the mechanism of deglution, Meltzer's method of anesthesia, Meltzer's treatment of tetanus, Meltzer-Lyon test for biliary disease, and Meltzer's law of contrary innervation.

THE HEBREW IMPACT ON WESTERN CIVILIZATION

W. H. Welch wrote of Meltzer as follows: "He had remarkable influence in furthering scientific research in both theoretical and practical medicine, especially upon young men." Bruno Z. Kisch (1890-   ), formerly professor of experimental medicine, physiology and biochemistry at Cologne, made important contributions to his specialty. He discovered a reflex closure of the eye, the law of irradiation of autonomic reflexes, and introduced a new test for toxic goiter. Alfred Fröhlich (1871-   ), formerly professor of pharmacology at Vienna, has done pioneer work in pharmacology and physiology. He flourished for half a century as an experimenter, teacher and author in his chosen field, and some of his discoveries have been accepted throughout the world. He describes the so-called Fröhlich syndrome in 1901. In 1910 he and Otto Loewi discovered that adrenalin following the administration of cocaine produces more intense effect. As a result of this discovery, the common use of adrenalin in combination with cocaine has been established in medical practice. In the same year Fröhlich and Hochward found that injection of hypoglysin produces powerful contractions of the non-pregnant uterus, and they recommended obstetricians to use hypoglysin during delivery, and it has been accepted in obstetric practice. He was the first to describe the stimulant effect of radium-emanation on the heart, and its protective action against anoxia in certain aquatic animals. David I. Macht (1882-   ) of Baltimore made fundamental contributions to pharmacology. Among other things he discovered a test and treatment for pemphigus.

One of the greatest anatomists of all time was Jacob Henle (1809-1885), a rabbi's grandson, who was professor of anatomy in Zurich (1840-1844), Heidelberg (1844-1852) and Göttingen (1852-1885). His contributions to medical science are of an epoch-advance in medicine. He was the founder of modern knowledge of the epithelial tissues of the human body. His name is associated with many structures of the body, such as Henle's loop in the kidneys, Henle's membrane, Henle's warts, Henle's layer, Henle's spine, Henle's fissures, Henle's cell, Henle's fibrin, Henle's sphincter, and the canal of Henle. In his *Handbook of Rational Pathology* (1846-1853) he overthrew antiquated systems and expounded new ideas. In 1840 he wrote a classical essay "Miasms and Contagia" in which he stated that infectious diseases are due to specific microorganisms. He searched for the pathogenic microbes with genius, but without technic but he did not discover them. He maintained that the germs are invisible because they differ so little from the tissues in which they are imbedded that they remain unrecognizable, and he stated that "before microscopic forms can be regarded as the cause of contagion in man they must be found constantly in the contagious material, they must be isolated from it and their strength tested." It was his pupil Robert Koch who thirty-two years later, confirmed Henle's theory by introducing his method of fixing and staining material films to discover the tubercle bacillus. Dr. Pagel stated that Koch was influenced in his epoch making discoveries by Henle. Victor Robinson pointed out that Henle laid the foundation of the germ-theory of disease. Dr. Rosen wrote that Henle gave a hint of the Virchow's cellular pathology and that Koch in later life admitted how deeply he was grateful to his great teacher Henle. Benedict Stilling (1810-1879) of Copenhagen introduced a new technic for the microscopic examination of the nervous system. His name is associated with the so-called Stilling canal, Stilling nucleus, and Stilling raphe. He also made valuable contributions to the physiology of the nervous system. Emil Zuckerkandl (1849-1910), professor of anatomy in Vienna, made significant contributions to anatomy. He described the aquaeductus vestible, discovered a gland near suprahyoid and the so-called Zuckerkandl bodies.

Jews distinguished themselves also in the field of medical history. Max Neuburger (1861-   ), formerly professor of medical history in Vienna, enriched the literature of medical history. He is the author of a classical book *History of Medicine* (2 volumes, 1906-1910) which is the most authoritative on the subject. He founded the Institute for the History of Medicine in Vienna. He is considered the dean of medical historians. Charles Singer (1876-   ), professor emeritus of history of medicine in London, is the author of a great deal of studies on the history of medicine in antiquity and the Middle Ages, and has been the leader of the modern medico-historical school.

Jews have demonstrated their capacity as medical organizers in all its phases. As directors the Jews introduced high standards in medical institutions. Some of the greatest medical centers in the world were developed under the direction of Jewish doctors. Thus, the Frankfurt Institute reached its culmination under Prof. Paul Ehrlich's directorship; the Institute of Experimental Therapeutics in Dahlem, and the Experimental Laboratory of the Kaiser Wilhelm Institute in Berlin were ably directed by Prof. August Wassermann and other Jewish celebrities; the Pasteur Institute of Paris flourished under the directorship of Prof. Elie Metchnikoff and the collaboration of Prof. Alexander Besredka; and the Rockefeller Institute for Medical Research in New York developed under the skill and guidance of its director, Prof. Simon Flexner. Sigismund S. Goldwater (1873-1942) was a recognized authority on administrative medicine and public health, and rendered great service to the United States and many European countries in the field of hospital construction. From 1914 to 1917 he served as commissioner of health for New York City. He was the first to suggest dividing the city into health districts. He also established the first bureau of public health education in many health departments in the country, issuing newspaper releases and bulletins. From 1917 to 1929 he was director of the Mount Sinai Hospital in New York. An organized unit was formed at this hospital that served as a section of the medical department of the U. S. Army during World War I, which afterwards became known as Base Hospital Unit No. 3. Goldwater became chairman of the hospital division of the Council of

National Defense, and greatly influenced the methods of organizing army camp hospitals. Prof. W. H. Welch wrote as follows: "Mount Sinai Hospital has become an important world centre for the advancement and diffusion of medical knowledge." Jews distinguished themselves as co-founders of international institutions that serve humanity. Thus, Adolphus S. Solomons (1826-1910) of Washington, D. C., was co-founder of the American Red Cross in 1881. He is listed as a charter member of the American Red Cross, served as its vice-president, and was a delegate to the International Red Cross Conference in Geneva. He also was a founder of the Mount Sinai Hospital and Montefiore Hospital in New York, the Columbia Hospital in Washington, D. C., and the first training school for nurses.

The foregoing record shows that the medical work done by Jews since the 19th century was most efficacious in these countries, where the admission of Jews to universities and teaching positions was more freely practiced. It also demonstrates that the Jews acted as creators, pathfinders, discoverers, systematizers, teachers and leaders in modern medicine. The Jewish physicians advanced all phases of medical science and art, and their medical accomplishments are of significance and of a permanent nature.

BIBLIOGRAPHY

CUSHING, HARVEY, *Life of Sir William Osler*, Vol. 2, pp. 403-405, 1926.

GARRISON, FIELDING H., *History of Medicine*, p. 129. Philadelphia: 1922.

GOLDMAN, E., *Palestine Medical Research Aid in Rebirth of Country*, Jewish Advocate, p. 6. Boston: September 25, 1947.

KAGAN, SOLOMON R., *Jews as Nobel prize winners in Medicine*, The Hebrew Medical Journal, Vol. 2, p. 95. New York: 1944.
———, *Jewish Contributions to Medicine in America*, Second Edition. Boston: 1939.
———, *The Modern Medical World*, p. 31. Boston: 1945.

MAJOR, RALPH H., *Classic Descriptions of Diseases*, pp. 203-208. Charles C. Thomas, 1932.

NEUBERGER, MAX, *Jewish Physicians in the History of Medicine*, Medical Leaves, Vol. 5, pp. 64-66, Chicago: 1943 (translated by S. R. Kagan and F. K. Neuburger).

ROBINSON, VICTOR, *The Life of Jacob Henle*, pp. 106-107. New York: 1921.

ROSEN, GEORGE, *Jacob Henle*, Bulletin of the History of Medicine, Vol. 5, pp. 528-529. Baltimore: 1937. *Ibid.*, Vol. 6, p. 909, 1938.

SINGER, CHARLES, *The Jews, their History, Culture, and Religion*, Science and Judaism, Vol. 3, pp. 1076-1077. Philadelphia: Jewish Publication Society of America, 1949.
———, *The Jews, their History, Culture, and Religion*, Vol. 3, p. 1089, 1949.

The Jewish Contribution to the Exploration of the Globe

By Hugo Bieber

FROM antiquity up to the present times, Jews have taken an active, often a leading part in exploring the world.

As early as in the sixth century B.C.E., Jews, living in dispersion, undertook long and dangerous travels to Jerusalem, the center of worship and the destination of numberless individual pilgrims and of missions sent by remote Jewish communities which wanted to maintain spiritual connection or advice in matters of religious rites and doctrines. These travels through countries inhabited by hostile peoples and often through unknown areas, induced the Jews to collect information about the safest ways and the opportunities to buy provisions or to repair their carriages, in order to facilitate pilgrimage. Very soon commercial interests joined the spiritual purposes. When Xerxes was king of Persia, a steady traffic between that country and Jerusalem was established. The more the Roman empire extended its domination, the more frequently the leaders of Jewish communities had to go to Rome for political reasons, whether to obtain privileges or to prevent anti-Jewish measures. Akiba Ben Joseph, the founder of rabbinical Judaism, who lived from about 40 to about 135 C.E., visited all places of Palestine, and wandered to Arabia, Cappadocia and Media to support his coreligionists morally and materially. He went to Rome to defend successfully the cause of the Jews before emperor Nerva, and to Parthia to perform religious ceremonies. Until Christianity became the official religion of the Roman empire, Jewish missionaries visited all of its provinces to win adherents to their religion. According to a statement in the New Testament (Matt. 23:15), the Pharisees compassed land and sea to make one proselyte. All these traveling activities involved investigations of the local, economic and social conditions of the visited places.

In the Middle Ages, Jewish merchants were the first to dare travels to the wilderness of Northern Europe and Central Asia for the exchange of goods, for tracing new avenues of trade and commerce, and often for diplomatic purposes in the service of non-Jewish rulers. In Asia and Africa they met with Jews who lived in places unknown to Europeans, understood Hebrew, supported their itinerant coreligionists and provided them with goods and information. In this way, the Jewish travelers often combined their commercial interest with more or less scientific aims while collecting economic and geographical lore, acquiring books or oral intelligence, above all learning from foreign mathematicians and astronomers. In the times of Charlemagne who sent the Jew Isaac as ambassador to Bagdad, the Radanites, Jewish merchants, organized commercial expeditions which went to China in regular intervals. A Jewish adventurer, Eldad Hadani who lived from 880 to 940, wandered through East Africa and struck the imagination of his audiences and readers with reports claiming to have discovered the descendants of the Ten Lost Tribes. While large parts of his story, translated into several languages, met with skepticism, some of his reports on Ethiopia proved to be reliable. Abraham ibn Ezra, a versatile poet and scholar, born in Toledo, Spain, in 1092, died probably in Rome in 1167, wandered in France, England, Italy, Palestine, Egypt, and eastward to India, studying peoples, their languages, their way of living, the state of learning, mathematics and astronomy in Islamic countries. The most famous Jewish explorer of that epoch was Benjamin of Tudela, Spain, who started his journey in 1160 in Saragossa, Spain, to return only thirteen years thereafter. From Spain he went to Provence, Italy, Greece, Asia Minor, Palestine, Mesopotamia, Persia, India, to the frontiers of Tibet and China, and, on his way back, to Yemen. His vivid descriptions of about three hundred towns are of unique documentary value. The knowledge of several peoples that disappeared completely because they were destroyed by the Tatars, is based upon Benjamin's reports only. A Bohemian Jew, named Pethahiah, born in Prague but commonly called Pethahiah of Regensburg or Ratisbon, began his journey in that city about 1195. He traveled in Poland, Russia, Crimea, Armenia, Babylonia, Persia and India, and returned to his Bohemian homeland by way of Syria, Palestine and Greece. Estori Ben Moses Farhi who was born in Provence about 1282 and died in Palestine about 1357, became the first to investigate scientifically the topography, archaeology and folklore of the Holy Land, dealing with its history, geography, architecture, numismatics, weights and measures, and the way his Jewish, Christian and Moslem fellow inhabitants of Palestine used to live.

In 1375, Abraham Cresques, a Jew from the Mediterranean island of Majorca, accomplished his "Catalan Atlas", which is considered "one of the most prized maps in the history of geography". Mapmaking had been for a long period in the hands of Majorcan Jews, almost exclusively. Cresques utilized for his map the reports of Benjamin of Tudela and of numerous of the latter's Jewish disciples who had penetrated into Africa, opened unknown areas to European trade and crossed the Sahara from Algiers and Morocco to Timbuctu. Abraham's son Jehuda Cresques who, in 1391, during a pogrom, was forcibly baptized and assumed the name Jaime Ribes, was also a great scholar and an authority on geography. He founded the famous "School of Sagres", a center of studies that became of primary importance to explorers and navigators. Prince Henry the Navigator of Portugal was the protector of the school whose teachers, most of whom were Jews or crypto-Jews, gave the prince highly valuable advice for the preparation of his expeditions. Jehuda Cresques was also a famous maker of nautical instruments. Mecia de Villadestes, another crypto-Jew from Majorca, and a disciple of Cresques, was an expert of inner Africa. In our days, tanks and autocars use the road across the Sahara which was at first traced by Mecia de Villadestes. Among the Jews of Majorca were also Gabriel de Vallsecha whose map was used by Amerigo Vespucci, and Abraham Farrisol who explored Africa on camel-back, climbed high mountains and brought immense treasures to Europe in exchange for salt.

Jehuda Cresques was not the only Jew who excelled in making nautical instruments. Nautical science was in medieval Europe principally a Jewish domain. Already in the eleventh century, Jewish astronomers introduced the use of the astrolabe. Jacob Ben Mahir Ibn Tibbon, a Jewish professor at the university of Montpellier, France, who lived from 1230 till 1312, invented the quadrant. His astronomic tables were used by sailors until the middle of the eighteenth century. Of greatest importance and influence was Abraham Zacuto, professor at the universities of Salamanca and Saragossa until the expulsion of the Jews from Spain, then court astronomer of king John II of Portugal, finally a refugee in Tunisia. Zacuto was consulted before Vasco da Gama could start his expedition which succeeded in discovering the maritime route to India, and improved de Gama's astrolabe and tables. When Vasco da Gama landed at the Indian coast he was greatly surprised to be greeted by a Jew who had come to the same spot overland from his native town of Posen. This Jew later assumed the name of Gaspard da Gama and became famous because of his valor while participating in Cabral's expeditions to South America.

There are continued debates about the presumably Jewish descent of Columbus. But without any doubt, the men who prepared his first travel to America scientifically and financially, and a large number of his crew were Jews. Columbus was taught by Abraham Zacuto and carried the latter's works on his voyages. Crypto-Jews, of whom Santangel and Sanchez were outstanding, defended his cause before Ferdinand and

Isabella of Spain and provided the money for the purchase and equipment of his ships. Santangel and Sanchez were the first to receive the announcement of his success by Columbus. Luis de Torres, a Jew baptized shortly before the expedition started served Columbus as interpreter. He was the first European to set foot on an American island. Bernal, the ship's doctor had narrowly escaped death because the Inquisition had sentenced him for adhering to Judaism. Alonzo della Calle, Rodrigo Sanchez and Marco, the cook, were also Jews participating in Columbus's first expedition while the Jewish origin of other members of the crew is less certain.

A great Jewish contemporary of Columbus, Joseph Vecinho, was also a disciple of Abraham Zacuto. He is blamed by Columbus because he did not favor support of Columbus's project by the king of Portugal. But Vecinho aided him with scientific information. Previously Vecinho had been sent by king John of Portugal to Guinea to determine the altitude of the sun throughout that area, and was highly respected because of the accuracy of his measurements.

About 1586, the Marrano Pedro Teixeira began his long travels which were of major importance to the development of reliable geographical knowledge. Teixeira explored the Amazon River and other parts of America, furthermore China, the Philippines, India, Persia and the Middle East. His reports, written with literary skill and scientific solidity, were highly appreciated for centuries after his death. Tobias Cohen, one of the greatest physicians of his time and a precursor of modern medical science, who was born in Metz, France, in 1652 and died in Jerusalem in 1729, made use of his journeys in the Near and Middle East for careful and exact studies of diseases, plagues and hygienic conditions. As the representative of the Jewish communities of Palestine, Haym Joseph Azulai traveled, from 1753 to 1758 and from 1772 to 1778, in Turkey, Egypt, Italy, Germany, France, Holland and England, Tunisia and Algiers. His diary is full of highly interesting notes about the economic and cultural life of the Jews of his time in Europe and Africa, interviews with rabbis and scholars, and descriptions of libraries and manuscripts. At the end of the eighteenth century, Samuel Aaron Romanelli explored North Africa, and acquired especially intimate knowledge of Morocco. His book on that country, published in Hebrew in 1792, was translated into English as late as 1887, and attracted even then general attention.

Search of the Lost Ten Tribes induced Jews continually to explore remote countries. In the seventeenth century, the Marrano Antonio de Montezinos penetrated into Ecuador for that purpose. From 1831 to 1834, Baruch Ben Samuel of Safed, Palestine, went to Yemen to trace there the Tribes until he was killed by the Imam. For the same purpose, the Roumanian Israel Joseph Benjamin who called himself, in memory of Benjamin of Tudela, Benjamin the Second, traveled from 1845 to 1853, in Syria, Kurdistan, India, Afghanistan and Algeria. His reports aroused the interest of the great explorer Alexander von Humboldt and numerous geographers.

Frequently it was longing for adventures that dominated itinerant Jews. Thus Simon van Geldern, a grand-uncle of the poet Heinrich Heine, and originally an excellent scholar, wandered, in the second half of the eighteenth century, from town to town, from country to country, visiting all capitals of Europe, delivering lectures and becoming implicated in various plots and affairs. In his diary he proved to be a keen observer. He died on the road. Jacob Philadelphia, a physicist and mathematician, born in Philadelphia, Pa., probably in 1720, enchanted many European princes as well as his learned audiences in the most important cities of Europe. He tried to promote trade between Prussia and the United States, and, in 1784, king Frederick II of Prussia adopted Philadelphia's ideas in his commercial treaty with this country. Philadelphia's successes, however, stirred up jealousy and caused him adversity on the part of many enemies. The last years of his life are veiled by legends. Perhaps the most fortunate Jewish adventurer was Alexander Salmon. He was the son of a banker in London but refused to enter his father's business. He became a sailor, and for many years he was on board a whaler. Then he came to the island of Tahiti, married the female ruler of that paradisic island, and was the principal adviser of the ruler. His daughter became a queen. His son was the intimate friend of Robert Louis Stevenson who made Tahiti famous in world literature. Salmon wrote important books on the social and economic conditions of Tahiti.

The eras of enlightenment, liberalism and democracy, removing many disabilities and discriminations, facilitated also the activities of Jewish explorers in many regards. The heroic age of the itinerant Jew, traveling alone and being exposed to greater dangers than his non-Jewish colleagues, came to an end. Instead Jewish explorers began to cooperate with scientific institutions, academies, learned societies, governmental enterprises, and their exchange of knowledge with non-Jewish scientists as well as their contributions to learned reviews became more frequent. While the exploring activities of the Jews became more and more integrated into the general progress of science, their individual initiative and adventurous spirit remained existent and effective.

The first Jew to participate in a modern scientific expedition which was undertaken by non-Jews was Israel Lyons, noted mathematician, astronomer and botanist. In 1774, he accompanied Captain Phipps who later became Lord Mulgrave, on his expedition to the North Pole, serving as chief astronomer. In the nineteenth century, five arctic expeditions were accompanied or led by American Jews. Isaac Israel Hayes was surgeon in the second Grinnell Arctic Expedition, commanded by Captain Kane, which, during the years 1853 to 1855, made investigations in Smith's Sound. In 1860, Hayes himself led a Polar expedition to Foulke Fjord, and proceeded from there to regions never before reached by a white man. In 1869, he directed an expedition to Greenland. Emil Bessels who previously had participated in a German voyage to the Arctic Ocean, was, in 1871, appointed surgeon on the *Polaris,* commanded by Captain Charles Francis Hall whose attempt to reach the North Pole ended tragically. It was Bessels who proved, on the ground of tidal studies, that Greenland was an island. After being associated with the Smithsonian Institution in Washington, D.C., Bessels participated in the voyage of the United States steamship *Saranac,* bound to make ethnological studies on the northwest coast of America, but wrecked in Seymour Narrows, British Columbia. Edward Israel, astronomer of the Lady Franklin Bay Expedition under the command of General A. W. Greely, became a victim of his daring spirit before the expedition went home. Angelo Heilprin, after exploring the geological structure of Florida, Mexico and the Bermudas, became world-widely famous in 1892 when he led the Peary Relief Expedition to Greenland. Later he explored the island of Martinique after the eruption of Mt. Pelee, North Africa and Alaska. Another famous relief-expedition was led by the Russian Jew Rudolph L. Samoilovich which, in 1928 rescued Umberto Nobile and the crew of his dirigible in the Polar region. Previously Samoilovich had explored Spitzbergen, and subsequently he directed an expedition to Franz Josef Land, each time making important discoveries.

Jews also contributed to the exploration of the Americas in modern times. Arthur Poznansky discovered antiquities in remote and almost inaccessible areas of Peru and Bolivia. Eight important expeditions were conducted by Charles Leopold Bernheimer who began as an office boy in New York City, and then became of national renown as an arbitration authority. Bernheimer explored the "bad lands" of Northern Arizona and Southern Utah, and excavated prehistoric settlements in New Mexico. He extended his investigation to southern Mexico, Yucatan and Guatemala. Leo Joachim Frachtenberg, from Atlanta, Georgia, studied the life, customs and history of North American Indians. Morton C. Kahn and Melville J. Herskovits did the same in Surinam and the Caribbean islands. Kahn also studied tropical diseases in Costa Rica and British Guinea, and became an authority on the life and history of the Bush Negroes. Herskovits was respected as an expert on Haiti and American Negroes. Julius Popper, born in Roumania, made a trip around the world, and finally concentrated his studies upon the island of Tierra del Fuego on the southern tip of South America, previously unexplored. He took possession of the island, ruled it as a sovereign, exploited it commercially and described it with scientific exactness from the geographic and geological point of view. Paul Radin excelled in geological and anthropological research. He discovered important traces of American aborigines and threw new light upon the psychology and the social life of American Indians. Franz Boas, the greatest anthropologist of his time, had previously become renowned because of his meteorological expedition to Baffin Land in 1882. Then his interest turned to the culture of the Eskimos, and subsequently the American Indians. In 1886, Boas began to study the life of the northwestern tribes of Canada. From 1900 to 1905, he was the leading spirit of the Jesup North Pacific Expedition whose principal scientific result was the proof of the cultural relationship between the Siberians, Eskimos and American Indians. This and several other expeditions conducted by Boas to Mexico and Porto Rico gave him the broad fundaments for the development of his anthropological and sociological theories.

In the Far East, Heinrich Agathon Bernstein explored the Moluccan islands and New Guinea for the Dutch government, and died on one of the islands in 1865. Samuel Fenichel, noted ornithologist and entomologist, observed the fauna of New Guinea, discovered numerous birds and butterflies unknown until then, and made valuable contributions to the knowledge of the native population. New Guinea was also the object of Lamberto Loria's investigations. Loria, descending from an old Italian Jewish family, also traveled through the Australian continent. The results of his studies were deposited in the Ethnographical Museum of Florence, Italy, which was founded by Loria. Charles Gabriel Seligman, British physician, ethnologist and anthropologist, was a member of the Cambridge Anthropological Expedition to Torres Straits and Borneo, and turned his special attention to native medicine and surgery, and gave interesting information about popular rites and customs. Married to Brenda Z. Salaman, noted zoologist, who assisted him in his anthropological research work, Seligman directed expeditions to New Guinea, Ceylon and the Sudan. His books on *The Veddas* and *The Races of Africa* which became standard works show the steady enlargement of his point of view. Seligman embraced physical anthropology, archaeology, comparative religion and sociology. Elio Modigliani, member of a well-known Italian Jewish family, explored the island of Sumatra and the neighboring regions, penetrating into areas on which no European had set foot, and describing both the peoples and the fauna with artistic skill and scientific accuracy.

The exploration of Northern Asia is of special interest because the Russian Jews who contributed to it began their scientific careers as political convicts, exiled to Siberia. A rare exception was Georg Huth, born in Krotoshin, Poland, who was invited by the Russian Academy of Science to make an expedition, intended to investigate the language, history and ethnography of the Tunguses in the Yenisei region. Thereupon Huth participated in an expedition to Eastern Turkestan. Vladimir Jochelson, sentenced to three years' imprisonment and ten years of exile to Siberia because of his revolutionary activities, studied there the language and folkways of the Yokashirs, and published the results of his research work after he had served his time. Subsequently, Jochelson took part in expeditions to Kamchatka, the Aleutian islands, Alaska and Eastern Asia. His wife, Dina Jochelson-Brodsky, assisted him in his research work. Leo Sternberg, a member of the Russian socialist party, was sentenced to ten years of exile on the island of Sakhalin in 1910. There he studied the language of the Gilyak, Orok and Ainu tribes. He made expeditions to the Amur region which yielded valuable results. Sakhalin and the Amur region were also explored by Berthold Laufer, curator of anthropology at the Field Museum in Chicago. Laufer collaborated with Boas as a member of the Jacob Schiff Expedition to China, the Blackstone Expedition to Tibet, and the Field Expedition to China.

A daring explorer of Central Asia was Ney Elias. In his early years he traveled without any companion or escort from Pekin to St. Petersburg, crossing the desert of Gobi by a route hitherto completely unknown. Thereupon, Elias was sent by the British government to Yunan, to Ladakh, India, and to Chinese Turkestan. In 1885, he undertook a long and dangerous journey, along the Pamir mountains, through Badakishan and Afghan Turkestan to Afghanistan. In 1889 he was entrusted with demarcating the frontier between Siam and the Burman Shan States, and accomplished this highly difficult task with bravery, energy and fairness. The inquiries of Sir Marc Aurel Stein made epoch not only in the history of scientific exploration of Central Asia but also in the general history of archaeology and art. Stein had been appointed principal of the Oriental College in Lahore, India, in 1888, and registrar of Punjab University. After making antiquarian investigations in various parts of India, Stein began, in 1900 his great expeditions to Central Asia which completely changed the aspects of the historical studies of art. Traveling from the Near East to China, Stein discovered the ancient frontier wall of China; in the "Cave of the Thousand Buddhas" he picked up very old paintings and manuscripts. He traced the campaigns of Alexander the Great on his way to the conquest of India, penetrated into unknown territories, rediscovered forgotten periods of art and civilization, and saved an immense number of works of arts from oblivion or destruction. Sven Hedin, another explorer of Central Asia who became popular because of his vivid narrative of his adventures, was of Jewish descent.

In the Near East, Joseph Judah Czorny was one of the earliest explorers of the Caucasus which he investigated for ten years, from 1864 on. He also made journeys to Daghestan, Persia and Afghanistan. Eduard Glaser contributed to the topography of Southern Arabia by conducting four expeditions to that country, where David Heinrich Mueller discovered important inscriptions and literary documents. Joseph Halévy, born as a Turkish subject, later a naturalized French citizen, made a dangerous journey to Yemen to study the Sabean inscriptions, of which he brought about 700 to Paris. He also explored Ethiopia and inquired into Babylonian and Assyrian antiquities on the spot. In the disguise of a dervish, Arminius Vambery traveled in Persia, Turkey and Armenia. Gottfried Merzbacher, an international banker and trained Alpinist, did much to explore the Northern Caucasus. He also climbed mountains in Africa and America, and became famous because of his ascents in Central Asia. A chain of the Tian Shan Mountains was called, in his honor, the Merzbacher Range.

In the nineteenth century, Africa, called the "dark continent", attracted the explorers particularly, first because its map showed many and large white spots, and above all because political aims were combined with scientific interests. African soil was considered as unclaimed property to be annexed by those who were the first to set foot on it. In this way, the explorer was bound to become a conqueror in the name of his nation. He had to meet with armed resistance on the part of the native population, and was exposed to intrigues on the part of competing colonial powers. Emin Pasha whose original name was Isaac Eduard Schnitzer, penetrated into inner Africa beyond the Sudan, after reaching the sources of the White Nile. At first he served the Khedive of Egypt, then he went over to Germany, and planned to conquer a great African empire for emperor William II. He was, however, assassinated before he could realize this idea. By far more successful was Louis Gustave Binger in his efforts to enlarge the colonial possessions of France. Binger was one of the greatest explorers of his time. He was an eminent geographer and philologist, an outstanding expert of African languages and dialects, a far-

sighted organizer, tactful and energetic administrator, a pains-
taking scholar and a steadfast and intrepid man. He was devoted to both science and conquest, to the enlargement of
human knowledge and to the great aims of French colonial
policy. For many years, the French government had deliber-
ated upon the plan to consolidate its African possessions by
linking the Sudan and Senegal with the Guinea Coast. Binger
was the man to accomplish this task. In 1887, he proceeded
from Senegambia to regions until then unknown, concluded
treaties with the native chieftains, and, after two years
of extremely dangerous and adventurous marching through
the wilderness, reached a French outpost on the Ivory Coast
which, due to Binger, was completely annexed by France in
1891. In the latter year, Binger began to explore the territories
along the Niger river and thereupon, by a travel of more than
twelve hundred miles, he took a decisive part in determining
the frontier between the French Ivory Coast and the British
Gold Coast. Binger's books on Africa, the history of geography
and the explorer's calling are considered classical, and his
maps of unsurpassed value.

Another French explorer, Edouard Foa, descending from a
distinguished Italian Jewish family, traveled through Morocco, Central and Southern Africa. He made highly valuable
contributions to the study of the Congo river and the territories of Dahomey and neighboring areas. His great performance was the careful investigation along the Zambesi river.
The expeditions undertaken by Nahum Slouschz, a native of
Odessa, Russia, who became a French citizen and lecturer at
the Sorbonne, Paris, were mainly devoted to researches on
the history and antiquity of the Jews in North Africa and the
vestiges of Phoenician civilization. Slouschz became intimately
acquainted with the population of Tripoli, Algeria, Tunisia
and Morocco, and discovered many inscriptions, manuscripts
and documents of forgotten civilizations. Later on, he directed
excavations in Palestine. After daring adventures in Indo-
China and Malaysia, Raimondo Franchetti, a member of a

widely ramified Jewish family, concentrated his exploring activities upon East Africa. The accounts of his perilous journeys in Ethiopia and Kenya made him famous as "the Italian Lawrence". Franchetti, born in Venice, was killed in an airplane accident in 1934, while on a mission for the Italian government. Valuable contributions to the knowledge of the Islamic populations and the Jews in North-Eastern Africa and the Middle East were made by Hermann Burchardt who was murdered in Southern Arabia in 1900.

The exploration of South Africa was initiated by Nathanael Isaacs, a native of Canterbury, England, who was a pioneer settler in Natal. He was called by the Zulus "Tamboosa", the valiant warrior, and was wounded on the battlefield more than once. Besides penetrating into unknown territories, Isaacs took an important part in the foundation of the city of Durham, South Africa.

A daring American Jewess, Sarah Lavenburg Straus, the widow of Oscar S. Straus, American ambassador to Turkey and cabinet member, financed and accompanied, in 1929, an expedition of scientists to explore the African fauna for the American Museum of Natural History. She traveled more than 15,000 miles and collected thousands of specimens many of which were of greatest zoological importance.

The development of the modern sciences, especially astronomy and meteorology, requires that the scholar sometimes has to leave his study or observatory to confirm statements or theories on remote places. Thus the theory of Einstein was confirmed by expeditions to exotic countries. A pioneer in this field was Sir Arthur Schuster, who, in 1875, was chief of the "Eclipse Expeditions" to Siam, and, in 1878, 1882 and 1886, directed, or participated in, the Solar Expeditions to Colorado, Egypt and the West Indies. Maurice Loewy, director of the Paris Observatory, had to undertake long travels to determine the longitude of many important cities more precisely.

Modern journalism called forth a new type of investigating traveler, the reporter and foreign correspondent whose profession often involves adventure, hardship and risk of life. The first modern journalist who succeeded in being present wherever something of political importance happened, was Henri Oppert de Blowitz, for many years foreign correspondent of the London Times. He was an eyewitness of revolutions and wars, an eavesdropper at international conferences of leading statesmen and secret plots, and seemed to be ubiquitous. He had many successors who combined rapidity of reporting with solid knowledge of the history of the countries on which they had to write and who showed sound judgment on the political, economic and cultural situation, and described their experiences with artistic skill. In the French language Joseph Kessel became noted because of his faculty in narrating both his adventures and contemporary events in a cultivated form. Arthur Koestler impressed even more readers by his experience, views, ideas and sentiments. In America, Hermann Bernstein, Isaac Don Levine, Elias Tobenkin, Isaac Marcosson became renowned as war correspondents and subsequently reporters on foreign affairs. They were followed by Louis Fischer, Eugene Lyons, Waldo Frank, I. F. Stone and many others who made American readers acquainted with the situation in various countries. The youngest roving writer who feels the pulse of the peoples of Europe, while traveling from country to country, is Cyrus L. Sulzberger.

BIBLIOGRAPHY

ADLER, ELKAN N. *Jewish Travelers.* London: 1930.

——, Introduction to *The Itinerary of Benjamin of Tudela.* Oxford: 1907.

BAKER, J. N. L. *A History of Geographical Discovery and Exploration.* Boston: 1931.

DE MADARIAGA, SALVADOR. *Christopher Columbus.* New York: 1940.

EDMUNDSON, L., "The Voyages of Pedro Teixeira", *Transactions of the Royal Historical Society.* Vol. 3. London, 1920.

GERSHENFELD, LOUIS. *The Jew in Science.* Philadelphia: 1934.

GILLESPIE, J. E. *History of Geographical Discovery.* New York: 1933.

GRAETZ, H., *History of the Jews.* Philadelphia, 1927.

GRAYZEL, SOLOMON, *A History of the Jews.* Philadelphia, 1947.

JACOBS, JOSEPH. *The Story of Geographical Discoveries.* London: 1899.

JOHNSTON, HARRY H. *A History of the Colonization of Africa.* London: 1913.

KAYSERLING, M., *Christopher Columbus and the Participation of the Jews in the Spanish and Portuguese Discoveries.* New York, 1894.

KEY, CHARLES EDWARD. *The Story of Twentieth Century Exploration.* New York: 1937.

KIMBLE, GEORGE. *Geography in the Middle Ages.* London: 1937.

KOMROFF, MANUEL, *Contemporaries of Marco Polo.* New York, 1931.

LEBESON, ANITA LIBMAN, "Jewish Cartographers", *Historia Judaica.* Vol. 10, No. 2, October 1948.

ROTH, CECIL, *A Short History of the Jewish People.* London, 1948.

——, *The History of the Marranos.* London, 1932.

The Jew as Soldier, Strategist and Military Adviser

By William B. Ziff

During the recent campaigns in Palestine, there were few of the experts who were not startled by the military prowess demonstrated by the Jews in their successful defense of the new State of Israel against the invading armies of six neighboring Arab nations.

It had been commonly held that the Jews would be pushed into the sea in a swift and easy campaign, with the converging Arab armies making juncture before the indefensible Jewish city of Tel Aviv, and dictating the peace there with bombs and artillery. Not only were numbers, strategic situation and weight of arms overwhelmingly on the side of the invaders, but the Jews appeared to have neither weapons nor organized forces, and indeed, no organized government. From the conventional military view, they were neither an army nor a state, but a disordered rabble composed of tradesmen, farmers, and shattered refugees who had fled Europe in panic. Even more important, an almost universal bias ascribed to them qualities of meanness, servility and cowardice which would make any calculated defense virtually impossible.

When by unaided raw courage and brilliant tactical capacity, the Jews demonstrated an ability first to hold their ground, and then to rout their opponents completely in a series of successive engagements, the gentlemen in the chancelleries and the top military echelons still could not conceive the situation. With an almost superstitious reverence for the traditional misinformation in which their opinions had been anchored, they were at the beginning disposed to credit the wildest of rumors to explain the miracle—Russian generals; Russian heavy tanks, munitions and airplanes; overwhelming

[240]

superiority in fighting planes and pilots somehow smuggled out of the American and British air forces.

Yet any competent survey of the history of the Jews would indicate that as a fighting people they have not been excelled anywhere.

It is true that as the traditional People of the Book, and as a race which has been scattered, ghettoized, and imprisoned everywhere in the iron chains of prejudice, they did not give the appearance of a military people. They seemed to lack much which is deemed essential to the warlike spirit. Their generally mild demeanor and high disproportion of intellectuals and tradesmen, for whom the military mind has had an habitual contempt, easily fitted into the legend of Jewish weakness and slavish self-seeking. In Palestine itself, the British commander, Sir Evelyn Barker, angered by the guerrilla exploits of the Jewish underground, epitomized this belief in the remark that he would force the Jews to their knees by a boycott of Jewish tradesmen, thus "hitting the race where it would hurt them the most—in their pocketbook."

What must be recognized is that in organized warfare, battles are not necessarily won by individual truculence and ferocity alone. As far as the human factor is concerned, the preponderant weight of arms is determined rather by organizability, skill, fortitude, determination, know-how and the capacity for strategy and maneuver. Here devotion, high intelligence, and the will to endure, give the martial spirit its real meaning. The superior capacity of a gifted and endowed people thus is as much reflected in the art of war as in any other type of human activity, and rests on exactly the same elements of character which allow for success in other competitive human endeavors. The whole history of the Jew, his intellectual resource, his tenacity, his quiet determination in the face of adversity, and his willingness to sacrifice well-being and life itself to his spiritual beliefs, all bear witness to this fact.

In the perspective of human affairs, it is perfectly clear that the Jews have always been a great military people, and given opportunity, excel both as soldiers and military organizers.

The Hebrew people were originally a colonizing offshoot of one of the great fighting peoples of antiquity, the Chaldeans.[1] The neighboring Phoenicians and their descendants of Carthage, were of identical stock, speaking a like language, possessing and displaying the same traits and the same adventurous fighting spirit.[2] The Old Testament *Apocrypha* declares the kinship of the Jews with still another great military people, the Spartans. In a letter to the High Priest Onias, Arius, King of the Spartans remarks "concerning the Spartans and Jews, that they are kinsmen and that they are descended from Abraham." The High Priest Jason, forced to flee for his life, is described as "crossing the sea to the Lacedaemonians, hoping to find protection there because of his relationship to them."[3]

However one may accept the accuracy of these accounts, it is certain that the Jews were among the ablest soldiers of ancient times. Inhabiting a little state caught in the pathway of many huge military juggernauts, their record is a saga of human endurance, of military ingenuity and boundless personal courage. Throughout their history they had to fight powerful and aggressive nations, far better equipped, situated and numerous than they, including the successive lords of the earth, the Egyptians, Hittites, Babylonians, Assyrians, Greeks and Romans. Access to metal for armor and weapons was poor. An even greater weakness from the aggressive viewpoint of the ancients, was the Jewish preoccupation with moral problems under a philosophy of living dominated by what the baffled Romans described as "the superstition of an invisible god". As a people the Jews were thus diverted from the prime business of enslavement and conquest which galvanized the purposes of ancient society.

Whether in their own land of Israel or in their collective history later as "dwellers among strangers", their dependence in military contest had to be on a superiority of tactics, mobility, courage and discipline.[4] In ancient Palestine, as later in the Twentieth Century, when Jews again fought as organized bodies under their own banners, their arsenals had largely to be built by seizing them from the enemy.

Ancient Hebrew military prowess must be considered of far greater importance than as a mere unique incident for historical reference. Its impact on Western civilization had decisive effects; for had the Jews succumbed to the massive forces around them as did the Hittite Empire, Moab, Edom and Philistia, Hebrew thought would have perished from the memory of men; Christianity and Moslemism would never have been born, and the course of Western history would have been unrecognizably different. The resistance of the Maccabees alone to the victorious march of Hellenism in the ancient world, possessed a determining influence on the final course of world events.[5]

Recent archaeological findings, plus the internal evidence of the Bible stories, indicate that the Commanders of ancient Israel anticipated by long centuries the military planning which distinguished Greece and Rome. Fleischer in his *From Dan to Megiddo* insists that the tactical formation of Jewish armies during the Exodus was later copied by the Romans. The British major, Vivian Gilbert, declares that during the Allenby campaign in Palestine, he and his commanding officer "were inspired by the Biblical account of the strategy used in the Battle of Micmash, and reproduced it exactly, and with the same excellent results."[6]

It was the Hebrew King, Uzziah, who first invented engines of war, some 500 years before the advent of Philip of Macedon. Similarly, Uzziah was the author of the general staff, and planned campaign, as well as the use of uniform military equipment for his entire host. Even Philip's use of the first standing army not composed of mercenaries, seems to have been long anticipated by David. The attack principle used by Titus against Jerusalem, that of a mound built in a moat, had been used by Joab as early as the Eleventh Century B. C. in his successful investiture of the fortified city of Abel.[7]

As early as Joshua, we find a very real mastery of the importance of thorough intelligence work preparatory to a campaign, and his understanding of espionage and reconnaissance were unique for his time. The training and organization of his men has been described as "a model of military art." The crossing of the Jordan into a bitterly hostile country, "points to a carefully planned, completely successful exploit such as had never been seen. An entire nation passed over a major topographical obstacle, without loss or confusion, and under perfect discipline."[8] The fall of the Walls of Jericho was a minor masterpiece of military operation, starting with the intelligence obtained from the spies who visited the local harlot, Rahab, and ending with a perfectly contained sapping operation. Joshua's capture of the fortified city of Ai showed the same understanding of the value of early and thorough reconnoitering, and of the type of strategic deception used so ably later by Alexander at Tyre and Hannibal at Cannae.[9]

Almost the entire principle of modern guerrilla warfare was anticipated in the ancient wars of the Jews. We shall see that this is particularly true in the desperate struggles against the Romans, but it was already the case in the feats of the Maccabees against the Greco-Syrian conquerors. After the crushing defeat of Judas Maccabaeus at the Battle of Elasa, the Greco-Syrian victor, General Bacchides, nevertheless found himself exposed to an endless succession of small raids, surprise attacks, ambuscades, and planned disruption of his communications, until "he was worn out and his army almost completely destroyed."[10]

II

Throughout the long course of their existence as a nation, the Jews enjoyed the reputation of being the finest fighting men in the ancient world. Overwhelmed time and again by the enormous forces of great world empires, they never yielded, and fought on to the last. Almost alone among the peoples of the earth they were not cowed by the power of Imperial Rome. The Jewish wars against Rome were epic in their proportions. Time after time, this small nation, pitting itself against the mightiest empire of the world, broke out in bloody armed rebellion.[11]

In the earliest of these, led by Judah the Galilean, the rebel watchword, never to be abandoned, was: "We have no master but God." Resistance to Roman rule culminated in a violent upheaval under the reign of the Emperor Nero. The Roman general Cestius Gallus who invaded from Syria, was thrown back with immense slaughter, the worst disaster to Roman arms to occur since the defeat at Varus. Nero promptly appointed the celebrated general, Vespasian, to prosecute the war. The rebels were led by a simple Galilean farmer called John of Gischala, and another independent force by an intellectual named Simon Bar Giora.[11a]

After six terrible years of struggle in which quarter was neither given nor asked, the Jews finally retreated to their capital, Jerusalem. The attack was now in the hands of Titus, famous son of Vespasian, who had under his command five Roman legions, together with 340 catapults. Titus in a series of magnanimous gestures, offered to parley with the insurgents. The Jewish answer was always the same—a contemptuous refusal of any terms save unconditional freedom and the total withdrawal of Roman troops from their country.

The Jewish troops conducted their campaign with such determination and ability, that twice Titus came within a hair's breadth of disaster, and once was himself almost taken. "So unconquerable was the ferocity of the Jewish soldiery," comments Dr. Adams, "that it may be doubted whether even the stern discipline, the high military spirit, and the overwhelming numbers of the Romans would not have been compelled ultimately to give way before them," had Rome not acquired two new and invincible allies—famine and dissension among the ranks of the defenders themselves.[12]

The Roman side of the war was conducted by an apostate Jew, Tiberius Julius Alexander, General of the Army and Chief of Staff, considered one of the outstanding military geniuses of his time. It was he who conceived the device of heaping up a mound against the fortifications so as to enable the Romans to bring their engines of war to bear, perhaps based on his memory of the traditional Jewish account of Joab's maneuver at Abel. Even here the defenders gave a terrifying account of themselves.[13] Dion states that the "Jews made night and day sallies as often as the occasion offered, set fire to the engines, slew numerous combatants. . . . As for the rams, they lassoed some of them and broke the ends off, others they seized and pulled up with hooks . . ."

When after six months of siege the city finally fell, the Jews still refused to capitulate. As they were later to do in the Battle of the Warsaw Ghetto, they fought for every house. The last resistance took place on the hill on which the Temple stood. Again, says Dion Cassius, "Titus made a new proclamation offering them immunity. They, however, even under these circumstances held out." The Roman writer relates almost in awe that "Though they were but a handful fighting against a far superior force, they were not subdued" until the Temple itself was on fire. "Then they went to meet death willingly, some letting themselves be pierced by the swords of the Romans, some slaughtering one another, others committing suicide, and others leaping into the flames. It looked to everybody, and most of all to them, apparently that so far from being ruin, it was victory and salvation and happiness to perish along with the Temple." Thus, this sober, pedestrian Greco-Roman got an inkling of something strange in the ancient world—of a great moral victory in the face of physical defeat.[14]

The reduction of Jerusalem was perhaps the most difficult undertaking in Roman military annals. Returning to Rome after seven years of grueling and costly warfare, the weary conqueror was honored by the erection of an arch to mark his achievement, a recognition only given to commemorate a victory over the most formidable of enemies.[15]

As a result of this deadly struggle, Judea was reduced to ashes. Yet a scarce forty-five years later, during the reign of Trajan, the Jews again found the strength to revolt. In Cyrene, Egypt and Cyprus, as well as in Judea, the rebellion blazed in uncontrollable fury, throwing the entire Empire into an uproar. Two hundred and forty thousand Greeks were alleged by Dion Cassius to have been slain in Cyprus alone. Before the rebels were shattered in Cyrene, the country was turned into a desert.[16] In Egypt, the Jews after driving their opponents to take refuge in Alexandria, were finally crushed by the Roman prefect, Q. Marcius Turbo. Meanwhile in Judea itself, under the generalship of a remarkable leader named Bar Kochba, the Romans were beaten everywhere. In one year, the Jews had reconquered fifty fortified strongholds and 985 towns and villages, and had even succeeded in reoccupying the ruins of Jerusalem.

Again the Romans did not take this contest lightly. Hadrian put the war in the hands of his greatest general, Julius Severus, who was recalled from Britain with his legions for the purpose.

When the resistance of this small land ceased after four years of unrelenting struggle, Judea had become a wilderness, almost without people. Says Dion Cassius . . . "fifty-eight myriads of men were slaughtered."

Even these disasters did not quell the fighting spirit of the Jews. Under the reign of the Emperor Constantine in the Fourth Century A.D., there was another of the usual desperate rebellions, which was put down by a powerful Roman army with indiscriminate slaughter. Still later when King Chosroes made war against Byzantium, the Jew, Benjamin of Egypt, created a Hebrew army of 30,000 men, which managed to reconquer Palestine and to hold it under Jewish rule for fourteen years. After the conclusion of a treaty of amity with Emperor Heraclius of Byzantium, that ruler, on the urgings of the Church, ambushed the Jewish troops without warning and succeeded in destroying them.

III

The hatred of the Church for the scattered remnants of the Jewish nation was without let. Throughout the civilized world, Jews found themselves scarcely in possession of the most elementary human rights, reduced to sunless ghettos, and treated with all the indignity of a pariah people.

It will be observed that the ancient legend concerning the Jews indicts them as an incorrigibly quarrelsome race, given to reckless violence and only happy in armed contention. Dion Cassius accuses them of every manner of atrocity against the Romans. Tacitus, too, refers dourly to the fighting qualities of this most irreconcilable of Roman foes, crediting them with almost superhuman truculence, obstinacy, and reckless desperation. Their indifference to death and ferocity in battle were a byword in the Roman world. Jewish captives were the favored gladiators in the arena, and Jewish mercenaries were highly regarded as professional soldiers until the end of the Fourth Century. They were numerous in all of the Roman wars. The Roman writer, Macrobius, declares that a large contingent of Jewish fighting men served in Caesar's legions. Both the Persians and Egyptians utilized Jewish mercenaries in considerable numbers. The Ptolemys relied heavily on Jewish fighting men. The founder of the dynasty, Ptolemy Soter, entrusted all of the major fortresses of Egypt to Jewish hands, settling Jewish military colonies in conquered areas he was anxious to hold. This was a system followed in turn by Ptolemy Philadelpus and his successors. Josephus tells us that Ptolemy II, called Philometer, and his wife, Cleopatra, "committed his whole kingdom to the care of Jewish troops" commanded by the Hebrew generals, Onias and Dositheus.[17]

The contrary legend that the Jews were a mild and nonmilitary people, or actually a cowardly and servile race, was fostered during the long dark period when the power of the medieval church consigned the race to the dark confines of the ghetto, and forbade them to take any active part in the life of the countries in whose midst they lived. Just as Jews might not own or cultivate land, or participate in the normal life around them, generally speaking they also were barred from the military profession everywhere.

Even under these withering conditions, however, there were indications that the Jewish fighting spirit was far from dead, and that the character of the race had by no means changed.

When Italy was invaded by Theodoric, King of the Ostrogoths, the suppressed Jews flocked to his banner. When his successor, Theodohat, was attacked by Emperor Justinian, whole units of the defending armies were formed of Roman Jews, who gave a magnificent account of themselves. When Justinian's troops landed on the toe of the Italian peninsula, the people of Naples, dejected and frightened, sought to surrender unconditionally. The Jews of Naples, however, refused to allow the city to submit. Led by Isaac Mender and Saar ben Gutta, they vigorously repelled the assault. When Justinian's great fleet attempted to occupy the port, every Jew up to the age of 70 served, holding positions along the entire coastline, and forcing the fleet to retire. Justinian's historian, Procopius, concedes that it was the stubborn Jewish resistance which gained badly needed time for Theodohat and thus postponed Justinian's conquest of Italy for another 20 years.

The conquest of Mauretania (Morocco) by the vandal king, Genserich, was largely due to the presence in his ranks of a strong body of Jewish troops. Shortly after, these *Bahuzim,* or Berber Jewish warriors, succeeded in consolidating the mountainous zone, or Jebel area of North Africa, into a strong confederacy. Under a noted fighting queen known as the Damia al Cahina,[18] they even succeeded in beating back the first waves of the great Arab invasion. The Cahina was subsequently defeated in pitched battle and slain. Many of the Jewish tribes were then converted to the creed of Islam, and participated in the later Moslem conquests. The Cahina's two sons are reputed to have been among the Moslem commanders during the military reduction of Spain.

Many Jews served in the Arab armies during the period marking Arab capture of both North Africa and Iberia. According to Arab writers of the time, conquered Spanish cities were often as not left in charge of Jewish garrisons. The Moorish invader, Tariq Ibn Zeiad, from whom Gibraltar takes its name,[19] was himself described as a Jewish Berber and former officer of the Cahina, and his Moslem army as a Jewish Berber force, augmented by a few Arabs.[20] In the Eleventh Century, the noted Samuel Hanagid was State Minister in charge of military affairs for the Moorish kingdom of Granada and Malaga.

In Christian Spain, where for a period the Jews were a reasonably free people, they participated actively in the military life of the nation. In Tulaitula in 838, they rose in revolt together with the Arabicised Christians against the tyranny of Moslem rule.[21] At the Battle of Zallâka in 1086, King Alfonso VI of Castile is reported to have had 40,000 Jews in his armies, an extremely large force for those times. The opposing armies of Moslem Seville also contained so many Jews that among other considerations the day of the battle was mutually arranged so as not to fall on the day of the Jewish Sabbath. Jews fought fiercely for Pedro I, a king who had always treated them well. They made up a large proportion of Pedro's armies "and great numbers fell fighting in defense of their king and country."[22] Pedro's chancellor and major strategist was the Jew, Don Samuel Ben Meir Allavi. The city of Toledo in a historic siege, is described as having been defended by Jewish troops fighting on the side of Pedro. Under Alfonso VII of Castile, Judah ibn Ezra was raised to the position of commander of the important frontier fortress of Calatrava and later became Court Chamberlain. Alfonso VIII, who also treated the Jews well, was repaid amply by them in loyalty and service given in his wars against the Moors.

During the earlier Medieval period there were many exceptions to the general rule which sought to forbid Jewish military service, and many instances of outstanding Jewish heroism and quality on the battlefield. It was only in later Medieval times, when the strictures of church and state against them became so rigorous that Jews no longer were allowed to bear arms for any cause, that history presents us with a blank page as far as Hebrew military genius is concerned. Even here, however, we occasionally find the names of converted Jews in high military position.

Jews were considered to be especially proficient as crossbowmen, and in some countries were admitted in considerable numbers to the noncommissioned ranks. Abramo Colorni was famous as an innovator in military defense works. We read that Hanuchim, a French Jew, was given special license to live in England because he had fought so gallantly in Normandy under King John. King Philip is reported to have had 30,000 Jews in his army in the war against Count Guy of Flanders. The Bohemian chronicler, Hajek, reports that in 995 A.D., it was armed Jews who decided the great victory of the Bohemians over the pagans. Even during the mass pogroms conducted by the armies of the Crusaders on their way to the Holy Land, the attacked Jews, though overwhelmingly outnumbered and largely without arms, defended themselves well. At Halle in Germany, in the year 1096, they succeeded in defeating the Crusading armies and in a pitched battle with the Crusaders at Carenton, France, forced the attacking knights to withdraw. In other cities where they were assailed by these wandering armies, they sold their lives dearly.

There were many Marranos (secret Jews) who figured prominently in the ranks of the *conquistadores* in the conquest of the New World. Among these was Luis de Torres, who sailed on all four trips with Columbus and was killed in a battle with the Indians in Haiti. Nunas Cabeza de Vaca, who adventured from the Texas coast southward, was the conqueror of Peru. Luis de Carojal y de la Cueva fought in Mexico, and was famous for his feat in capturing Hawkins' buccaneers. Gil Gonzales, a sanguinary ruffian of the stripe of Cortez, discovered Nicaragua in 1519, and at the head of a small body of infantry and horse, wiped out a considerable share of the Indian population of Central America. Alonzo Hernando fought for five years at the side of Cortez. Also well-known in the conquest and sack of Mexico was Alfonso de Avila, cousin of Gonzales, who was killed in a battle with the Indians in 1537. In the following generation, another Gil Gonzales and Alfonso de Avila, of the same family, were executed as rebels in the early abortive attempts to secure the freedom of Mexico.

Among the long list of adventurers of the period was Simon Fernando[23] who sailed the seas with Sir Francis Drake, and was captain of the Admiral's ship, and who before this was reputed to have been a pirate. Many Marranos also participated in the Portuguese expeditions to India and the Far East as well as to the New World, and their names are still perpetuated among many distinguished military families in Latin America.[24] Antonio Vaaz Henriquez prepared and led the Dutch expedition which captured Pernambuco in 1630. Another Jew, David Peixotto, was in command of the eighteen vessels sent for the relief of that city. Francisco de Silva, a Marrano fighting in the Spanish service, was instrumental in defeating the French at the siege of Treves in 1673. Simon de Caceres was military adviser to Cromwell, and the Portuguese emigre, Edward Brandon, was a Yorkist hero during the Wars of the Roses.

In far away Surinam, Jewish settlers, rejoicing in their new-found freedom, became famous for their military prowess. Under Samuel Nassy, they fought brilliantly against the French assault in 1688-9, and again in 1712, under the noted Captain Isaac Pinto.

IV

The Napoleonic conquests, which smashed with cyclonic force against the stockades of feudal Europe, brought into these twilight areas the bright light of French equalitarianism. Once more Jews were allowed to bear arms and to take part in the general military life. Learned debates now took place throughout the continent as to whether this queer race of Jews who had just been released from the crushing enervation of the ghetto, were physically or morally capable of fulfilling the role of citizenship, and particularly that of military service. It was certainly true that the stamina and physical strength for which the Jew once had been famous, had deteriorated under the blight of the ghetto. Abject poverty, enforced degradation, and the type of occupation to which the race had been relegated, had left their cruel marks on the Jewish personality; but these effects vanished with miraculous rapidity under the warm sun of freedom.

Jews were first admitted to the Prussian army in 1813. The historian Buchholz remarks upon the outstanding quality of Jewish valor in the wars with Napoleon. The much decorated Prussian war heroine, Esther Manuel, fought against the French Emperor disguised as a man, in a regiment of lancers. How well Jewish soldiers acquitted themselves may be judged from the fact that the Chancellor, Prince Hardenberg, found himself writing much to his surprise (January 4, 1815), that "young men of Hebrew faith prove to be excellent fighting comrades of the Christian soldiers, and we have seen in their midst examples of true heroism and of most praiseworthy disdain of the dangers of war."

In the Franco-Prussian war of 1870, more than 100 Jews were commissioned officers, and 373 decorated for valor. Though they constituted a fraction of less than 1% of the total population, 5,000 Jews fought on the Prussian side, 10% of whom were killed or wounded.

In the War of 1866 the Jewish general, Von Henikstein, was chief of the Austrian General Staff. The situation in Austro-Hungary was such as to cause the Emperor Franz-Josef to write to his minister, Dunayevsky, that to him the anti-Semitic movement in Austria was actually painful when he considered the heroic service rendered to the throne by Jewish soldiers in the wars of 1878 and 1882. "Even now", he exclaims, "in my desk are piled up numerous orders rewarding Jewish soldiers for their distinguished deeds." It is interesting to note that by 1893, though Jews composed some 3.9% of the Emperor's army, roughly corresponding to their percentage in the general population, those in the officers corps constituted 8%, including the celebrated naval engineer, Rear Admiral Siegfried Popper, and the Austrian Naval Chief, Rear Admiral Ludwig Tobias Freiherr von Oesterreicher. By 1909 there were on active duty in the Austrian army one Jewish lieutenant general, three major generals and a large number of lesser officers. Among the Jewish officers of the period was Lieutenant Field Marshal Joseph Singer, who was responsible for the complete reorganization of the Austrian officers corps.

In Italy, Jews enjoyed complete equality since 1848. Until the time of Mussolini's conversion to Hitlerism, the familiar type of social anti-Semitism could scarcely have been said to have existed. From Jewish ranks was drawn the distinguished General Giuseppe Ottolenghi, known as "the father of the Italian army," who, after a brilliant military career which included a professorship of military history and tactics in the Royal Military School at Modena, became Minister of War in 1902-03. In 1911, there were some 500 Jewish officers in the Italian army, an almost fantastic ratio when one considers the minuscule Jewish population of that country.

In all of the states but Imperial Russia, the story was much the same during this period. Jews played a role in all wars and in all revolutionary movements. They fought behind the barricades with Kosciusko. A Jewish enlisted man named Wolff died in the Alamo. Captain Ullman of the 5th Cavalry fell with Custer in the Indian massacre of Little Big Horn. Jews stood with Houston in all the battles for Texas' independence and earned immortal glory at San Jacinto, Goliad and Neches. Among these was the noted Captain Levi Charles

Harby, who later commanded the Neptune during the Civil War; David Kauffman, who had a Texas county named after him; and Moses Albert Levy, who was Surgeon General for Houston's army throughout the Texas-Mexican War. A Jewish regiment served under Kossuth in the Hungarian Revolt of 1848, and two Jews, Michael Heilprin and Fishel Friend, were among the Hungarian leaders' principal lieutenants. In the Greco-Turkish War, 1,500 Jewish soldiers served in the Greek ranks and carved out an undying name for themselves in the Battle of Previsa. Among other Jewish soldiers, General Jacob Baiz fought in the Central American battles for freedom, and Captain Luis H. Brie in South America. The records of all the Spanish-American wars for independence are heavily sprinkled with the names of fighters descended from old Marrano families, though these were no longer identified as Jews.

Ernesto Nathan, later to become Mayor of Rome and to enlist for active service in World War I at the age of 70, was an associate of Mazzini. The Italian revolt against Austria of 1848-9, centering in Venice, was led by the converted Jew, Daniel Manin. In his service were many Jewish enlisted men and a dozen Jewish officers. High in the upper echelons of Garibaldi's command were Giuseppe Ottolenghi, Giuseppe Finzi, Enrico Guastalla and a number of lesser officers. Jewish military adventurers include the unique Elias Pasha (Elias Cohen) who was at one and the same time general in the Turkish army and vice admiral in the Turkish navy; General Mazar Pasha (Stephen Lakeman) who fought professionally in the Turkish army and also served in South Africa, India and Britain; and Simon Bolivar's fighting comrade, General Isidore Borovsky, later to fall in battle while soldiering for the Persians.

In Bulgaria, saturated with virulent anti-Semitism, Prince Alexander Battenberg found it necessary to address his Jewish soldiers after the victory at Pirota as follows: "Valiant

Jews, your heroic conduct today proved that you are direct descendents of the Maccabees."

Russia of the Czars remained untouched by the great broom of the French Reformation. Its Jewish population continued to be herded into the restricted area known as the Pale, and made the subject of repressive laws up to the time that Kerensky took power. Jews, who had reason to detest the monarchy, nevertheless fought ably in its behalf wherever they were called upon.

Advancement in the army, or recognition even of outstanding valor, were impossible to Jewish soldiers.

Jews in military service were subject to the harshest restrictions. They could not serve in fortresses, artillery, navy, border patrols or local reserves. They were not allowed to take examination for officer's rank, and though not specifically forbidden by law, in practice were denied the possibility of becoming non-commissioned officers. The usual encouragement given to soldiers, such as medals and promotions, were not allowed to them except for rare exceptions. Nevertheless, there were many instances of individual Jews surmounting these discouraging barriers, such as Chaim Zaitchikoff, who showed such lionlike courage at the defense of Sevastopol that the Supreme Commander singled him out for a ceremonial shaking of hands after the battle.[25] The famous partisan leader, D. V. Davydov, in his *A Diary of the Partisan Wars of 1812*, remarks on the brilliant exploits of a certain Uhlan, adding: "It is very strange that this Uhlan, having received the Cross of St. George for his heroism, could not wear it. He was a Jew from Berdichev." During the Russo-Turkish war, General Kuropatkin wrote that "the Jews showed that they knew . . . how to fight and die as heroically as the rest of the Russian soldiers."

The heroism of Joseph Trumpeldor became a byword in the Russo-Japanese War. Though Trumpeldor had lost an arm during the siege of Port Arthur, he wrote to his commanding officer, "I have but one arm left; but this one arm is my right arm. And, therefore, desiring to share as before the fighting life of my comrades, I beg Your Honor to petition for an issuance to me of a sabre and a revolver." Despite the fact that he was a Jew, Trumpeldor was promoted to junior non-commissioned officer's rank, decorated with all four classes of the Russian Military Order of St. George, and finally given command of a company which distinguished itself in the defense at Port Arthur—the first Jew ever to receive a commission from the Czar.

The Russians had some picture of the fighting quality of Jews when engaged in a cause in which they believed, during the Russo-Polish War of 1794, where many Jewish young men flocked to the banners of Kosciusko. The Austrian official, Anton Baum, reported to the Minister of War that these pale and narrow-chested denizens of the ghetto had nevertheless formed a corps of border patrols, incongruously dressed in the ghetto garb of the time, yet carrying sabres and pistols, and declared himself amazed at their heroism. In his book, *Berek Joselowicz,* the Polish author, Ernest Luninsky, recounts that during the siege of Warsaw, Jews showed miraculous courage in the face of the heaviest losses under fire. He comments of Berek Joselowicz's all-Jewish regiment of light cavalry, that though its members were pale, poorly-nourished men who still wore the caftans and somber raiment of the ghetto, the regiment "was impressive in its austere firmness and discipline." Almost the entire regiment perished in a single day during the terrible assault on Warsaw of November 4, 1794.[26]

For Holland, Belgium, and Britain, Jews served at all fronts. In the latter country, Sir Jacob Adolphus, after being baptized became a major general in 1770. In the early Nineteenth Century, both Sir George Aguilar and Sir David Ximinez reached the rank of lieutenant general. Jewish sailors fought under Nelson; and Wellington specifically cites for commendable performance, fifteen Jewish officers who served under his command at Waterloo. Major General Albert Goldsmid fought in all the British wars of the period, including those against

Napoleon.[27] In far-away India, where only a few thousand native Jews, known as Bene Israel, exist, "Bene Israel soldiers . . . constituted almost half of the number of native officers of each Regiment of the Bombay Presidency for nearly a century and a half of British rule".[28] During the Napoleonic wars, Vice Admiral Alexander Wilmot Schomberg[29] was considered one of Britain's ablest commanders. Colonel Sir David Harris took part in many colonial wars. Hugh Culling Eardley Childers was Secretary of War under Gladstone, and Ralph Bernal Osborne was Secretary of the Admiralty during the Crimean War.

A strong contingent of Jews served in the British army during the Boer war, including Colonel Albert Edward Goldsmid, Chief of Staff with the 6th Division. Colonel Sir David Harris commanded the Kimberly Guard. Major W. D. Karri-Davis was the first to enter Johannesburg and Mafeking. There was a whole Jewish regiment known as the Pietersburg Light Horse. Many Jews also served on the Boer side. Among these were the two French engineers, Léon Gruenberg and Samuel Léon, in charge of artillery and sappers, whose exploits became legendary in Afrikaans' patriotic tradition.[30]

It is one of the ironies of history that just as it was the Jew, Tiberius Julius Alexander, who was instrumental in bringing the Roman siege of Jerusalem to a victorious conclusion, it was the Jewish Minister of State, Farchi, who was the presiding genius at the defense of Acre, whose successful resistance frustrated Napoleon's plan to march east to India.[31]

In the ranks of Napoleon's armies were many Jewish fighting men, as well as a sprinkling of officers. Most famous of these was Andrea Menasse, whose name was later changed to Massena. He became Napoleon's most important marshal, and was referred to by the French conqueror as *"L'enfant chéri de la victoire."* Like almost all the Jews of his time, Massena came into prominence the hard way, with very little conventional military instruction. He had volunteered to the Italian army and later to the French army. His military career was one long succession of personal triumphs, including the conquest of the Maritime Alps in 1794, and the decisive victory over the Austrians and Sardinians at Loano. It was Massena who was credited with saving the day at Lodi, and with the victories at Castiglioni, Rivoli, Mantua, Friedland and Wagram. In his memoirs, Napoleon lauded him as "one of the greatest men of his age."

After the fall of Napoleon, a bitter reaction set in, swallowing up many of the Emperor's reforms. The European attitude toward the Jew once more hardened. France was no exception to the disease of anti-Semitism which once again swept over Europe to capture the souls of men, as was soon seen in the notorious Dreyfus affair.

At that time there were serving in the French army some 337 Jewish officers. L'affaire Dreyfus is too well known to be recounted here, but this conspiracy against a distinguished comrade by the ruling officer caste of France, offers the clearest evidence of the difficulties both Jewish soldiers and officers were under in attempting to requite their duty as citizens in the lands of their birth.

V

Even in America, deepseated social prejudice actuated against the Jewish population. The Governor of New Amsterdam, Peter Stuyvesant, refused arbitrarily to allow Jews to serve in the military guard duty of the colony, imposing instead a discriminatory tax. The Jewish population though minor, spiritedly resisted this affront. In 1655, Asser Levy demanded that Jews be allowed to stand guard. When Stuyvesant remained adamant, Levy bought uniforms for himself and other Jews, and proceeded to stand guard just the same.

From the scattering pre-Revolutionary records we learn that Captain Isaac Isaacs served with the first expedition against the French stronghold of Crown Point; Aaron Hart was on the staff of General Amherst at the capitulation of Montreal; and

Captain Isaac Myers and two Jewish enlisted men marched with Washington in the Indian expedition across the Alleghenies.

In 1776, there were less than 2,500 Jews in the Thirteen Colonies, including women and children. By ordinary standards, this meant perhaps 800 men capable of bearing arms. At least 600 of these fought through the entire War of Independence, serving on all fields from Valley Forge to Yorktown. Among a distinguished group of officers was the able Colonel David Salisbury Franks, who was later to fall in a fight against the Indians; Benjamin Sheftall of Georgia, whom the British referred to by official proclamation as "a very great rebel"; Francis Salvador of South Carolina, who became known as "the southern Paul Revere" and was later killed in battle; David Emanuel of Georgia, later to become Governor of the State; and young Isaac Franks, who enlisted at the age of 17 and later became a lieutenant colonel in the Pennsylvania militia. Isaac Nunez Cardozo, great grandfather of the late Supreme Court Justice Cardozo, was a member of a company of fighting men said to be almost entirely Jewish. Lieutenant Colonel Solomon Bush, Major George Bush and Major Lewis Bush fought with distinction; Captain Jacob Cohen of Virginia commanded a cavalry company. Isaac Myers of New York organized a company of men, of which he was chosen Captain. In South Carolina, there was a "Jews' Company" commanded by Captain Richard Lushington, the majority of whose members were Jews. Major Benjamin Nones volunteered from his native Bordeaux, France, and became aide-de-camp to Washington. Nones' Legion of 400 men attached to Baron de Kalb's command, was composed largely of Jews. When de Kalb fell mortally wounded at the Battle of Camden, he was carried off the field by three Jewish officers, Major Nones, Captain Jacob de la Motta, and Captain Jacob de Leon.

Among other figures was Mordecai Sheftall, Commissary General of the troops of Georgia, and the immortal Haym

Saloman, who is best known for having been instrumental in financing the Revolution and in its economic organization. What is less known is that he "displayed great personal courage also in carrying on daring enterprises to destroy the fleet and storehouses of the enemy,"[32] and that he once was tortured and condemned to be hanged for his Revolutionary activities, but managed to escape to Philadelphia.

During the War of 1812, it is probable that the number of Jews in the United States was around 3,000. In this war, too, they served with distinction.

One of the great fighting men of United States naval tradition was Commodore John Ordroneaux, who in one sea battle defeated and sank five British frigates. The British referred to him as "the terror of the seas". He is reported once to have halted a retreat on the part of his men in the face of a British boarding party, by lighting a match near the powder magazine and threatening "to blow the ship to hell" if his men retreated further. Another brave naval officer was Commodore Uriah P. Levy, who is also said to have been responsible for the abolition of corporal punishment in the Navy. Among Jewish officers in this war were Brigadier General Joseph Bloomfield, Major Abraham A. Massias, who was instrumental in the defense of Charleston, Colonel Nathan Myers, and a considerable group of lesser rank. Captain Mordecai Myers distinguished himself in many engagements, and wrote the stirring words: "Sum must spill there blud and others there ink. I expect to be amongst the former. . . ." Among the enlisted men was the grandfather of the author, Bret Harte; and Levi Myers Harby, who volunteered as a boy of 14 and later was to distinguish himself for heroism in the Mexican War. At the defense of Fort McHenry, whose triumphant resistance to heavy British battering inspired Francis Scott Key's *The Star Spangled Banner,* the records show a considerable proportion of Jewish names.

In the war with Mexico, General David de Leon who became known as "the fighting doctor", led cavalry charges as well as attended to the medical needs of the army. His gallantry in action caused him twice to receive the thanks of the United States Congress. There was the usual complement of lesser officers and enlisted men. One company composed almost entirely of Jewish immigrants from Germany was organized in Baltimore.

At the time of the Civil War, Jews constituted less than one-half of 1% of the 31,000,000 people then living in the United States. Their number in both armies was disproportionately large. John Seddon, Confederate Secretary of War at the time, is reported to have refused a request for High Holy Day furloughs for Jewish soldiers, on the ground that there were 10,000 to 12,000 Jews in the Confederate army and that "it would disintegrate certain commands if the request were granted." Observers at the time placed the number of Jews in the Union armies at fifteen to twenty thousand.[33] These figures include whole families of brothers, fathers and sons, as for example, the five Moses brothers of South Carolina, the five Wenk brothers of New York, and the Jonas family, which sent four brothers to the Confederate army, with the father and one brother enlisting on the Union side.

Among the Jewish soldiers serving in Blue and Gray uniforms were nine generals, twenty-one colonels, and 647 officers of lesser rank. The most prominent of these, perhaps, on the Union side, was General Frederick Knefler, a brilliant tactician who served on Sherman's staff in the famous March to the Sea in 1864.

The Union general, Oliver O. Howard wrote of the German officers and men under his command, that "so many were of Jewish lineage that I am unable to designate them. I had a Jewish aide-de-camp, one of the bravest and best, in the first battle of Bull Run . . . I had another aide who was killed at the Battle of Chancellorsville, a true and brave officer. Two of my brigade commanders answered to the above description." During the first two days of the Battle of Gettysburg, the brunt of the Southern attack was borne by the regiment under the command of Colonel Edward S. Solomon, which repeatedly repulsed the desperate charges of the Confederate cavalry leader, Pickett. The 27th Pennsylvania Infantry, which covered the retreat of the Union army in the first battle of Bull Run, was commanded by Brigadier General Max Einstein of Philadelphia, and included 30 Jewish officers and a considerable number of Jewish enlisted men. William Durst, a sailor on the Monitor, so conducted himself in the historic battle with the Merrimac,[34] that the ship's commander, John Lorimer Worden, on receiving the thanks of the Congress for his valiant action, observed that Durst, too, was "eminently worthy to be recognized by some action on the part of Congress." Among others who served with distinction was General Leopold Blumenberg, who commanded the 5th Maryland Regiment and who left one of his legs on the field at Antietam, and the legendary captain, J. B. Greenhut, of the famous 82nd Illinois. Among other citations and awards for heroism, seven Jewish soldiers won the coveted Congressional Medal of Honor, the highest award for bravery. Leopold C. Newman was promoted from colonel to brigadier general during a personal visit by Lincoln, as the former lay mortally wounded in a military hospital.

On the Confederate side, Jews served with equal gallantry, and considering their small numbers, left a most remarkable record. There were at least twenty-three Jewish staff officers in the Confederate forces. Judah P. Benjamin of Louisiana, became Secretary of War and later Secretary of State for the Confederacy. There were two assistant adjutant generals, J. Randolph Mordecai and Lionel Levy. The Surgeon General of the Confederate armies was David Camden de Leon of South Carolina, the gallant officer who had so distinguished himself under fire at the Battle of Chapultepec in the Mexican War. Captain L. G. Harby, also a veteran of the Mexican War, became a commodore in the Confederate fleet and commanded the defense of Galveston.

The great Confederate military hero of his time was the Jewish soldier, Max Fronthall. His name became a synonym for heroic conduct under fire, so that any man cited for conspicuous bravery was described as "a regular Fronthall". During an account of the Spottsylvania Courthouse battle in which Fronthall took a conspicuous part, the writer, A. T. Watts, exclaimed: "I now understand how it was that a handful of Jews could drive before them the hundred kings; they were all Fronthalls".

In the Spanish-American war, Jewish fighters again were conspicuous, bearing their full share of the national burden. Five thousand[35] Jews saw service in this struggle, a ratio 20% higher than that applying to the American population as a whole.

Fifteen Jews went down with the crew of the battleship Maine. The executive officer of the Maine, and later vice admiral of the U. S. Navy, was Adolph Marix. The first to fall in the Battle of Manila was a Jewish sergeant, Maurice Juster of California; the first to capture an enemy flag was Sergeant Morris J. Cohen of the 20th Kansas Volunteers, later killed in action; the first American sailor killed in an engagement with the Spaniards was the Jewish seaman, Ernest Suntznich, during the bombardment of Cienfuegos; and the first to reach the top of San Juan Hill in the famous charge of Colonel Roosevelt's Rough Riders was Irving Peixotto of the 6th U. S. Infantry.

VI

In view of the brutal anti-Semitism which was to engulf them immediately after World War I was concluded, the heroism of the Jews in this terrible struggle, and their passionate faith in its purposes, comprise one of the bitterest gibes the Fates have ever written into mortal history.

The estimated total of men under arms on both sides was 65,000,000. The number of Jews engaged was about 1,506,000 or 2.3% of the total under arms. The proportion of Jews to the total population of the countries concerned, approximated 1%. The Jewish dead totaled 171,375 or slightly over 2.6%. Over 100,000 were decorated for valor.

Even in Germany, where pre-Nazi anti-Semitism was already real and crushing, the ratio of Jews in the armed services was more than 12% greater than the ratio of Jews to the total population.[36] Of the 100,000 Jews in the German army, at least 78% served at the front, and some 35,000 were decorated, including 900 who received the Iron Cross, 1st Class, and four who were awarded the rarely bestowed Prussian Gold Medal for exceptional heroism under fire. About 23,000 were promoted to non-commissioned ranks, and over 2,000, not including the Medical Corps, were commissioned, a remarkable record since previously no Jew could be commissioned in the Reichswehr.[36a]

Of the handful of German fliers, 200 were Jews. Among these were the celebrated ace, Lieutenant Frankel, who was killed in action, and the gallant Lieutenant Weill, also killed in action. The oldest German flier was 48-year-old Jakob Wolf. The leading instructor in the German naval air service was Ellis Dunitz. The famous Baron Manfred von Richthofen and his brother, Lothar, would have been liquidated by Hitler as non-Aryans. So would General von Mossler, commander of Wilhelm's Hussar Guards; General Max Hoffman, who played a leading part at the great German victory at Tannenberg; and General Otto Liman von Sanders, who won the title of "Lion of Gallipoli" for his successful defense of that strategic spot, and who later was defeated by Allenby in 1918 while commanding the Turkish army in Palestine.

The first member of the Reichstag to fall in battle was the Jewish Social-Democrat, Ludwig Frank. The youngest German volunteers were all Jewish lads, Joseph Steinhardt, 15, Richard Bing, 14, and Joseph Zippes, 13, the latter losing both legs on the field.

Outside of the armed services, the German Jews gave themselves fully to the war effort. The work of Walter Rathenau in mobilizing the Germany economy for war was instrumental in keeping German resistance alive for so long. So was that of Fritz Haber, Director of the Kaiser-Wilhelm Institute for Physics and Chemistry, and in charge of German Chemical Warfare. His discovery of the means for extracting nitrogen from the air kept Germany from military collapse long before her final defeat at the hands of the Allies. Karl Arnstein was chief builder and designer for the Zeppelin works, and the principle of the rigid airship itself was discovered by David Schwartz, a Hungarian Jew, whose widow subsequently sold his plans to Count Zeppelin who named the ship after himself.

In Austria-Hungary there were 320,000 Jews in the armed forces, or more than 14% of the entire Jewish population. More than 12% of the Jewish servicemen died under fire. In the Austrian divisions alone, 6,000 were decorated for conspicuous heroism. Although anti-Semitism was ineradicable in the Dual Monarchy, the policy of Emperor Franz-Josef was completely opposed to discrimination. In his service were two Jewish field marshals, six generals and 691 other officers. These included Lieutenant General Felix Schreiber, who led the Emperor's armies in the advance on Serbia, Colonel Joseph Knerber, the first Austrian officer to be killed at the front, and the noted General Emil von Sommer, who later had his medals torn from his uniform by Hitler's minions because he was a Jew.

In almost all of the countries engaged in the war, including Greece, Rumania, Serbia and Turkey, "the Jews furnished a greater proportion of fighters and a greater proportion of dead and wounded."[37] In Belgium, 6% of the Jewish population served as against 3.6% of non-Jews. Twelve percent of the Jewish soldiers were killed in battle as compared with 5% of the non-Jews. More than 25% of the Belgian Jewish soldiers received one or more decorations. Among the Jewish officers in the Belgian army were General Louis Bernheim,[38] valiant defender of Antwerp, and Leopold Wiener who entered the war a major, and came out a general, with eight decorations for bravery.

In the British Empire 2.3% of the total population was mobilized. Among the Jews of the Empire, 12% served in the armed forces. Twenty per cent of the Jews in the armed forces were volunteers. Of the non-Jewish subjects of the King, only 2.3% volunteered. Before conscription came into effect, a total of some 10,000 Jews were in the British Army, of whom 1,130 were officers.[39]

Ten per cent of the fighting British Jews fell.[40] The figure for non-Jews was 4.8%. Of the comparatively few Englishmen who received the Victoria Cross, five were Jews. All told, Jewish fighters received 1,596 awards and citations. Many gained distinction as aviators.

Voluntary enlistments in the Dominions were high. Canada, with 80,000 Jews sent 6,000 overseas. In Australia, out of a Jewish population of 17,000, there were 2,000 enlistments. Of these, 260 died in action. The proportion of Jewish volunteers was 11%, against 9% for the country as a whole. The commander of the Australians was the brilliant Sir John Monash, who was in charge of the great offensive which finally crushed the spirit of the German army in the summer of 1918. Next in command in the Australian forces was Major General Sir Charles Rosenthal. Another Jewish soldier, who was also to distinguish himself in the fighting in World War II, was General Bernhard Cyril Freyberg, who commanded the New Zealand troops. A tough, fighting officer, Freyberg had become a brigadier general at the age of 27, was wounded in action no less than nine times, and among other decorations, wore the Victoria Cross.

Jewish officers in the British forces included Brigadier General H. J. Seligman who commanded in the Royal Artillery from the beginning to the end of the war. Lieutenant Colonel Solomon J. Solomon was instrumental in converting the British army to the use of camouflage. Chaim Weizmann, later to become President of Israel, played a key role by finding a way to produce acetone, indispensable to the production of cordite. Lieutenant Colonel Sir Albert Stern was the first to recognize the immense potentials of tank warfare; and the engineer, Sir Alfred Yarrow, was responsible for the design and building of the high speed torpedo boats and destroyers which so greatly affected the nature of naval warfare.

Also fighting under British command in the Middle East were a number of wholly Jewish units, who marched under the blue and white banner of Israel.[41] Joseph Trumpeldor and the Zionist leader, Vladimir Jabotinsky, had offered to form a Jewish legion to fight on the Allied side against the Turks. At Cairo, the British commanding general, Maxwell, refused the offer, but suggested instead a Zion Mule Corps for service at Gallipoli. Jabotinsky was indignant but Trumpeldor philosophically decided to make the best of the situation and accept. The Mule Corps was placed under the command of the noted British soldier, Dublin-born Colonel J. H. Patterson. For the first time in modern life, 720 volunteers, though recruited for non-fighting service, marched proudly under the ancient flag of David. Shortly, the Zion Mule Corps found itself in the thick of the fighting. Trumpeldor, whose characteristic cry was "Kadimah!" (Forward!) and who was again wounded on the field, was described by Colonel Patterson in his reports as "the most courageous man and the best soldier whom I ever met."

The failure of the Gallipoli expedition resulted in the disbanding of the Mule Corps; but with the issuance of the Balfour Declaration in November 1917, Jabotinsky finally succeeded in obtaining permission for the organization of a Jewish battalion recruited for Palestinian service, the 38th Royal Fusiliers. Colonel Patterson again was placed in command. Two other units, the 39th and 40th Battalions, commanded respectively by Lieutenant Colonel Eliazer Margolin and Frederick Dudley Samuel, soon followed. It was the 38th Battalion, known as "The Judeans", which held the difficult position on the extreme right flank of the British army, at the Wadi Mellahah, and which participated together with the 39th and 40th Battalions in the final drive which resulted in Turkish collapse. It was they who pursued the Turks across Jordan, finally capturing Es Salt.

In France, over 55,000 Jews, comprising 22% of the Jewish population, fought. Seventeen percent of this number were killed. Of the non-Jewish French population, 14.9% fought, with a casualty record of 16%. Over 2,000 Jewish soldiers received war decorations. One hundred and one Jews received the Croix de Guerre; 140, the Medaille Militaire; and 311, membership in the Legion d'Honneur.

A like pattern existed for the Empire as a whole. The 11,000 Tunisian and Moroccan Jewish troops who joined the Tricolor were all volunteers. Not being French citizens, they were not subject to the draft, and not being Moslems, they could not be recruited in the native contingents. Many of the best fighters in the Algerian Zouave regiments were native Algerian Jews. The Jewish population of Algeria was about 65,000. There is no documentary evidence to establish the exact number called to the colors, but, preliminary lists showed 29 decorated with the Legion d'Honneur, 94 who received the Medaille Militaire, and about 800 citations for heroism under fire. Whole regiments of Algerian Zouaves who conducted themselves so remarkably in the war, were found under analysis to be made up one-third to one-half of Jews.

The foreign Jews residing in France in 1913 numbered 30,000, including women and children. Of this number, 12,000 volunteered for service in the French Foreign Legion. In the attack on Carency of May 9, 1915, the regiments of the Foreign Legion which bore the brunt of the fighting, consisted mainly of these Jewish soldiers, less than 20% of whom survived the battle.

At the start of World War I, there were two Jewish generals in active service. Four in the Reserve Corps resumed service. Eight other officers became generals, making fourteen in all.

General Georges Valabrégue, head of the Artillery School and the Paris Military Academy, commanded the 3rd Army Corps. General Heymann who had reached the over-age limit, had the 15th Region of Marseilles. General Lucien Lévy commanded the engineers of the 4th Army Corps, General Geismar, the artillery of the 4th Army Corps, Brigadier General Camille Lévi, a division of shock troops, Brigadier General Dennery, a territorial division of infantry, Brigadier General Grumbach, the brigade of infantry which performed so heroically at the Marne, and Brigadier General Mayer, the expeditionary forces to French West Africa. Lieutenant General Naquet-Laroque was a member of the Superior Council of Inventions at the Ministry of War. General Francfort commanded the fortress of Epinal and was killed in action. General Bloch was one of the chiefs of the garrison of Maubeuge which defended itself so well against siege. General Mordecai Valabrégue was a member of the Supreme War Council. General July Heym commanded the 15th Army Corps. The Artillery General, Paul Edouard Alexandre, is generally credited by military men as being the real hero of Verdun, not the vacillating Pétain. Any list of French military leaders of World War I must also include the superb tactician, Brigadier General Chanville Levy, and the formidable General Andre Weiller, who was wounded eight times and received six decorations. Alexandre Millerand, the great French Minister of War, also would have been liquidated under Hitler's Aryan laws.

A long list of lesser officers commanded and fought in all the combatant branches. That these were for the most part field officers rather than desk sitters, may be judged from the fact that some 250 French Jewish officers were killed, exclusive of alien Jews, Algerians, Moroccans and others who served under the Tricolor banner.

Even though Russia had been the land of pogroms and violent Jewish persecution, the Jews of that state rallied to her defense during the war. Though with rare exceptions Jews previously could not be commissioned as officers in the

Russian army, "there were several hundred Jewish officers in 1916-17, indicating that they had achieved this rank by sheer merit on the battlefield," [42] By July of 1917, 60,000 Jews in the Russian army had been decorated and 2,600 recommended for commissions. The figures necessarily must be pieced together due to the destruction of records following the Red Revolution, but the indications are that some 650,000 Jews, or 9.4% of the Jewish total in the Czar's Empire, fought in the armed forces, as compared to a general total for all Crown subjects of 7%. Jewish casualty figures "have been estimated as at least 100,000 dead, or over 15% of the Jewish enrollment."[43]

In Rumania where the Jewish population constituted 3.19% of the total population, they nevertheless made up 4.6% of the mobilized forces. The anti-Semitic bias against Jews was largely identical in Rumania with that of Russia. Nevertheless, at least 900 received war decorations and 218 became commissioned officers, achieving this rank through valor in the field.

In Italy, whose entire Jewish population was only 43,929, or slightly more than one percent of the total population, there were no less than 700 Jewish officers, including two full admirals, one rear admiral and eleven generals, two of whom, Aristide Benedetti and Allegro Pavia, were killed in action.

Jewish officers were also prominent as air fighters and submarine commanders. The Gold medal for valor, given to only 57 men, was won by four Jews. Over 500 Jewish soldiers received decorations. Baron Sydney Sonnino, Italy's wartime Foreign Minister, was killed in the Air Corps. Lieutenant Colonel Benedette di Benedetti died in action at the age of 77. Among the outstanding heroes of World War I were Admiral Umberto Pugliese, and General Achilles Levi-Biancini.

Some 250,000 Jewish soldiers served in the U. S. armed forces during World War I, constituting 5.7% of the total American mobilization. The Jewish proportion of the total American population at the time was 3.27%.[43a]

More than 20% of the Jewish contingent, as shown by the files of the American Jewish Committee, were volunteers.

In the A.E.F. the infantry, artillery, cavalry, engineers and signal-aviation branches together constituted 60% of the total personnel. The distribution of Jewish soldiers in these branches, however, was 75%. The infantry was 26.6% of the entire army but constituted 48% of all Jewish soldiers. The signal-aviation corps represented 6.5% of the U. S. army total, but 15% of the Jewish fraction. The proportion of Jews in the medical corps was 8%, as compared to the general average of 9%. In the marine corps, 3.4% proved to be Jewish.

There were nearly 10,000 Jewish commissioned officers. These included Rear Admiral Claude C. Bloch, in charge of Naval Transport, and later commander-in-chief of the U. S. Fleet, Rear Admiral Joseph Strauss, Rear Admiral Edward David Taussig, Major General Milton G. Foreman, who became the first commander of the American Legion, Brigadier General Abel Davis, and Brigadier General Charles H. Lauchheimer of the marine corps. The navy had at least 900 Jewish commissioned officers, and the marine corps another hundred.

The total of Jewish dead was more than 5.7% of the total American death roll. Of the 63 American volunteer dispatch runners who died in the performance of this exceptional duty, 37 were Jews. The youngest American in the war was thirteen-year-old Albert Cohen of Memphis, Tennessee, who fell in the Meuse-Argonne offensive. Altogether, 1,100 Jewish soldiers were cited for conspicuous valor. Of 78 Congressional Medals of Honor awarded during World War I, Jews received at least three.[44] Four received the rarely conferred French Medaille Militaire; 174, the Croix de Guerre; and 150, the Distinguished Service Cross.

The youngest American soldier to receive the Distinguished Service Cross was Louis Abend, who enlisted at fifteen and was already a corporal when he landed in France at seventeen. Another Jewish soldier, Sergeant Sam Dreben, was referred to by General Pershing as the "finest soldier and one of the bravest men I have ever known." Dreben received the Distinguished Service Cross for single-handedly rushing an enemy post and killing 23 of the 40 Germans located there. Another to receive the Distinguished Service Cross from the personal hands of Pershing was Abraham Krotoshinsky, an immigrant from Poland, cited for his spectacular heroism in the battle of the Argonne Forest.

Sergeant Sydney Gumpertz, on a mission to silence a machine gun nest, found his companions killed, but went on alone in the face of heavy fire and succeeded in capturing a crew of nine Germans at Bois de Forges. For this, he won the Congressional Medal of Honor. Sergeant Ben Kaufman, later to become a Brigadier General in the Army Reserve, advanced alone with an empty gun upon a German machine gun nest, despite a shattered right arm, took one prisoner and scattered the balance of the crew. For this his country gave him the Congressional Medal of Honor.

Numberless instances of heroic conduct on the part of Jewish fighting personnel dot the records. All told, they gave a proud account of themselves and served their country well. On another front were still other patriots, advising in the war effort and doing the thankless work of organization back home. The most illustrious of these was Bernard Mannes Baruch, Chairman of the War Industries Board and the author of the American system of wartime controls. During this period, Felix Frankfurter, later to become Associate Justice of the Supreme Court, was an Assistant Secretary of War.

VII

One of the most remarkable military thinkers of our time was the Polish Jew, Jean de Bloch. Although largely forgotten today, his exhaustive six-volume work, *The Future of War in Its Technical, Economic and Political Relations*, written in 1897, was a matter of great controversy in his time, and was translated into many languages. The well-known British military writer, Major General J. F. C. Fuller, comments on the fact that aside from Bloch, neither Von Moltke nor Foch, nor the other military geniuses of the past, had grasped the meaning and nature of modern war, especially in its relation to industrial world interdependence. Whenever Fuller mentions some radically new military development, he states that "even Bloch could not have foreseen it." He remarks that Bloch's "description of the modern battle is exact, for it is exactly as it was fought seventeen years later, and his prediction of the coming war is no less so."[45]

Bloch's estimates of the course of the Boer War were so accurate that R. E. C. Long, writing in the *Fortnightly Review*,[46] declared that Bloch "had predicted, even in number and detail, the course of events in the South African war." Bloch clearly foresaw both the tactical and strategic functions of the modern air arm. He recognized the obsolescence of cavalry and the gradual obsolescence of navies, as well as the regrouping of power potentials which has destroyed the war-making ability of minor states. Almost alone, he foresaw that the day of cold steel was over, and predicted with uncanny insight, not only the trench fighting in World War I, but the precise conditions under which the battle would seesaw back and forth, as well as the ultimate role industry, science and civilian production would play in military decision.[47]

The collapse of the Russian state and the almost complete disintegration of the Russian armies in 1917-18, brought into prominence the brilliant organizing genius and great military gifts of another amazing figure, the Communist theoretician, Leon Trotsky. Together with his chief lieutenant, Efraim Markovich Skliansky, a Jewish physician with as little practical military experience as Trotsky himself, the Communist leader was responsible for hammering the Red Army into an effective military instrument, despite the deadly chaos which gripped Revolutionary Russia.[48]

Trotsky was easily one of the pre-eminent military figures of our time, not only for his practical achievements in the organization of the Red Army, but for his deep insight into the future of military operations. In an article written several months before Munich, he estimated with amazing accuracy the course, nature and outcome of World War II.[49] He foresaw that the English theory of the small army would have to give way to conscription, despite the advent of high mechanization, and visualized in essential detail the "totalitarian character of the next war," though in this respect, he may possibly have been influenced by the writings of Bloch.

In the revolutionary and turbulent post-war period, Jews served prominently in all of the fighting movements, with the exception of that of the Nazis. Even here, there were outstanding figures such as Colonel Dusterberg, one of the co-leaders of the powerful ex-servicemen's organization, the Stahlhelm, who had to retire because of Hitler's racial laws, though his organization in the pre-election campaigns collaborated with the Nazis. There were also others who might be presumed to be at least half-Jewish by blood, as for example, Goering's Chief of Staff for the Luftwaffe, Field Marshal Eberhard Milch, who legally had himself declared a bastard in order to disacknowledge his Jewish father.[49a] Nor did Hitler neglect to utilize the work of Jewish military inventors and thinkers on behalf of his warrior state, or disdain to have the important German psychological warfare branch rest on principles evolved by such men as Hirschfeld, Stern, Lippman, Bergson, Freud, Lazarus, Steinthal and Stransky.

In the Irish Rebellion, one of De Valera's top lieutenants was Robert Briscoe of Dublin.[50] The Jewish general, Morris A. Cohen, known as General Ma, organized the first modern Chinese army, and for a period of time was virtually Minister of War for Chiang Kai-shek. Jews marched with D'Annunzio in the seizure of Fiume. In the Spanish civil war of 1936-39, among the foreign volunteers who rallied to the side of the Republicans, the Jewish percentage was high. Of the American contingent of 3,500, 630, or about 20%, were Jews. Two hundred and seventeen of these were killed and 90% of the rest wounded. Both of the leaders of the Abraham Lincoln Brigade were Jewish boys, Lieutenant Colonel John Gates, and the battalion commander, Milton Wolff.

Just as Jews were numerous in the leadership of the Red Revolution, so they were also disproportionately so in Mussolini's march on Rome. Half a dozen Jews were among the small group of leaders who founded the Fascist party. Three were among the "martyrs" who gave their lives in its early struggle for supremacy. The Duce's righthand man during the whole early period was Aldo Finzi, the airman. Another Jew, Carol Foá, as editor of the official Fascist journal, Gerarchia, was instrumental in molding the party's opinions and policy and Marghereta Sarfatti was the Duce's literary collaborator and close adviser during the whole early Fascist period.[51] Even after the Aryan laws which Mussolini had placed into existence at the insistence of Hitler, some Jews had to be called back by him for wartime service as advisers. Among these were the noted General Modena, Admiral Pontremoli, and Admiral Umberto Pugliese, considered Italy's greatest naval designer. Though Jewish participation in the armed services was thus rigorously brought close to zero, a Jew, Bruno Jesi, nevertheless managed to win the rarely bestowed Gold Medal "for outstanding valor under fire," in 1939.[52]

VIII

World War II as is well-known, proved to be the graveyard of a large section of the Jewish people. More than 6,500,000 were wiped out in the Nazi extermination camps alone. During this time, anti-Semitic calumny reached a pitch of fury hitherto known only to the darkest period of the Middle Ages. Jewish patriotism was assailed, and the quality of their soldiering made the butt of vicious jibes. Even in those parts of the world where Jews had not been deprived totally of human rights, the mass effect of carefully nurtured propaganda was to derogate them in the eyes of their neighbors as a craven people. Yet the records which exist indicate that in this war, too, Jewish soldiers bore themselves with dignity, and fought with all the fine courage and manliness which has distinguished the registers of the race over the centuries.

It is known that a total of more than 1,000,000 Jews served in the armies of the United Nations; but the collapse of the various governments in the death struggle over Europe, and the virtual disappearance of organized Jewish life on that continent, has made exact data on the fighting forces of many countries almost impossible to secure. By far the best information available on the performance of Jewish soldiers as patriots and fighting men, is from the United States, the British Empire, and the Soviet Union.

Though the Soviets showed an increasing tendency to restrict the participation of Jews in the higher circles of state leadership, they were by no means allergic to Jewish fighting intelligence and skill. Among the Soviet generals warring against Hitler, 313 were Jews. These included General Isserson, whose infantry tactics were greatly admired by German military leaders and copied by them in the initial campaigns of World War II; Lieutenant General Jacob Kreiser, master strategist of the Battle of Moscow; General Lev Dovator, victor in the crucial first Battle of Rostov; General Michael Rabinovitch, commander of the tank troops; and Marshal Jakob Smushkevich, commander of the Soviet Army Air Forces. The Jewish poet, Israel Fisanovich became the most feared of all the Russian submarine commanders. The development of guerrilla warfare, so important to the final outcome of the war, may largely be credited to heroic Jewish officers.[53]

Although the Jews were hardly 2% of the population of the Soviet Union, they took fourth place among all the national groups decorated for gallantry in battle during World

War II. Altogether, 185,000 Soviet Jewish soldiers were cited by the Soviet High Command for bravery.

In the American forces during World War II, there were 550,000 Jews in uniform, or approximately five per cent of the total under arms. The Jewish proportion of the whole American population at the time was 3.55%.[33a] Of the Jewish total, 80.59% were in the army, and 19.41% in the navy, coast guard and marine corps. In the quartermaster corps, a traditional source of anti-Semitic ridicule, despite a familiarity with this type of work which should have qualified them for a far higher proportion, the percentage of Jewish servicemen was only 3.43%, whereas 33½% of the Jewish army men were with the Army Air Forces. Jewish flyers constituted close to six per cent of all AAF flying personnel.

Jewish voluntary enlistments were extremely high. A survey of Jewish refugees made early in 1945, showed that 10% had entered the armed services. At the identical period, 8.9% of the total American population was in the service. A survey of 22 cities covering 3,050 physicians, of whom 20% were Jewish, showed that 44% of the Jewish physicians were in service against 25% of non-Jews.

The grand total of awards to American Jewish soldiers, including citations and awards by foreign governments, was 61,448.

Jewish officers were about 20% of all Jewish men in uniform. These included seven major generals, thirteen brigadier generals, one admiral and two rear admirals.

Jewish names were sprinkled throughout the news of the war, including such men as Sergeant Barney Ross, one of the heroes of Guadalcanal; Sergeant Meyer Levin, the bombardier for Captain Colin Kelly, whose plane put the Japanese battleship, Haruna, out of commission; and Major General Maurice G. Rose, commander of the famous 3rd Armored Division, the first American unit to reach German soil, and who was killed in action in western Germany. The last American word sent from Corregidor was wirelessed by a young Brooklyn soldier, Sergeant Irving Strobing. Rear Admiral Ben Moreell, later to become a four star admiral, organized and command-ed the Seabees, who played so important a part in operations in the Pacific.

Among a long list of heroic officers, Lieutenant Colonel Robert S. Levine, air squadron commander, of Columbus, Ohio, received 16 decorations of valor, the Distinguished Fly-ing Cross, Silver Star, Air Medal, and Croix de Guerre, to-gether with eleven oak leaf clusters to the Air Medal. Lieu-tenant Raymond Zussman of Detroit, a tank officer who had been a street fighting instructor at Fort Knox, proceeding on foot in a hail of hot lead, when his tank bogged down in the Rhone valley drive, wiped out two snipers' nests in succession, killed 17 Nazi soldiers and captured 32, together with a quantity of antitank guns and other war materiel. For this feat, he received the Congressional Medal of Honor.

In the fields of communications, engineering and scientific discovery, so vital to modern warfare, the record is studded with Jewish names. It was Professor Raymond D. Mindlin who was the main designer of the proximity fuse. The atomic bomb itself, on which America relies so much for its security today, is largely the product of Jewish minds. It was Albert Einstein and the Russian-born economist, Alexander Sachs, who successfully urged upon President Roosevelt the practi-cality of the research upon which the bomb was founded. It was Einstein, together with other men and women of Jewish blood, such as the professors Isidore Rabi, Niels Bohr, Lise Meitner, O. R. Frisch, Rudolph Peierls and Franz Simon, who supplied the all-important theoretical work in nuclear physics, and another brilliant Jewish physicist, Professor J. Robert Oppenheimer, who planned, organized and directed the subsequent work which produced the bomb itself.[53b] It is worth mentioning, too, that it was Rear Admiral Joseph K. Taussig who predicted before the Senate Naval Affairs Committee in December 1940, the subsequent Japanese attack on Pearl Harbor. His warning at that time caused him to be looked on as a firebrand, and to be passed over for promotion.

In the United Kingdom, out of a Jewish population of 400,000, over 60,000 served in the British armed forces. Fourteen thousand were in the Royal Air Force, and 15,000 in the Royal Navy. These figures do not include Dominion personnel, or the 30,000 men and women who volunteered for the British forces from Palestine.

Among a prominent list of others, Leslie Hore-Belisha, Minister of War, 1937-1940, was chiefly responsible for the mechanization of the British army at the beginning of the hostilities. Sir Philip A. G. D. Sassoon, who had been Under Secretary of State for Air, is generally credited with responsibility for molding the RAF into an effective fighting arm. There were a number of generals, including Major General R. H. Lorie, Brigadier W. R. Beddington, Brigadier E. F. Benjamin, and Brigadier F. H. Kisch. Among the pilots killed in the air struggle over Britain was the son of Chaim Weizmann.

The names of Jewish fighters figured prominently in the dispatches during the early battles in France, the evacuation at Dunkirk, the air war over Britain, and in the subsequent fighting over the globe. Lieutenant A. N. Abrahams who had fought in both the Boer War and World War I, was killed in action while on patrol duty in the North Sea, though over 70. Lieutenant Colonel Claude Beddington fell at sea during the Dunkirk evacuation, at the age of 72.

In South Africa, where Jews constituted 4.7% of the population, they contributed 10% of the total enlistments. They were especially numerous in the RAF and the armored divisions. In Australia and New Zealand, out of an estimated Jewish population of 35,000, provisional figures show 3,872 in all services. In Western Australia, the single place where complete figures are available, Jewish enlistments were 14% of the total Jewish population of 2,200. In Canada, out of a

Jewish population of 176,500, there were 16,883 serving in the armed forces, 5,889 of whom were in the Royal Canadian Air Force. An additional 1,631 Canadian Jews fought under the flags of other state members of the United Nations.

The number of awards for gallantry to Jewish soldiers of both the United Kingdom and the Dominions, was substantially large.

Authoritative information on Continental Europe for World War II is scattering. Among the details which are available, we note that in Greece, 100% of the Jews eligible for military service joined the colors. There were 7,000 Jewish soldiers from the single city of Salonika, who took part in the heavy fighting on the Albanian front. Six thousand five hundred Greek Jews registered for military service with their consulate in Jerusalem alone. The first officer in the Greek army to be killed in battle was Colonel Mordecai Frizis.

Jews, strangely enough, formed an actual majority in the Czechoslovak army fighting in France. Twelve hundred of these volunteered from Palestine. Gervasi observes that "a high proportion of the Polish army's officers are Jews."[54] These included at least one high-ranking officer, General Mond. Jews are declared to have been prominent particularly in the Polish air forces.

On October 9, 1939, the Polish General Staff announced that 32,216 Jews had already fallen in defense of Poland. The Polish army organized in France was 12% Jewish. Two of its Jewish members received the Order Virtuti Militari, an award comparable to the American Congressional Medal of Honor. General Anders, head of the Polish army in Russia, declared that more than 15% of his troops were Jewish volunteers, certainly an under-estimate, since the Polish corps which marched from Russia to Iran and the Middle East, is believed to have been no less than 30% Jewish.

The French Foreign Legion again had a heavy proportion of Jewish members. In June 1940, a regiment of the Legion composed entirely of Polish Jews, showed such violent resistance to the German advance that out of 3,000 only 400 survived.

More than 80,000 Jews, of whom half were foreigners, served in the defense forces of France, a truly astounding figure. Forty thousand of these were volunteers. The French armed services included a large complement of Jewish officers, with at least eleven generals and two admirals. The names of Generals Darius Bloch and Charles Huntzinger were particularly outstanding in the pre-Vichy dispatches. The leader of the first French company to cross the frontier into German territory was the Jewish captain, Pierre May; and the last official resistance, continuing for two weeks after France signed the articles of capitulation, was that of 1,300 men led by the Jewish colonel, Schwartz, who held out on the Maginot Line until Pétain forced him to lay down his arms.

After the fall of Europe to the German Wehrmacht, Jewish soldiers were numerous among those who rallied to the support of De Gaulle in London. When the Free French began recruiting in the Middle East, "the highest response was from the French Jews."[55] There were many Jews also in the ranks of the Free Dutch. The same is true of the Belgian Army-in-Exile as is noted from the statement of Baron Silvercruys, Belgian Minister to Britain, who called attention to the fact that "many Jewish names appear in the list of Belgian martyrs," and that a great number of Belgian Jews "risking not only their own lives but those of their families, had joined the Belgian forces in Great Britain."

IX

It was the Jews principally who resisted the Nazis in occupied Europe. Even though Jews were relentlessly hunted down, and automatically herded into small concentration areas, they were an important factor in the guerrilla resistance everywhere. Their percentage in these forces throughout the Continent was phenomenal, and their courage and ingenuity outstanding. Whole Jewish guerrilla units became famous for their exploits. Their desperate courage in battle was such that the Germans were said to have feared them particularly.

Judge Leon Meis reported that at least 40% of the French Maquis were Jewish, including whole independent Jewish units.[56] The number of Jews among the Maqui fighters is indicated in the reproach made by collaborationist Radio Paris to the French Committee of Liberation in Brazzaville, for acclaiming ten saboteurs in Paris as "liberators and true Frenchmen." Expostulated Radio Paris: "Is Grieswachs, the perpetrator of two outrages, a Frenchman? No, he is a Jew, a Polish Jew. Is Elek, who was responsible for eight derailments and the deaths of dozens of people, a Frenchman? No, he is a Polish Jew. The other terrorists are also Jews: Lifshitz, Fingerweiss, Stockwerk, and Reiman."[57]

A French Jew, Roger Carcassone, became the leader of the resistance movement in French North Africa, which played a decisive part in causing Algiers to fall into American hands. José Aboulker, Pierre Smadja, and Raoul and Edgar Bensoussan, also Jews, organized the underground itself, while still another Jew, Bernard Karsenty, became the liaison officer between the underground and the Allied Military Intelligence. The record here is superb. When the appointed hour arrived, the underground methodically seized and arrested enemy officers and leaders, occupied police and staff buildings and cut telephone wires. Raphael Aboulker commandeered the main radio station and broadcast the news of General Giraud's return. José Aboulker seized the Central Police Office. Alfred Pilafort, another Jew, blockaded and held the main street; and when the regular army rose in opposition under the influence of Vichy dictates, still another Jew, Lieutenant Jean Dreyfus, led the partisans into battle to protect the work of the underground. He and his men fought successfully until dawn, when the American troops landed. In this action Dreyfus was killed.[58]

Four thousand Jews succeeded in escaping the systematic extermination in Greece and took to the hills, fighting as guerrillas.

In Yugoslavia, Jewish partisans liberated whole concentration camps. There were 68,000 Jews in Yugoslavia in World War II, of whom 6,000 fought in Tito's forces. Other thousands fought with Mikhailovich. One Jewish officer was Mikhailovich's aide-de-camp, and another directed operations of 50,000 men.[59] General Velebit, head of the Yugoslav military mission in London, said in January 1945: "The leaders of the National Liberation Army feel deep gratitude for the magnificent contribution of the Jews in their ranks." One of the leading figures of the Yugoslav resistance, and later one of the three Vice Presidents of the Provisional Government, was Moische Pijade. Another was Dr. Alkalay.

An extremely high percentage among the Czech guerrillas were Jews. A much feared, purely Jewish guerrilla group, known as the "Jewish Patriot Brigade," operated from a mountain stronghold.

Reports coming out of Hungary through underground channels at the end of November 1944, indicated that the armed resistance against the Nazi Government in Budapest was largely carried out by Jews.

In Poland, the guerrilla fighters had a high percentage of Jews who had escaped the ghetto, men who distinguished themselves by their resourcefulness and reckless courage in action. Jewish partisans out of all proportion to the existing numbers, served in every one of the raids on German outposts, estates and communications. Cases of extreme individual heroism and daring were numerous. Baruch Goldstein who brought the first flame thrower into the ghetto, was responsible for the wrecking of four German ammunition dumps. Engineer Isaac Ratner ingeniously contrived delayed-action chemical gadgets by which many German gasoline reservoirs were wrecked. A Jewish partisan group which called itself "The Avengers," became a minor scourge, wrecking trains, destroying bridges, factories and German ammunition dumps. When the Red Army began its attack on Vilna, the first to enter the city were the Jewish partisans, who engaged the barricaded Germans in a bloody encounter in which neither side expected, or received, mercy.

The savage struggle of the Warsaw Ghetto was not a battle in the ordinary sense. It was more than that—a kind of terrible epic which occurs seldom in history, a last supreme test of human dignity, courage, endurance, and moral strength. Originally the overcrowded ghetto area had held some 200,000 people. An influx from the provinces in the wake of the German army brought it to 400,000. About 50,000 died in a nightmare year of disease and deliberately induced starvation. In July 1942, mass deportations began to the Eastern extermination camps, which had been described to the deportees as mere labor camps. More than 300,000 Jews from the ghetto had thus perished before the horrible truth dawned upon those who remained.

Now within the ghetto walls were 45,000 human creatures, without human rights, sick, emaciated, ragged, inexperienced in war, and without arms. The leaders of the ghetto remnant met, and despite the disheartening conditions the determination was made to fight.

The plan of defense was astonishingly well-conceived, and in an area filled with German informers, involved a miracle of discipline and secret organization. The Polish underground, made aware of the impending struggle, refused to help, regarding the moment as inopportune. However, a secret tunnel was built from the headquarters on Muranowska Street, into the Aryan sector, through which weapons were smuggled, to be stored in underground arsenals. Jewish partisans from the forests infiltrated into the area to furnish military instruction. Weapons and bombs were manufactured right in the ghetto.

The Germans meanwhile had gotten wind of the fact that something was brewing. On April 18, 1943, the ghetto was surrounded by heavily-armed battalions of S. S. Elite guards, and regiments of their Lithuanian, Latvian and Ukrainian allies. The blue and white Jewish flag was suddenly raised and the Germans were met with machine gun fire, hand-grenades, Molotov cocktails, knives, clubs and stones. More than 250 Germans fell in this first full-scale rebellion against Nazi rule and outrage. The rest retreated in wild disorder. The next day, a special Jewish shock troop group broke through the walls of the ghetto, attacked German arsenals and factories and took possession of a considerable quantity of Nazi uniforms and war materiel, together with badly-needed food stores. The following night a body of four hundred Jewish commandos dressed in German uniforms, stole out of the ghetto through the secret tunnels, and stormed the great Pawiac prison, liberating several thousand Jews and a number of Christian Poles, who joined the fighters.

Now followed an amazing struggle which lasted for forty-two bloody days, in which an untrained rabble army, overwhelmingly outnumbered and outweighed, and more resembling emaciated scarecrows than men, held out against the most powerful and best equipped army in the world.

The tactics, discipline and organization would have done credit to any professional army, much less to the ragged tubercular ghetto men, women and children who constituted the defenders. The Jewish plan of organization utilized every street corner and every house as a point of support for a general blueprint of defense. All possible tactics were foreseen and prepared for. Barricades were improvised, a system of medical stations created for expected casualties, and even a commissary provided by which orderly resistance could be maintained. Everything that could be used in a fight, including vitriol and boiling water, was utilized against the heavily-armed enemy.

During the course of the battle, Colonel von Sanmern, commanding the S. S. troops, was removed, and Police General Stroop placed in command. He sent an ultimatum to the defenders ordering them to give up "the senseless fight" and release German prisoners, threatening otherwise to destroy the ghetto in a day. The Jews replied that they would be glad to exchange prisoners—ten Jews for one German, and refused to discuss the other points of the ultimatum.

The gates of the ghetto were mined. The Germans now came in with heavy artillery and tanks. When they crossed into the ghetto, the mined gates blew up causing dreadful havoc. The German armor was met by well-camouflaged anti-tank guns, resulting in the annihilation of the advance guard of tanks. The tanks which had been able to retreat were stopped by Jewish men in German uniforms who jumped on board, throwing hand-grenades inside, and often blowing themselves up with the enemy. Again the Germans hastily retreated with heavy casualties. That night, Jewish hand-picked troops in German uniforms attacked Gestapo guardhouses, liquidated the occupants, commandeered arms and brought them back to their own headquarters on German trucks. Now the fight went on in deadly earnest, with the Germans bringing up their heavy cannon, using flamethrowers, bombers and poison gas. Hundreds of German tanks and cannon were destroyed in a single day. Every house was fought for and had to be burned out before the defenders could be routed. Throughout the struggle, fighting within a veritable sea of roasting corpses and stinking flesh, the Jews counterattacked in orderly ranks against the guns and heavy armor with which they were met.

Ceaselessly blasting artillery and incendiary bombs, rained on the ghetto from attacking planes, finally turned the entire area into a roasting inferno of flames. A desperate last appeal to the Polish underground to join the battle was met by renewed refusal, and the Jews determined to fight it out to the bitter end alone.

By June 3 only one house was left standing amid the ashes of what had once been the great Jewish ghetto of Warsaw. With the exception of its occupants, and some 300 who had managed to escape into the forests to join the partisans, all the defenders had been killed. They had laid down their lives in a battle, not for victory, which the Jews knew was a hopeless dream, but for the honor of their name. This remaining structure was defended stoutly, floor by floor. The last survivor, a young Jewish boy of 14, was finally trapped on the roof, his ammunition gone. In a last incredible gesture of defiance, he grasped the blue and white Jewish banner which still floated from the roof, wrapped it around his body and leaped to his death in the smoldering ruins below, rather than surrender.

German losses had been heavy, both in men and material. It is said that they used more fire power in liquidating the virtually defenseless ghetto than during the entire siege of Warsaw.

Revolts followed in other cities, including Sobibor, Bendin, Minsk, Vilna, Slutsk, Rovno and Bialystok. In Bialystok alone, 40,000 Jews, men, women and children, fell after eight days of desperate fighting. The Germans learning from their costly experience in the Warsaw battle, no longer took the Jewish defense lightly. They brought up their big guns at once, coordinated with a massive weight of incendiaries dropped from the sky, systematically turning the entire ghetto into a flaming furnace. The Battle of the Ghetto of Vilna lasted for a full week, with the Germans using bombing planes and heavy artillery to break down the walls.

X

It is in Palestine, the ancient cradle of the race, that the Jews have relived the heroic days of the Maccabees, of David, Gideon, and that host of heroes who have been for the Christian world the very symbol of valor in battle. It was this vanguard of returning expatriates whom Britain's foremost military expert, Captain Liddell Hart, was finally to refer to with unstinted admiration as that "fine fighting race . . ."

During the period following the Balfour Declaration, the Jews of Palestine had learned a deep distrust and hatred for their British overlords, whom they had come to regard as tyrants and conspirators bent on destroying the fetal Jewish state before it could be born. Immediately upon the outbreak of war, however, practically every able-bodied Jewish man and woman eligible for service volunteered, and offered themselves to the British War Office as a body, to fight under the Jewish flag. Altogether, over 137,000 individuals registered for military service in September 1939.

The British, notwithstanding the peril of their own position, refused the offer. The explanation was that to accept the Jews without a compensating number of Arabs, would "disturb the delicate balance of Jewish-Arab relationship." The British attempted instead to organize a Palestine division, half Arab and half Jewish. The Arabs, however, would not enlist in substantial numbers, so the project had to be abandoned. The British thereupon decided to accept a limited number of Jews into the British armed forces themselves. Some 10,000 were promptly inducted into the RAF, including mechanics and air crew specialists. After the collapse of France, this first Palestinian pioneer unit was suddenly dispatched to that country, where it was given the ungrateful task of covering the retreat of the British expeditionary force, a job it discharged with so much daring and courage that it became known as the "Suicide Squad."

On the whole, British reluctance to accept Jewish servicemen from Palestine continued for more than a year. Only a limited number were taken, and at the beginning these generally were assigned "to shoveling dirt and truck driving, but not to combat duty."[60] Although they were forbidden to fight under their own banner, 30,000 Palestine Jews finally were permitted to join England's fighting forces.

By the Summer of 1942, the situation of the British army in Egypt had become little short of desperate. It had lost more than half its manpower and the better part of its mechanized equipment to Marshal Rommel, who confidently expected to be in Cairo in a matter of weeks.

Farouk of Egypt had refused to fire a single shot in defense of his invaded country, and was openly pro-Nazi. Iraq had revolted in favor of a Nazi alliance. The German timetable envisaged a descent through the Caucasus and thence down the ancient pathway of the Middle East, to make final juncture there with the seemingly unbeatable Japanese war machine. To the north, the Vichy regime was preparing Syria as a base for a German invasion.

In response to a request from the worried British authorities, twelve young Jews volunteered to blow up the all-important oil establishments in the Syrian port of Tripoli, well knowing that they would never return. Dashing off at night in a speed boat loaded with high explosives, they succeeded in overpowering the French guard and demolishing the refineries. All were killed.

The Jews specialized in these suicidal expeditions, where their record as fighting men is literally incomparable. Before the reconquest of Iraq, the British received information that a German crew was arriving to destroy the vital Mosul oil wells and installations. They had in jail David Raziel, leader of the Jewish underground. Raziel was released and given the assignment to protect the Mosul installations. With 24 of his picked fighters, he made his way to Bagdad in Bedouin disguise. The little band managed to locate the special crew of 150 German engineers and mechanics who had been landed by German transport plane and were waiting on the outskirts of the city to complete their job of demolition, if the British were to advance on Iraq. Raziel possessed only ten machine guns, a number of cases of hand-grenades, and one revolver for each man. Commandeering five cars, he ambushed the German crew that night, destroying almost all of them together with their trucks and equipment. Raziel was killed as were almost all of his men, but "a fantastic mission had been successfully completed—a mission upon which hinged the life and death of the British Empire."[61]

In 1941, with the Germans poised in Greece, and ready to make juncture with the Vichy French in Syria, 50 Jewish volunteers dressed in German uniform crossed the Syrian border, mingling with the collaborationist soldiers, contacting Free French forces behind the enemy lines, sabotaging valuable military equipment, and transmitting by wireless the intelligence necessary to the success of the forthcoming Syrian campaign. Not one of the 50 volunteers was ever seen again. Two days before the British invaded, another group of fifty young Jews led by Moshe Dayan, who previously had been jailed by the Mandatory Government for possessing "unauthorized arms," was sent on a mission to seize three essential bridges. Their task was to prevent the destruction of these vital arteries by the French, an action which well might have turned the invasion of the Australian spearhead into disaster. The Vichy stronghold, Fort Gouraud, which dominated the approaches to these bridges, was built on the site of an ancient crusader's castle, and manned by a garrison of 300. Dayan and his boys took the fort by a ruse, and in a fierce, uneven struggle in which the greater portion of them were killed, managed to hold until the Australians and Free French came up.

Another group of thirty-two Jews was dropped from British planes into Yugoslavia, Rumania, Slovakia and northern Italy, under instruction to organize Jewish resistance groups and train them in sabotage. Among these was the famous girl officer, Hanna Szenes, who was shot by a Nazi firing squad in Budapest in 1944.[62]

It was Jewish desert scouts, able, daring, acquainted with the type of terrain, and speaking German so that they could mingle undetected with German troops, who provided Montgomery with his military intelligence and guides. It was Jewish engineers who organized and manned the coastal defense and signal services of the entire Middle Eastern coast, and the Jewish coast guard which ran the hundreds of speed boats along the dangerous Mediterranean line.

Until Montgomery took over from Auchinleck, the British at no time had more than 45,000 men on the African front. Of these almost a full quarter were Jews. In the crucial battle of Egypt, which was won by the British 8th Army, the 30,000 Jewish volunteers from Palestine played an indispensable part. There were 2,500 Palestine Jews who served "with the Royal Air Force as bombardiers, pilots and observers. Six thousand more Jews were in the ground crews of the Egyptian airdromes."[62a] Under the direction of Brigadier General Frederick Hermann Kisch of Haifa, chief engineer of the 8th Army, Jewish engineers constructed Britain's so-called impregnable forts at El Alamein. It was Kisch and his men who organized the tremendously difficult supply line which enabled Montgomery to undertake his successful 1,300-mile trek through Libya and Cyrenaica to Tripoli. It was at the gates of Bizerte that Kisch himself was killed.

In June 1942, a company of Jewish engineers at Mechili in Libya, led by Major Felix Liebman of Tel Aviv, disrupted Rommel's inexorable advance for the first time. Laying down a mine field to prevent Rommel's forward thrust aimed at turning the flank of the 8th Army, which stood with its back to Alamein, they were spotted by German scouts. The Germans immediately attacked in strength with Stukas, heavy bombers and tanks. Liebman wirelessed the British for antiaircraft and antitank guns, reinforcements and instructions. The guns and reinforcements did not arrive, but instructions did—to finish laying their mines and hold the position at all costs.

The ill-matched contest lasted for almost a month, with the Jews tenaciously holding their ground. Surrounded on three sides by enemy armor, the engineers received a German emissary who demanded that they hoist the white flag of surrender. Liebman replied that he had no white flag, that he only had the blue and white flag of Zion, and that he was going to fly it. He did. His camp was promptly assaulted by three German columns totaling 110 tanks, together with a number of Stukas. The Jews replied with Molotov cocktails and tommy guns, conserving their ammunition by waiting for close combat before they counterattacked. One sergeant alone accounted for seven tanks. Daily the German assaults against these obstinate men continued in mounting intensity, with Liebman and his remaining men forced back into a deep central dugout, where they made their final stand in the intense desert heat. Their food was gone, and small amounts of water were dropped to them in cans by the RAF.

When they were finally rescued by a column of Free French under General Koenig, the Jews had managed to destroy a considerable portion of Rommel's armor, and had held their position. Only 42 of the 500 remained alive.[63]

It was Major Richard Perach who led the battalion which turned the flank of the Mareth line at another critical juncture in the war. It was a Jewish suicide task force of 85 men, carrying only machine guns and small arms, which at another dangerous moment in Montgomery's campaign, under instructions to create a diversion behind Rommel's lines, instead accomplished the impossible by capturing the important stronghold of Bardia intact, together with all its military booty and 9,000 enemy prisoners. Jewish suicide task forces landed in Tobruk and helped take that city as they had captured Bardia earlier.[64] The expendables used by General Sir Archibald Wavell as the spearheads for the capture of Sidi Barrani, Solum, and Fort Capuzzo, were Jews from Palestine.

There were no engagements in Africa or the Middle East in which Jewish boys did not play a prominent part. In Eritrea, it was Jews who covered the left flank of the advance to Karen, which cut off the Italians. In Ethiopia, they operated as advance suicide squad spearheads, and played a vital role in the capture of Gondar, the last Italian stronghold. Among the 10,000 British troops reported missing in Greece and Crete, 1,023 were Palestinian Jews.

At the moment when he was facing a seemingly invincible Rommel, Montgomery himself had stated privately that only a miracle could save him. "Jewish Palestine," remarks Van Paassen, "was part of that miracle."[65] In addition to the participation in the military forces, the Jews turned all of Palestine into an industrial bastion for the British armies, supplying them with the precision instruments and vital equipment of all types which are needed by modern armed forces. With typical ingenuity, the Jews created almost overnight some 432 new industries for war, furnishing as well the skilled technicians, medical, meteorological and other experts required by a modern mechanized army.

On the plea that such a course was necessary "to avoid inflaming the Arab-Jewish question," the extraordinary and significant service of Jewish Palestine was virtually ignored in the wartime acknowledgments released by British leaders and information services. Nor were Jews allowed to serve as Jewish nationals until September 1944, when intense pressure from the United States and elsewhere forced Britain to agree to the formation of a Jewish infantry brigade group under its own flag. Commanded by Brigadier E. F. Benjamin, this brigade moved into Italy in November 1944, becoming a complete combat group and winning for its personnel many citations for distinguished conduct in the field.

XI

The fighting record of the Jewish Yishub, standing on its own as the new State of Israel, in repelling the invasion of the armies of six Arab countries, trained, equipped and led by the British, is almost without parallel.

Over the years, the sharp clash which had developed between the aims of restive Jewish Palestine and those of its

British rulers, had resulted in deep tension, and a bitterness bordering on hatred. The growing Jewish underground, described to the writer by the French military as the finest guerrilla force this age has produced, had succeeded, after a series of daring operations, in destroying both the peace and security of the British stationed in the Holy Land, together with the all-important prestige of the British raj elsewhere in the Colonial areas. Forced into a dramatic action, London announced its intention of withdrawing from Palestine, leaving the Jews to contend alone with the combined armies of the suddenly bellicose Arab states. When the British finally evacuated, it was confidently expected by most military men, and certainly by those in the British Foreign Office, that there would be a quick end to Jewish pretensions.[66]

For years, the British had made possession of arms by Jews a criminal offense. Regular searching parties had raided Jewish settlements in an unending search for military contraband. At the beginning of the Israeli-Arab war, it may safely be said that there were not enough small arms and ammunition in Jewish hands to equip 2,000 men. The departing British had deliberately drained all known stocks of oil out of the country in an effort to freeze its vehicular services. Administrative services were left in chaos. There was not even a postal service; the phone service was in a hopeless jangle. No effort had been made to train and turn over to the new Jewish authority any of the departments of government. A world wide blockade had been instituted, allegedly for the purpose of localizing the conflict, but operating with massive force against the hopes of the Jews in particular. The key points in Palestine's military economy had been transferred to the Arab Legion, nominally headed by Abdullah, but up to the final moment of withdrawal, used as an integral part of the British policing operation against the Jews. Not only did the British assist the Legion in fortifying itself in the very heart of Palestine, but placed at its disposal the large amount of war material concentrated in the Transjordan British bases.

[295]

In addition to the Palestine Arabs themselves, the armies of Iraq, Transjordan, Syria, Lebanon and Egypt were poised on the borders. Saudi-Arabia was prevented from marching[66a] only by a distrust of Ibn Saud's intentions on the part of Arabs occupying intervening territory.[67] The Arab armies possessed heavy armor and squadrons of modern military aircraft. They had the expert advice of top British military personnel, and in the case of the Transjordan Arab Legion, were equipped, financed and led as a virtual arm of the British military forces themselves.

Pitted against this imposing host was a hastily organized volunteer militia, with some broken-down, antiquated aircraft,[67a] almost without a central authority, and possessing only a few makeshift, home-armored vehicles, a few home-made mortars, and a limited quantity of small arms and ammunition.[67b]

The territory the Jews occupied was not only attenuated but lay in lowland country caught within the surrounding hills; strategically it could be regarded as being in an almost impossible position.

That any people could have successfully survived this crushing set of circumstances is a phenomenon from beginning to end. The Jews were always short of arms and munitions. At the time of the first big Arab Legion assault on Jerusalem, the total Jewish arms in that city consisted of a small quantity of rifles, and three 3-inch mortars with a daily ration of 16 shells delivered to an improvised airfield by light plane. There were two Beza machine guns which arrived on May 13, but only one man in the city was found who knew how to handle them. A considerable stock of Molotov cocktails were discovered, however, providentially left behind by the departing British. Against these meager arms stood an iron wall of heavy guns, ringing the city almost completely. The attacking Arabs were estimated at two infantry brigade groups, supported by a field artillery regiment and strong armored elements, two batteries of 25-pound cannon, two batteries of 4.2-inch mortars, large units of tanks and armored cars, and various small artillery units.

For the most part, the Jewish militia was green and inexperienced. Months later, the American, James F. Metcalf, remarked that if the recruit received instruction "for twenty days between conscription and combat, he has had a lot more than the earlier trainees."[68] He described the Israeli troops as "a fighting element reduced to its barest essentials, a man and his weapon, with little in the way of artillery or other support." He observes that though "the invaders were driven from positions that appeared impregnable," there was never any parity of weapons, and that these striking victories were achieved by small detachments of determined men "relying almost entirely on surprise, dash, night attacks and a will to win."[69] The greatest weapon the Israeli soldier had was what Captain Liddell Hart described as the fact that the Arab was "more careful of his own skin than the Jew."

Desperately lacking munitions and arms, the Jews attacked at night with cold steel. The Arabs proved to have little stomach for this type of campaign. In every case of hand-to-hand fighting the Arabs gave ground, abandoning their equipment in headlong flight. The Jews also benefited by a superb and daring intelligence service which allowed them to peg the movements of their foes in many cases well in advance.

Meanwhile by a combination of circumstances, including the capture of war material from the Arabs, raids on British arms trains and depots, and the acquisition of arms purchased in many countries abroad and run in one way or another through the blockade, the quality of Jewish equipment improved enormously, though at no time did it compare with the heavy armor, artillery and planes in the hands of the invaders. Within a matter of weeks, the impossible had occurred, and the beleaguered Jews, fighting tanks with rifles, and bombers with machine guns, relying largely on their courage, initiative, endurance and resourcefulness, succeeded in passing to the offensive. Jaffa, a city of 70,000 Arabs, bulwarked by a considerable army of irregulars from Iraq and Syria, was attacked by some 400 men of the Jewish underground. As the Jews advanced in the narrow streets, British artillery began to shell their positions. Nevertheless, after heavy street fighting and a series of brilliant tactical operations, considerably aided by the panic which had overtaken the Arabs, the Jews succeeded in running up their flag over the central part of the city. The great bulk of the Arab inhabitants fled, together with the irregular units who had been the advance guard of the Arab armies.

Haifa fell in a similar lightning attack, and again the British opened up on Jewish troops with cannon and tank fire, as they evacuated. The overwhelming majority of Haifa's 66,000 Arabs bolted, both before and after the battle was joined.

At Safed were 1,200 Jewish inhabitants, in a town containing 16,000 Arabs, and completely surrounded by 40,000 Arab fellaheen and tribesmen. Confident that the Jews had no arms, the Arabs attacked in force. From hidden recesses the Jews dug up some old shotguns and rifles secreted against this very need. When the struggle was over, a small number of Jews and Arabs lay dead; the balance of the Arabs had hurriedly packed what they could and ran, leaving the entire area in the undisputed possession of the surprised Jews.

Quite different from the circumstances which clogged the roads of Europe before the German advance, and which caused the numerically preponderant Arab population of Palestine to flee almost in a body, the Jews yielded nowhere. Isolated outposts and farming communities dug themselves in and held out against whole armies.

The typical case of Negba, known as the "underground kibbutz," became an Israeli legend. The village lies in a hollow one kilometer below fortified heights which were handed over to the Egyptians and Iraqians by the British military. The whole area of the Negba settlement was hardly more than 150 acres, and its able-bodied male population not more than 90. These were equipped with 80 rifles, 35 machine guns, five two- and three-inch mortars, one short-range anti-tank gun and several hundred hand grenades. In possession of the attackers, in addition to regulation armament, were several batteries of heavy artillery, numerous Bren carriers, planes, tanks and other heavy armor. On one day alone more than 6,000 shells are reported to have fallen into the settlement. All houses were completely demolished by constant shelling. The settlers dug themselves underground, holding their fire until the enemy was within rifle distance. During the five-month siege, the settlement was swept daily by heavy artillery shells and aerial bombs. On a single day four waves of Egyptian infantry led by ten tanks, thirty-six armored cars, and supported by heavy artillery, mortars and the Egyptian air force, attacked. On June 12, 1948, the Egyptians opened an all-out assault on this obstinate settlement, strafing it from the air and advancing on it with infantry and artillery units behind a spearhead of twenty-four giant Sherman tanks. The Jews replied with machine guns and their single anti-tank gun. They concentrated with this and with Molotov cocktails, hitting seven of the armored vehicles in the first column. The Egyptians turned back.

At Ramat Naftali, Yad Mordecai, and other tiny communities, the Jews defended themselves with the same fierce determination. In this battle of armor versus human flesh, a typical report states: "One of the settlers stood at his post, absolutely exposed, working his Bren gun as though he were punching a time-clock in a factory. Another went straight up to an enemy tank in the closing phase of the battle, throwing a hand-grenade into it, and blew himself up together with the enemy."

During the shelling of Jerusalem, there were 4,300 casualties out of the city's 100,000 population. Food, fuel and water were scarce, and a large part of the city reduced to rubble. But the Jews held.

The enterprise and valor by which the Jews contrived to supply the "New City" of Jerusalem with badly needed food and arms for defense, must literally be described as Homeric in its dimensions. Jerusalem was totally cut off from the rest of the Jewish territory. The single tortuous road passed through Arab-held areas. Each time supplies were run, the road itself had to be cleared by a frontal attack. The Jewish supply trucks were compelled to run a gantlet of fire down this narrow ribbon of road whose surrounding heights were manned by Arab sharpshooters and artillery. The road was quickly littered with the blasted shells of Jewish trucks and cars. The casualties were heartbreaking, but the Jews kept coming.

Meanwhile the Arab Legion, already anchored in the old City of Jerusalem with the help of its British mentors (who had also given the Legion possession of Jerusalem's source of water supply as well as the important military positions and approaches to the city) made a supreme attempt to take the all-but-isolated New City.

In addition to confiscating Jewish weapons, disclosing Jewish positions to the enemy and blocking Jewish lines of communication, the British opened up on the Jewish defenders with their own mortars and artillery. It was British heavy guns which dislodged the Jews from the strong defensive position they held at Sheikh Jerrah.

The single strong point remaining to the Jews which would hold back the Legion long enough for the defenders to consolidate their positions in the New City, was the Kfar Etzion Bloc in the heart of the Hebron hills. The entire fighting force consisted of 100 Jewish women and 400 men. These were surrounded by a well-armed Arab population of 60,000, stiffened by the Arabs of Abdullah's Legion. The Jews possessed no antitank weapons nor heavy arms of any kind. Only one-half of the Jewish defenders could be equipped with the arms available. The function of the defenders was to engage the thousands of villagers and Legionnaires who would otherwise have converged upon the city with irresistible force.

Strong assaults by the Arab "liberation army" were beaten back with heavy losses. The Arab Legion finally began an offensive under cover of a merciless ten-hour bombardment from the surrounding ridges. The Arabs used among other vehicles heavy British Sherman tanks, numerous infantry and a large complement of guns. Wave after wave of this armored assault was repulsed. A large proportion of the defenders were killed outright or badly wounded, but the enemy nevertheless was thrown back. The Jewish tactic was always to permit tank advance until the attackers were within range of rifle fire and hand-grenades, and if possible, to turn the battle into a hand-to-hand encounter.

On the morning of May 12, after a protracted defense, the Arabs opened up an all-out attack employing two Legion battalions, thousands of villagers and 40 armored vehicles. In this fierce and bloody struggle, positions continuously changed hands. Kfar Etzion finally capitulated after the Jews had run out of ammunition completely. Only a handful of the 500 defenders survived this ordeal, but they had played their part well. They had held long enough to give Jerusalem's Jewish defenders the breathing spell they needed to dig themselves in. And meanwhile, too, the resolute Israelis had accomplished another minor miracle by cutting a new road along the southern flank of the Judean Hills which linked up Jerusalem with Tel Aviv through wholly Jewish-held territory.

In the end, each of the Arab armies was beaten in detail, beginning with the forces of the Iraqian adventurer, Fawzi Bey Kauji, who was shattered in the battles of Tirat Zvi in the Jordan Valley, and at Mishmar Haemek, scene of the Biblical Armageddon, losing most of his armor to the Jews.[70]

In the decisive Second Battle of the Negev, the Egyptian army was broken with crushing rapidity. By a lightning attack, Jewish jeep units had taken the desert center of Beersheba. In the final movement, perhaps the most daring operation of the war, swiftly moving Jewish troops swept around a wide arc over the southern desert to completely outflank the Egyptians, turning up in Egyptian territory at its rear.

The Egyptian forces lay in two arms, one based on the "impregnable" fortress of Asluj, and extending to Auja, and the other along the southern coast to Gaza. Occupying what apparently was an unbeatable strategic position, the 30,000 Egyptians had at their disposal two modern armored regiments in addition to numerous aircraft.

The Israelis secretly managed to make a circle through the desert, bypassing Asluj and exposing Auja to direct assault. Their desert scouts had found the course of an all-but-obliterated Roman road. This narrow desert track with its dangerous soft sand shoulders, was followed silently through the black night by the Israeli army train, whose travel-weary soldiers were scheduled to arrive after fifteen hours of foot-slogging, at an early morning hour on the main Auja-Rafah road.

Appearing unexpectedly like the very wrath of God, these ferocious, wraithlike warriors descended on Auja, putting the defenders to immediate rout. The road to the south of Asluj was cut at El Musharafa and the position of the supposedly impregnable fortress rendered hopeless. With one of their armored regiments trapped between Auja and Asluj, and completely annihilated, the Egyptians fled across the frontier pursued by Israeli troops, who penetrated 50 miles to the great Egyptian base of El Arish. From this base, the Israelis systematically destroyed Egyptian airfields, capturing some aircraft, and shooting down others. The greater part of the fine Egyptian air armada was smashed on the ground. Hundreds of tanks and armored vehicles were left a twisted and blackened mass of iron or abandoned, together with gasoline, ammunition, small arms and other booty to the triumphant Jews. The remaining Egyptian forces in Palestine found themselves suddenly cut off from all communications with their home bases.

This operation introduced Israeli marine commandos for the first time. In addition to developing a small war industry of their own, the Jews had succeeded in running the blockade with enough materiel to produce a small but efficient air force, and a swiftly moving jeep unit. In an operation perfectly synchronized with the movements of the ground troops, Jewish aircraft simultaneously hit all enemy strongpoints, destroying railroads, munition dumps, troop concentrations and airfields, and took complete control of the air. At the same time, the fledgling Israeli navy took over command of the coastal waters, and in its sole naval contest sank the Egyptian flagship and pride of the Egyptian navy, the King Farouk.

The same total victory was achieved over the Lebanese army which had advanced into Palestine headed by a mechanized column. This was attacked, cutting off the Lebanese armored vehicles, and throwing the entire column back into Lebanon in precipitate retreat. Similarly, the Syrians were soundly trounced in the Jordan and Huleh valleys and forced to turn back into Syria.

The Arab Legion itself, despite the carefully nurtured British legend to the contrary, was decisively beaten in every encounter it had with Israeli troops. The Legionnaires fled in disorder from Lydda and Ramleh, which the Israeli army took in a series of sharp blows. In a few days of fighting, the Legion lost some 20% of its personnel and a whole squadron of armored vehicles. At the time of the final truce, which was insisted upon by the great nations of the world, the Legion's military position was a precarious one. During the nine days of battle between the first and second truces, the combined Arab armies lost about 22% of their total strength of approximately 56,000, together with much of their armor. It is conceded that the Armistice forced on the Jews by British pressure in the United Nations, saved the Arabs from complete annihilation. There is little question in the minds of competent military observers that had the Israeli Prime Minister, David Ben-Gurion, given the word, his forces could have marched successfully on Cairo, Amman, Beirut and Damascus at any time in the latter days of the campaign. The British, in fact, felt compelled to warn the Jews that if they crossed over into Trans-Jordan, they would be met there by the British army. This perhaps deterred the top echelon of Israeli planners. The fighting Jews, however, were not intimidated when armed British reconnaissance planes appeared over the battle area in the Negev, for they promptly shot down five of them.

XII

In a century trembling under the impact of stirring events, none has been more impressive than the succession of victories by which Palestine has disappeared forever. In its place stands Israel, inhabited once again, as if the continuity of their residence had never been broken, by a fighting people who have taken up again where their forebears in the militant days of antiquity had left off. The cost has been heavy, for there is scarcely a home in Israel which is not draped in mourning for loved ones who have fallen in the field. It is this record which speaks for itself in reply to the calumnies which have assailed the character and martial qualities of the Jewish people; for here the record is clear, and may be read without debate as to the value of comparative figures.

Elsewhere the evidence amassed over the centuries would appear to point indisputably to the conclusion that the record of the Jewish fighting man is among the best the world has produced. It is the record of a stanch and devoted people whose loyalty to all causes to which they have been pledged has been proved on all of the battlefields of Western civilization.

FOOTNOTES

[1] See Sir Leonard Woolley, *Abraham*; see also *The Apocrypha*, Book of Judith, and Josephus, *Antiquities,* Book XIII, Chapter 5. The remnants of the Chaldaic-Assyrian nation, still living in the Middle East, acknowledge this relationship to this day, and still speak Aramaic, the language of the Jews during the time of Jesus and the Apostles.

[2] Joseph J. Williams, *Hebrewisms of West Africa,* pages 188-196.

[3] Mentioned in both the First and Second Books of Maccabees.

4 It was only in the time of Solomon that a really well-equipped Jewish army existed. According to I Kings, 10:26, the great philosopher-king had 1,400 chariots and sufficient horses for 12,000 horsemen, together with a navy whose principal port was Eziongeber at the present site of Aqaba on the Red Sea.

5 The triumph of Judas Maccabaeus over Nicanor at Adasa in the Judean War of Independence "was certainly as decisive as the victory of General Gates at Saratoga over Burgoyne in the American Revolutionary struggle, over 2,000 years later. The effects of Judas' success were still influential when Mother England retired from the contest with her daughter colony across the Atlantic."—Israel Abrahams, *Campaigns in Palestine*, page 3.

6 *The Romance of the Last Crusade.*

7 " . . . and they cast up a bank against the city, and it stood in a trench; and all the people that were with Joab battered the wall, to throw it down." II Samuel, 20:15.

8 Rogers MacVeagh and Thomas B. Costain, *Joshua*, p. 91-165.

9 How well advanced the early Jews were in the military arts may be inferred from Lyn Montross' observation that "by the fifth century B. C. the Greek line of battle consisted of a hedge of spears bearing down upon the enemy . . . it was seldom that either general resorted to surprise, maneuver, flank attack or any other variation from the plain frontal assault."—*War Through the Ages*, page 9.

10 Joseph Kastein, *History and Destiny of the Jews*, page 101.

11 Describing the quality of Jewish character which led to these conflicts, Dion Cassius observed in his *Annals*: "the race is very bitter when aroused to anger . . ."

11a Bar Giora, or Bar Gurias, as his name indicates, was said to have been the son of a convert to Judaism; hence, at most, he could only have been part-Jewish. The interesting and oft-mooted question as to whether the term 'Jew' connotes a religious, racial or purely social definition, cannot be answered here. However, the question does pose certain difficulties in reference to the purposes of the present study. In the case of a famous American general killed on the battlefield, his wife is alleged to have declared that he could not be Jewish because he was a Protestant, notwithstanding the fact that he was the son of a Jewish rabbi. On the other hand, if Hitler's definition that a single Jewish grandparent was sufficient to confer Jewish identity were to apply, the list of known Jewish military figures would be enormously enlarged. It may be added, also, that absolute records often as not, were not kept at all. It is also a fact that numerous military figures have concealed their Jewish antecedents, which under circumstances of the prevailing anti-Jewish bias, were felt to be prejudicial to their careers.

12 Rev. H. C. Adams, M.A., *The History of the Jews*, page 34.

13 The military writers, Spaulding, Nickerson and Wright, remark with true insight into the stream of Jewish history: "They resisted the Romans desperately, with the intense determination familiar to modern students of Jewish character."—*Warfare: A Study of Military Methods from the Earliest Times,* page 205.

14 "So they fell," writes Tacitus, "with swords in their hands, contending for liberty, and, in the act, preserving it . . . "—*History* VII:13. After this unmitigated catastrophe to Jewish arms, the fortress of Masada, at the southwest corner of the Dead Sea, continued grimly to hold out. Dr. Adams, who regarded the rebels with as little sympathy as did his Roman sources, remarks that Masada was "garrisoned by men as fierce and resolute as the defenders of Jerusalem itself." (*The History of the Jews,* page 38). After a protracted and harrowing siege, the Romans succeeded in breaching the outer walls of the fortress and firing the inner wall. When they entered finally, a terrifying silence greeted them. The defenders, men, women and children alike, had taken their own lives during the night rather than capitulate. There had not been a single outcry to act as a sign to the Romans as to what was transpiring.

15 This arch has endured the destructive hand of time and still stands in Rome.

16 Before they were finally beaten by the Roman legions, the Jews had held the greater part of Cyrene and had even proclaimed their leader, Andreas, as king.

17 *Treatise Against Apion,* Book II, Chapter 4. See also Nathan Caro Belth, Universal Jewish Encyclopedia, Book IX, page 597.

18 She is referred to by French scholars as the African Joan of Arc.

19 *Gebel al Tariq,* or Rock of Tariq.

20 Joseph J. Williams, *Hebrewisms of West* Africa, page 210.

21 A short decade before, they had erupted against the Caliph in Andalusia in a characteristic bloody rebellion against repressive taxation, and were put down with great slaughter.

22 E. H. Lindo, *The History of the Jews of Spain and Portugal,* page 153.

23 Fernando also sailed with Sir Walter Raleigh on four voyages to America, and was the discoverer of Virgina in 1584.

24 When the Portuguese explorer Vasco da Gama arrived in India, he found there a Jew from Posen, who had made his way to India years before, and was now admiral in the fleet of the Viceroy of Goa. Cecil Roth, *The Jewish Contribution to Civilization,* page 9.

25 A special monument was erected at Sevastopol to Jewish soldiers who fell in defense of that city.

26 Joselowicz, its leader, managed to escape and later took a prominent part in the Napoleonic Wars, falling in combat finally at the battle with the Austri-

ans at Kotzk in 1809. He was known at the time as "the famous Polish colonel". In 1830, Berek's son, Joseph Berkowitz, again called his fellow Jews to revolt in the cause of Poland; and in 1860-63, Jews stood stanchly beside their Christian compatriots in the abortive revolution.

27 Goldsmid belonged to another well-known British military family. His three brothers were officers, as were his sons after him.

28 H. S. Kehimar, *The History of the Bene Israel of India*, page 218.

29 Sir Wilmot's father, Sir Alexander Schomberg, was also a noted naval officer, as was the latter's cousin, Captain Isaac Schomberg. A brother of Sir Wilmot attained the rank of rear admiral, as did two of Sir Wilmot's sons. A third son was General Sir George Schomberg.

30 Jewish captains had earlier commanded pioneer militia forces in the wars against the native tribes. Among these were Elias de Pass and Joshua Davis Norden, killed in the Kaffir wars. Nathaniel Isaacs became military leader to the great Zulu king, Chaka, and principal Chief of Natal. He was called by the Zulus "The Brave Warrior." Part of Britain's claim to Natal was based on the charter received by Isaacs from King Chaka.

31 Bonaparte had announced his sympathy for the project of a renascent Jewish state in Palestine and had called on Jews to rally to his standards.

32 Universal Jewish Encyclopedia, Vol. IX, page 622.

33 Together with the figure estimated by Mr. Seddon for the South, this would come to the high figure of sixteen to twenty-one percent of the then 155,000 Jewish population. For this reason, and since exact statistics were not kept at the time, the estimates made then have been questioned later by Jewish sources.

34 On the luckless Merrimac, too, was a Jewish officer, Lieutenant Moses.

35 This constituted five-tenths of 1% of the approximately 1,000,000 Jews in the country, as against four-tenths of 1% for the population as a whole.

36 Jews constituted 1.1% of the armed forces; their population ratio in Germany was 0.93%.

36a These Jewish officers whose commissions thus were born on the battlefield, actually constituted 2.5% of all the officers of the German army. This figure comprises only officers of the Jewish confession, and not so-called non-Aryans in the Nazi sense of the word, who were also numerous.

37 Ralph Nunberg, *The Fighting Jew*, page 172.

38 It was Bernheim who held the Germans on the Yser for fifteen days until the sagging line could be reinforced, and who commanded the Belgian North Division when it made its decisive break-through.

39 The Sassoon family contributed ten officers, of whom three won the M. C. All five sons of Mrs. Arthur Sebog-Montefiore held commissions, and one

was killed at Gallipoli. The Beddington family contributed 37 members. One, Lieutenant Colonel E. H. Beddington, was mentioned six times in the dispatches. The Spielmann family gave 41 members, of whom one was killed in France, one at Gallipoli, and 12 were wounded.

40 "It is a striking fact," remarks the *American Jewish Yearbook, 1919-20,* "that a large majority of Jews engaged in active service belonged to the fighting units of the army, such as the infantry, artillery, tanks, machine-gun units, and the special brigades of the Royal Engineers who were in charge of gas operations." In the administrative departments, there appear to have been comparatively few.

41 After the Kerensky Government came into power, Joseph Trumpeldor, hero of Port Arthur, and the engineer, Pinchus Ruthenberg, conceived the idea of recruiting an army of Jewish volunteers who would invade and liberate Palestine through the Russian Caucasus. When the Bolsheviks came into power, they immediately declared their opposition to the "imperialistic war," and outlawed Zionism by decree as a counter-revolutionary movement. Five thousand Jewish volunteers who succeeded in reaching the ports of Vladivostok and Kharbin were disbanded, and both the doughty leaders were thrown into prison.

42 Bernard Postal, *The Jews in the World War,* page 12.

43 *Ibid.*

43a J. George Fredman and Louis A. Falk, *Jews in America,* page 78.

44 The Universal Jewish Encyclopedia lists six, but other sources authenticate only three. The latter figure though probably erring on the side of conservatism, is used by the author. Much of the same difficulty in absolute authentication of names undoubtedly has served to reduce the actual Jewish figures throughout.

45 J. F. C. Fuller, *Armament and History,* page 125. This tribute is all the more marked in view of the fact that Fuller is politically a follower of Sir Oswald Mosley.

46 Issue of February 1902.

47 A convert to Calvinism, Bloch became influential at the Court of Czar Nicholas II. The Hague Peace Conference is said to have been called at his instigation.

48 D. Fedotoff White in his book, *The Growth of the Red Army,* credits Trotsky with not only molding the Red Army into a powerful fighting force, but with the tactics and strategy by which it achieved its triumph over the White Guards of Denikin, Wrangell, Kolchak and Semenoff. He refers to Trotsky as the Soviet "père de la victoire."

49 *If World War Comes Again,* The Yale Review, June 1938.

THE HEBREW IMPACT ON WESTERN CIVILIZATION

49a The dean of German military men, *Generaloberst* Alexander von Linsingen, noted for having held the Russians on the Bug, and for having led the later advance into the Ukraine, though a so-called non-Aryan, had not, as a professed Christian, considered himself Jewish. The classic story was that after the ascent of Hitler, the doughty old general made application to the Reichs Union of Jewish War Veterans, with the following words: "Since Herr Hitler has promoted me to be a Jew, I have the honor to make application for membership in your Society."

The distinguished Prussian military writer, Adolf Caspary, himself of Jewish descent, observes in a letter to the author that Hitler was forced quietly to mitigate his actions against Jews under the "Aryan paragraph", where it came down to the officers corps in the Reichswehr, so that two Christian grandparents in practice were sufficient to make a man Aryan. Otherwise, remarks Caspary, the higher echelons of the Prussian military caste would have been disastrously affected, and the German army crippled. He points out that the Prussian nobility, among whom the military career was practically hereditary, provided the great bulk of high-ranking officers for the German army, and had since the days of the elder Von Moltke, inter-married in a powerful and steady stream with wealthy or important Jewish families.

50 Out of Ireland's minuscule Jewish population a number of Irish patriots of Jewish antecedents made themselves immortal in the wars for freedom. The best known of these was Charles Stewart Parnell, whose Jewish mother referred proudly to the fact that her famous son sprang from fine fighting Jewish stock.

51 Of the fifteen jurists who drew up the Fascist Constitution, three were Jews. Cecil Roth, *The History of the Jews of Italy,* page 509.

52 Among the tragedies caused by Mussolini's racial policy was that of Colonel Ascoli, scion of the famous military Ascoli family, one of whose members, Aldo Ascoli, commanded the Italian fleet in the Aegean, and another, General Ettore Ascoli, who was director of the Central Military School in Civita Vecchia. Colonel Ascoli in the presence of his regiment, draped the regimental flag over his shoulders and shot himself, rather than resign.

53 A particularly flaming figure was a girl, Reizel Teitelbaum, who led a famous guerrilla unit, and for her extraordinary exploits became known as "The Manager of the Bryansk Forests."

53a This figure is based on the general assumption that the American Jewish population was close to 5,000,000, a calculation arising from the 1937 estimate of the Jewish Statistical Bureau, of 4,771,000. The American Jewish Year Book for 1948, after systematically compiling the figures for 1,200 communities, suggests that the earlier estimate is an exaggeration, and that the true population figure may not exceed 4,000,000.

THE JEW AS SOLDIER, STRATEGIST, MILITARY ADVISER

53b The specially selected 20th Air Force group given the duty of organizing and carrying out the historic atomic bomb missions against Japan, included a high proportion of both Jewish officers and enlisted men. Among the officers were Captain Joseph Slusky, technical inspector and flight test engineer of the Group, Major Guy Geller, squadron adjutant, First Lieutenant William Schiller, armament officer, Captain Bernard H. Budmen, ammunition and delivery officer, First Lieutenant Meyer Rothenberg, adjutant of the maintenance squadron, First Lieutenant Richard Podolsky, electrical officer, and First Lieutenant Jacob Baser, who flew on both the missions to Hiroshima and Nagasaki. Also on the Hiroshima mission was radio operator, Sergeant Abe H. Spitzer. Flying as bombardier-navigator on one of the observation escorts was Captain Charles Levy. The navigator of the photo reconnaissance plane which followed to photograph the stricken city, was First Lieutenant Frederick Charnes.

54 Frank Gervasi, *The Jew as a Soldier,* Collier's Magazine, April 22, 1944.

55 Frank Gervasi, *The Jew as a Soldier,* Collier's Magazine, April 22, 1944.

56 *Black Book—The Nazi Crime Against the Jewish People,* page 416.

57 Marie Syrkin, *Blessed Is the Match,* pages 305-6.

58 The first American troops to land in Algiers were commanded by Lieutenant Colonel A. H. Rosenberg. Corporal Bernard J. Kessel of Brooklyn manned the guns of the first U. S. tank to enter Oran. It was Squadron Leader Julius Cohen who managed to bring Duff Cooper and General Lord Gort from Britain to Rabat, Morocco, to make contact with the refugee French ministers there. The New Zealand general, Freyberg, led the Anzacs in the North African campaign. The final surrender of the Nazis in North Africa by General Fritz Krause and his staff at Bizerte, was made to another American Jewish army officer, twenty-three-year-old Lieutenant Albert Klein. It is of some interest, too, that the leader of the American expedition, General Mark Clark springs directly from an old Jewish military family on his mother's side.

59 Israel Cohen, *Jews in the War,* page 77.

60 Frank Gervasi, *To Whom Palestine,* page 92.

61 Mac David, *Jews Fight Too,* pages 103-106.

62 Though this number does not appear large, at no time did the entire British Empire have as many as 250 parachutists working behind enemy lines.

62a Pierre Van Paassen, *The Forgotten Ally,* page 225.

63 Van Paassen gives a stirring account of this incident in his *Forgotten Ally,* pages 193-96. He recounts that Major Liebman himself, wasted with hunger and seriously wounded, was embraced by General Koenig, and then immediately took down the Jewish flag. "Why?" asked Koenig, astounded. Liebman explained that flying the Jewish flag was against regulations—he had only raised it because he thought everything was lost. The indomitable Koenig replied that

he did not give a damn about such regulations, and placed the Jewish flag next to the Tricolor on his own car, causing his men to pass it in salute.

64 In Tobruk, there is a street called Rehov Tel Aviv, honoring the Jews who were so essential a part of the defense of the city.

65 Pierre Van Paassen, *The Forgotten Ally*, page 232.

66 The tenor of the British view may be gained from Foreign Minister Bevin's contention to President Truman that if further Jewish immigration was permitted into Palestine, it would require a half million American troops to protect the Jews from the wrath of local Arabs.

66a A token force of Saudi Arabian troops consisting of several battalions of infantry, actually did accompany the Egyptian invasion armies, along with elements of the Defence Force of the Anglo-Egyptian Sudan.

67 There were at the time 650,000 Jews in Palestine, and about 1,100,000 Arabs. The attacking Arab states possessed a population of around 40,000,000.

67a The Jews had managed to buy 20 obsolete single-seated Auster trainers, which were in such poor condition that the British had considered them worth nothing except as scrap. By a great effort the Israelis were able to make a portion of these flyable. These rickety and almost wholly unairworthy planes constituted the nucleus of what was to become the Israeli air force. They were used for airlift of besieged settlements, and also for a type of primitive dive-bombing, and the strafing of enemy troops with Browning machine guns.

67b There were also a small number of homemade two and three-inch mortars, but these were extremely short on munitions, and their use had to be limited to the amount of captured British munitions which became available. The most important of these weapons, known affectionately as the Davidka, was a homemade Napoleon gun, which possessed no rifling and had to be muzzle-loaded. This primitive artillery piece had its principal value as a noise-maker. When the war started, the only artillery the Israelis had were two 75-millimetre guns mounted on Cromwell tanks, which the Jews had managed to get away from the evacuating British forces. The Jews possessed only a limited quantity of light weapons—rifles and homemade Sten-guns, though Jewish shops soon began turning out efficient submachine guns. Even the armed escorts on the vital supply road to Jerusalem, in the early fighting, had no rifles, and were compelled to use short-range machine guns.

68 Infantry Journal, March 1949.

69 *Ibid.*

70 Fawzi Bey with the blessing of the Arab League, had appeared in Palestine with his well-equipped "volunteers" from all of the Arab countries, with an ultimatum addressed to all Palestine Jewry: "Surrender, or we wipe you out." Fawzi Bey's army consisted of 3,000 Syrians, Iraqis and other trained volunteers, assisted by German, Yugoslav, Syrian and British officers. The Israeli forces engaged at Mishmar Haemek consisted of less than 2,000 members of the Haganah, the Israeli militia.

BIBLIOGRAPHY*

ABRAHAMS, ISRAEL, *Jewish Life in the Middle Ages*

American Jewish Historical Society, Publications Nos. 3, 26 and 33

American Jewish Yearbooks, 1919-1920, 1920-1921, 1946-1947

American Jews in World War II, (Jewish Welfare Board)

BERG, MARY, *Warsaw Ghetto*

Canadian Jews in World War II, (Canadian Jewish Congress)

CASPER, BERNARD M., *With the Jewish Brigade*

DUKER, ABRAHAM G., *Jews in World War I*

EMDEN, PAUL H., *The Jews of Britain*

FREDMAN, J. GEORGE AND FALK, LOUIS A., *Jews in American Wars*

FRIEDMAN, LEE MAX, *Jewish Pioneers and Patriots*

GRAETZ, H., *History of the Jews*

JOSEPHUS, *The Jewish War*

LEVY, HERMANN, *Soviet Jews at War*

McCALL, SAMUEL WALTER, *Patriotism of the American Jew*

MILLER, MADELAIN AND LANE J., *Encyclopedia of Bible Life*

NATHAN, DR. MANFRED, *Jews in the Boer War*

PARKER, JAMES, *The Jew in the Medieval Community*

RADIN, MAX, *The Jews Among the Greeks and Romans*

SHILLMAN, BERNARD, *The Jews in Ireland*

South African Jewish Board of Deputies, *They Answered the Call*

USOV, M. L., *Jews in the Army*

ZIFF, WILLIAM B., *The Rape of Palestine*

* Additional bibliographical material may be found in the footnotes.

The Fountainhead of Western Religion

By VERGILIUS FERM

IT IS strange when one comes to study the thought of a person or some ideological movement how much clearer it becomes when one sees and understands the sources out of which it emerges. Strange it is because one tends to think of a man's ideas or some thought current as an isolated phenomenon and then comes the almost surprising realization that these thoughts have a history which removes the illusion of utter novelty. Not do we mean to say that the genesis of an ideological current constitutes a full explanation; for, nature and growth have a way of adding novelty to history. Nevertheless, it has become a truism that no man or movement is wholly cut off from its setting.

How much, indeed, is missed in Platonism, for example, apart from an understanding of its natural setting in the Greek view of life, from the Socratic method and conclusions preceding it, from the great Pythagorean movement which taught the doctrine that forms and patterns underlie the structure of the world and give meaning to it. How little of Aristotelianism can be understood apart from the Platonism which preceded it and which undergirds the whole tenor of its approach. How much of the Old Testament literature remains obscure without a knowledge of the borrowings, the imitations and reactions which the ancient Israelites carried over from the Canaanites from the day they entered the Promised Land. How little of later Mohammedanism is understood apart from the acknowledged influences of the religions of the Jews and the Christians.

In this essay, we set our limitations to that phase of Western religious thought commonly called Christian which carried on, consciously or unconsciously, the great religious tradition of the Hebraic-Judaistic culture. It is no surprise to be reminded of how great was this influence since, for the most part, Christians have acknowledged their commitment to the ancient Jewish Scriptures; but it is surprisingly strange how much of it that came to be called Christian was, in fact, the lengthening shadows of Hebraic ideas and influences.

Strong was the consciousness of these ancient people of a destiny to which they felt called and around which so much of their lives revolved. This characteristic alone makes any people genuinely religious. For it is of the essence of the religious mind that it is aware that life has a meaning which reaches out beyond the everyday tasks of living to something big and great and momentous. Ancient Israel was not the only group in the old world that possessed this consciousness strongly. The Hindus and the Iranians had a consciousness of destiny equally strong; in fact, all ancient peoples took the hinterlands of life seriously as witness the rituals and cult-practices and the gropings for an understanding of life's meaning.

Why the Hebrews had this sense of destiny in such striking measure and why they were able to pass it on to successive generations so persuasively calls for a number of interpretations. The ancient and persistent explanation was that the God of the Universe had especially selected them to convey His message and direction to all sons of men. But an equally strong conviction was in the minds of devout Hindus who also claimed the doctrine of a universal insight to which all the peoples of the earth are called. The traditional *religious* explanation of the Jews—accepted even by Christians—is a matter that cannot be settled dispassionately since it belongs to whatever religious commitment favored by the interpreter. For a more objective interpretation one must not overlook the fact that time and circumstance and sheer quality of offerings play their rôle in the measure, the reach and the breadth of a people's influence.

THE FOUNTAINHEAD OF WESTERN RELIGION

The descendants of the ancient Israelites lived strategically; they lived at the cross-roads of the world of their day; they moved about, willingly and forcibly, among other people and were relatively free from cultural isolation; they were made stronger in their religious convictions and commitments in the measure that they were politically weakened by invading conquerors; their experiences with unwelcome strangers of the world made them strong as extroverts in carrying on their difficult rôle in economic struggles and, at the same time, prevented their religious pattern to follow (as did the isolated Eastern Hindus) the path of inward isolationism and asceticism. And when Western civilization emerges it is Western and the Jews were there on its borders and in Roman and Greek centers to make their contribution—even though by subtle infiltrations. But this is not, of course, the whole story. They had a way of looking at life which caught the imagination of many of those whose own outlook was less satisfactory. Their dramatic picture of creation was not without appeal. Their religious commitments called for a welcome response because of a certain sanity which appealed to men of vigorous nature: they did not ask for withdrawal from life but called men to rise to their full stature as moral creatures with moral responsibilities in a moral Universe. The finer sensibilities of men have a way of responding to life as a noble adventure—in spite of life's crudities and absurdities. Their utter sense of destiny—in spite of the reverses of personal and political fortunes—kept their optimism high and never failed to impress others who lacked it. They were not easily to be removed in the struggle. They may have been down; but they never did quite count themselves out. Their experiences had been rough enough to cause them to forge for themselves an outlook which could carry over the rough edges. But what is more—they had great prophets who measured values with depth of insight. And they, as a people, were the ancestors of the greatest of their prophets, Jesus of Nazareth, who captured the imagination of not only the children of their own faith but those who by birth and circumstance had been strangers to it in the early generations and in the long generations which followed.

In spite of what traditional scholars have been saying, the Jewish people were as rich in philosophy as they were in religion. What is fundamentally the difference between the two? Only one factor: a religion represents a *commitment* to a way at looking at life and destiny; a philosophy is an exposition of what life is held to be. The two are ideally one in content. And surely the Jews excelled in trying to come to an understanding of the Universe. This was to them a serious matter, so that their philosophy was not a mere theory: it constituted a commitment which then became their religion. Extroverted in terms of a vigorous moralism as was their religion, it was not, like Confucianism, at the expense of an inward conviction of deeper philosophical meaning and cosmological significance. True, they were not scientists in the earlier day, but neither were the Greeks in any modern sense of the term. It is not true, as many historians would say, that Western philosophy began with the ancient Greek culture; it is equally untrue to say, as is heard from many sources, that high ethical insights began with the Hebrew prophets. Dating beginnings is always precarious business when one sees how far back lie the sources of men's insights and the origins of ideological movements and practices.

The theory of strongly marked racial characteristics, with attending socio-psychological distinctions, in so far as these are deep in the blood of peoples, is one that is today much in question. There is evidence, of course, that certain peoples have distinguishable biological characteristics such as stature-types and pigmentation. There is, for example, evidence too from recent genetic studies that the Negro race exhibits blood phenomena such as sickle-cell-anemia which points to some affirmative conclusion of group-blood characteristics. Although this question is an open one for biological and psychological studies, sociologists realizing the complex intermixtures of peoples are on surer ground when they speak of cultural heritages which distinguish groups from others. Cultural heritages are as distinguishable in the Hebrew lineage, even as they are among the Irish, the Nordics and even among smaller social units such as American Yankees or Southern aristocrats. Great cultural changes, it is clear, are now moving at a rapid rate due to an age of increased intercommunication and intermixture which technological advances have forced upon man.

The cultural inheritance of the Jewish people like any others is to be explained by climate, source and character of food supply, proximity to the great routes of communication, topography, strategic localization, isolationism or its opposite by virtue of geographical factors, and a thousand others. The strong feeling of Jews for loyalty to their own kith and kin can surely partly be explained by the geographical location of their homeland: for centuries their backyards were the highways between north and south and they must for self-protection fortify themselves and unite to survive. That their religious philosophy should be affected by this cultural circumstance is only evident: a strong protective nationalism, a conscious struggle to preserve self-integrity, the dynamic of the idea of a peculiar destiny. Any people fated to live closely together by circumstance will inevitably develop codes of cleanliness, regulations for the details of living, moral norms and some unified philosophy. For such people to believe themselves the elect of God was not the result of some mystic contemplation (as it could have been for others) but issued in the roots of insecurity of their homeland, of themselves and their families and the need for strong ties to bind when the temptation to falter was strong—as it often became. Even an intense monotheism has a cultural rootage.

For the Jews morals and religion were one. The Lord God was the focal point of an ultimate destiny and the promise of a better and securer day. Loyalty to the will of a father-God would pay delayed dividends far surpassing the sufferings of

[317]

this present world. To follow after the light of the Divine promise—vouchsafed to selected leaders—was the *summum bonum* of life. Man can not expect to strive to be less than the character of God demands; the holiness which is in God demands its reflection in man. (Lev. 19: 2) To sin against these promises and this high election of God's special revelation is no light matter; it is sheer rebellion which can only end in disaster both for the individual and the people.

Life with its concrete demands for living is a serious business before the God of the Universe. Hillel, a leader and patriarch of Palestinian Judaism of the early Christian era, taught the essence of the Judaistic faith to be: "What is hateful to thee, do not unto thy fellowmen; this is the whole Law; the rest is mere commentary." (Compare also Lev. 19: 18 which is the earlier expression of the Golden Rule.) The concrete virtues of life to which men are to dedicate themselves, according to Jewish religious thought and standards for ideal practice, were unsurpassable by any ethical standard: honesty, truthfulness, justice, mercy, purity, honor of parents, solicitude for the weak, reverence, obedience, love of fellowmen (brotherhood), kindness to animals, sexual purity and regard for family relations. All these were Jewish before they were Christian; even as (so we are coming very slowly to realize) they are a part of the bundle of teachings in other great religions of the world.

It is interesting to note how, centuries later in medieval Catholicism, the same list of the cardinal sins of men recurs as was taught in the developed Judaistic faith: the shedding of blood, sexual impurity and apostasy. A sturdy morality it was that issued from the voices of the ancient prophets of Israel and a strong respect for a sense of obligation to the moral order of the world lay at the heart of Israel's traditional teaching. It is wrong to accuse the whole of Judaistic religion of the extravagancies of the priesthood which fell victim to trivial requirements turning values upside down and preferring the lesser to the greater. This is the common fate of all priestly religions everywhere, including Christianity.

The Christian religion was born in the matrix of Judaism but it was born as a reaction not against essential Judaism but against its eccentricities. The three competing schools of Judaistic religious thought at the time of Jesus did not represent Judaism at its best any more than do the derivative cults of any great religion which shoot off into radical expressions. Pharisaism though soaked in the parent culture was not Judaism at its best, although its sincerity would match the sincerity of any religious cult. It was a priestly religion with meticulous observances made prominent, fanatical in behavior, in thought and expectation. Saducceism and Essenism, the one the religion of the privileged and charged with political intrigue to the point of advantageous assimilation, the other a semi-communistic Quaker movement strongly touched with ascetic motives, both fanatical, did not represent the best in the great tradition. Against these did the new prophet from Galilee pit his quiet strength, calling down a holy curse upon those who distorted values and calling for a return to the great prophetic religion of the fathers.

Not enough is objectively known about the beginnings of this modest religious movement to give a detailed and accurate picture. What is known can be gathered only from broad outlines and these, for the most part, by religiously committed witnesses. We do know that it was content with the anonymity of its disciples (with the exception of a few) and with no organization for its effective propagation. How far Jesus remained loyal to the religion of his fathers, in essence or in detail, and how far he launched a movement totally different from it, is a question which has been settled with prejudice on both sides. The Jews of broad appreciation would claim him as among the greatest in their prophetic lineage but would set certain limitations to what they would regard as extravagant claims of Gentile admirers. The Christians who followed soon after saw in him a person so unique that they tended to forget that whatever else he may have been, he was a Jewish prophet and belonged to the ages out of which he and his ancestors came.

A more balanced interpretation—doing no harm to the *essential* claims of either camp—would be, perhaps, to say that while he belonged—most strikingly, to be sure,—with the greatest Jewish prophets, both he and they belonged also to the prophetic world at its best; for many of the insights which they had in common concern all men of whatever the lineage and cultural background and to those prophetic voices which men may believe issue from Reality. Universality is the real *basis* of the greatest religious values. And no true judgment can be made without a sure sense of universality. One thing seems clear: He protested against the current religion of his day but, at the same time, he was as eager to recognize the truths and values of the religion· of his fathers as he was quick to recognize the qualities of values from whatever sources they came—even from those who were rooted in the less promising soil of official Gentilism.

The Christian religion did not emerge from Judaism with any pretense of founding itself upon a literature apart from the accepted literature of the Jews. True, it soon began to interpret that literature after its own heart and later to work out a literature of its own. But Judaism's Old Testament remained in this primitive period the only authorized literature, quite understandable to Palestinian Jewish Christians and more or less so to those far from the traditional Jewish centers. It would only be natural to expect that Hellenistic Jewish Christians would gravitate toward an understanding of the message of their Teacher in ways more adaptable to their own peripheral environment. The Peter Christians were Jews of one type; the Pauline Christians in that larger world out-beyond the holy shrines would be something different. Paul, most naturally, saw to that. And — what is more! — Hellenistic Christians without the Jewish background would see to it that their understanding would not be ignored. Gnostic Christians, for example, saw to that.

It was Paul, the Jewish Pharisee, who swung open the gate to allow interpretations wider than the strictly Jewish homeland would permit—except perhaps the Prophet himself. His earliest outlook upon life—although we cannot be certain—was presumably that of a normal Jew living outside the homeland but in contact with the traditional culture of his family. His parents were probably orthodox; for it is clear he knew well the keeping of the minutiae of the Law. But the open air of a more cosmopolitan commercial city, Hellenistic in influence, together with the privileges of Roman citizenship must have operated, however slowly and painfully, to release him from the religious fundamentalism of his heritage. Some scholars would point out the probability of the liberalizing influence, even indirectly, upon Paul of the contemporary Jewish philosopher, Philo of Alexandria, in coming to terms with Greek thought. We do know that he had not seen the Prophet of Nazareth in the flesh; but he had felt the breath of the Teacher from the heroic witnesses already bent on proselytizing their kindred. They say it was a miraculous conversion from Judaism to Christianity that saw the birth of Pauline Christianity. Paul himself may have been convinced of some sudden Divine intrusion upon his life. Certainly one would not expect a carefully worked out auto-psycho-analysis on his part. His own religious interpretation will be affirmed or denied only in so far as one's own religious commitment persuades. One thing is clear: a man of his varied gifts, training, cosmopolitan contacts, could hardly have failed to note in his maturing years the awareness of a strong dualism between the religion of his fathers on the one hand, and the wider religion (return to essential Judaism?) of the Prophet of Nazareth, of the provincialism of many of his kinsmen as compared with the wider world of everyday experience, of the impossible exactitude of a life of conformity to a circumscribed past with the freer air of a wider culture. Pharisaism must sooner or later come to look quite small in comparison with that other very real world of the Gentiles, also sons of God.

And so Paul receives his conversion (however gradual) and he begins to declare openly his convictions and to write letters and, unconsciously, to contribute to a new and sporadic sacred literature. A distinctive religious philosophy emerges in which the world outside and the world within are sharply distinguished, a world of flesh and a world of spirit, the old Adam and the New Adam, the here-and-now and the great hereafter, the Law and the Gospel, the works of righteousness and the grace of faith, principalities bad and principalities good. The religious philosophy of the Prophet of Nazareth was much more on the side of harmony and a world not too foreign to its God—much more monistic, in the terminology of philosophy. For Paul the world became split into a violence of disharmony; and there was need of effecting some ultimate harmony. Thus, the idea of salvation which implies a two-fold sphere (away from and toward) became accentuated (typical with the Greeks) in his thought and reflects his own torn personality. The Greek and Oriental mystery cults of the Roman empire furnish a dramatic fulfilment of this emphasis upon salvation and this was something Paul understood and certainly could incorporate into his religious experience and interpretations.

So secure in the early Christian tradition was the acknowl-edged link with the Jewish Old Testament by the early Chris-tian church that any movement to cut the church off from that tradition would find the going hard. The classic attempt, of course, was that of Marcionism (and, naturally, Gnosti-cism). According to the wealthy Marcion, Christianity had set its course in the wrong direction. That course was set by its too friendly relations with traditional Judaism, particularly in holding on to the cosmological faith as taught in the Old Testament Scriptures. It was his aim to correct this error and to launch the church on a course with a commitment to a

much simpler type of Scripture, a new canon, of which he was
to be the reforming editor. The Old Testament, he said bluntly,
depicts the God who is the Demiurge rather than the one
true God revealed by the Christos. Moreover, the religion of
the Jews, with its submission to the Law, belonged to a religion of yesterday, altogether inferior to that of the new faith
in the Gospel so emphasized by Paul.

Marcionism constituted a formidable threat to sever the
Christian religion from its deep roots in Judaistic thinking.
From the middle of the second century until its close, while
Catholicism was beginning to work out some self-conscious
organization, Marcionism continued to be the church's greatest
threat. Why did Marcionism fail? The answer seems evident:
Marcion, though earnest and committed to high morals and a
liberal, failed to take into account how deep in the consciousness of the early Christian Church was its dependence upon
the religion of the Jews. The unfailing emphasis of Jewish
monotheism would never permit a material world to be created by one God and a spiritual world as belonging to a
greater. The Greek mold into which his mind was cast, and,
for that matter, the minds also of many fellow Hellenistic
Christians of that time, while calling for an interpretation in
keeping with Gnostic philosophy could not, however strong,
cope with the mighty stream of Judaistic tradition. The shadows of a towering, historic Judaism fell across the Greek
Christians and they were unable to ignore them. Jesus did live
in Nazareth; his disciples were from that far-off Judean country; the Old Testament had long been the one Bible; Paul had
set forth his own message but Paul too was a Jew and belonged originally with the faith of his fathers; and, too, the
so-called Gospel could hardly be meaningful without the Law
which is emphasized as its contrast and which became interpreted as the stepping-stone.

The Roman stage was set for the post-primitive chapter in
the history of the Christian religion—a chapter which takes
into account the gains made and the way to preserve them.

Christianity must now be fortified. The presbyter-priests now take over and unruly prophets of reform are brought into subjection.

It was Tertullian (born c. 160 A. D.) who, in general outlines, drew the map of the future for Christian belief—a map which, although filled in here and there by different colors of crayon and sharper lines due to the changing theologies of time and the provocation of heresies, was to remain normative for subsequent Roman Catholicism. The Tertullian map (anti-Marcionite) revealed in bold strokes an acknowledgment of the unbroken Jewish heritage: its monotheism, its sturdy morality, the normative character of that whole tradition and the high place of the ancient sacred literature. He, of course, did more. Jesus of Nazareth had become the promised personal Messiah and the Christos. The mysteries of worship and ritual (e. g., communion) with their more or less fantastic and elusive interpretations as practiced by the mystery-cults of the Graeco-Roman world were put to sanctified use in the gathering tradition. Nevertheless the lengthening shadows of the Jewish faith continued to fall over the established church and to prevent the recurrence of another serious anti-Jewish threat like that of Marcionism.[1] It would be centuries before any radical reformation would appear—and then the church would have established for itself a mighty tradition.

The Judaistic heritage must remain secure if for no other reason than the simple fact that one cannot deny one's parents or the land of one's birth. But that was not, of course, all of it. Who would fail to discern the voice of a moral God in the moral passion of the Hebrew prophets? Who could deny that Deity was not to be found in much of the Jewish law, e. g., in the ten commandments? How could the function of the ancient priesthood be abrogated in view of the growing powers of a new priesthood in the Christian church? How could there be a divorce from the ancient sacred literature when the new carries on references to it on every scroll? Who would dare think that Abraham and Isaac and Moses were altogether strangers to the ways of God and as not forerunners of the new faith? If there be any trouble in making them a part of the developing drama of the new faith one need only a set of principles of interpretation to understand all this and make it clear to others. Clement[2] and Origen (born late in the second century)—and Philo before them with his interpretation of the Old Testament—helped to that end with their famous method of allegorization—a principle which was destined to bind the Old and New Testaments solidly together into one whole, *only if properly understood.*

By the end of the second century, the main body of the New Testament had been canonized. The canon of Jewish scriptures was also finally settled in the second century of our era by the rabbis at Jamnia. The Jewish canon included the three-fold division: the Law, the Prophets and the Writings.

It is interesting to note that a chief principle by which selections were made for this New section of the enlarged Bible was that the writings were supposed to show the mark of reversion to origins. A writing must be apostolic and carry some apostolic name (whether the authorship permitted it or not). Thus, the Christian mind had in the day of the canonization of its literature the will to proclaim that Christianity had roots which must never be forgotten. But what is more—these roots stretched far back into the Old Testament literature and beyond to the antecedent Hebraic culture. Many of the apologists of the second century stated their conviction that the great truths of Christianity had been taught before Christ, that Christianity was not something new but a confirmation of truths already known. Moses and the Hebrew prophets, they said, were teachers of Christianity.

When it came time to draw up its first ecumenical confession, the Christian Church at Nicea in 325 did not hesitate to proclaim its allegiance to Jewish monotheism in spite of its long practiced worship of Jesus as also somehow God. Moreover, it followed the lead of bishop Irenaeus (late second century) who insisted so strongly that the Old Testament was to be honored as part and parcel of the Christian faith (as well as the Jewish moral law). Said Irenaeus of the Christian faith: It is "in one only God, the Father almighty, who created heaven, earth, sea and all they contain." Said the Nicene creed: "We believe in one God, Father almighty, Maker of all things visible and invisible."

The Christians followed the pattern of the Jews who had come to regard the canon fixed and that further revelation could be, at most, only an illumination of what had already been given. Thus ended the age of revelation. Further generations needed only to look back for their religious norms and at the same time look around suspiciously upon any who would claim some new and even reformatory apocalyptic insight.

The unity toward which the church strove and which was brought to so successful conclusion in Roman Catholicism had its historic counterpart in the fundamental unity which underlay the religion of Israel. The idea of a chosen people with a special revelation and a destiny—so highly cherished in the minds of the Hebraic-Judaistic people—now became a fundamental doctrine of the Christian church—amended, of course, with emphasis upon the person of Jesus Christ as the Incarnation of the living God. The church, like Israel of old, was to be the homeland of its people, the anchor for every storm and the sure guarantee of Divine favor and prosperity. Cyprian (died, 258) used the symbol of the Ark of Noah for the church—outside of which no one can be saved. The institution of the church, in its very beginnings, had been modeled after the Jewish synagogue—even its form of worship[3]—(attested to by the literature of the earliest days). The older men naturally took the leadership. Time and circumstance were to bring changes—such as the pre-eminence of urban centers such as Rome giving prominence to priestly leadership—but the pattern was still there. Again, the lengthening shadows of Judaistic influence reached down and touched even the area of administration in the new households of faith.

The Jewish people were exiled from their own land in the year 70 A. D. Until recently they had been a people without their own country. Throughout the long centuries, their devout hope and prayer remained for a return to their ancient home as they believed was vouchsafed them by their God. Their ritualistic prayers never forgot the land of Israel. Not even the attempted suppressions by the two great competing religions, the Mohammedan and the Christian, could blot out this religious conviction.

During the Middle Ages the Jews were regarded as a nation and each Jewish community as a fragment of that nation. From the late eighteenth century they were granted the rights of citizenship and expected to become loyal members of nationalistic groups. Thus nationalism came in as a temptation to curb the traditional hope and desire to return to their own homeland of Israel. But to traditional Jews this conferred citizenship was still a temporary experience; they were still confronted with two loyalties. In the developing modern states they were expected to discard their allegiance to both their Written and their Oral Laws in favor of the reigning civil laws—all of which was an aggravated affront to their very religion since the revealed Word of God and its accepted interpretations (e. g., the Talmud) covered the rules for all living. Moreover, emancipated as the Jews were in the days of the Enlightenment their emancipation was not complete. They still suffered humiliation socially; and the worst offenders were those from whom it should least be expected, the Christians. Christians might have accepted the Jews had they forsworn their fathers' religion in favor of the church. Likewise the Mohammedans. Their Hebrew tongue was preserved in their sacred literature and in their rituals and holy festivities in spite of the necessity to use the language of the nation into which they became adopted. Compromise languages they created which shows the strength of their own group-feeling and at the same time their loyalty to the civil authorities. They created out of German the Yiddish; and out of Spanish came the Ladino.

It was their religion, however, which bound these people together. Their Torah was their chief group-interest and their rabbis continued to be the symbol of their unity in dispersion. They idealized the future and lived in it. And it was a future which stretched out into eternity.

Claim has been made that Mohammedanism has been strongly conditioned by the Hebraic faith. Not all scholars are agreed that Islam imported its strong emphasis upon monotheism from the first and great commandment of Israel. Mohammed's own ideas may have been affected more strongly by Jewish thought than by Christian; but the record is not too clear as to the development of his religious ideas. The *Qur'an* has numerous references to Judaism and the Old Testament but this is no proof of Mohammed's own early dependence upon those ideas. It is unquestionably true that Judaism (together with Christianity) prepared the way for Mohammedanism, negatively by weakening the traditional religions of Arabia and positively in the later formulation of Islamic ideas— especially in the interchange of peoples in the day of Moslem conquest. Both Jews and Christians had to be subtle in the propagation of their own faiths to avoid the penalties imposed upon them by the great Islamic victories. For the Moslem was as certain of the truth of his faith as others were of theirs. Although theoretically tolerant of both Judaism and Christianity the Moslem victors sought converts; and Jewish and Christian pagans had to make choice between refusal with burdensome taxation or conversion with its promise of death for apostasy. Neither choice was too good. From the seventh century on Judaism and Christianity were to suffer losses to their missionary enterprises in successive waves of Arabic victories. Islam by 1500 dominated the Western religious scene —even the sacred shrines and holy places of Israel. Not only Jews but Christians became minority groups by the avalanche of a new religion which claimed to be a corrective of both.

The close of the fifteenth century brought the final elimination of Islamic political power in Spain and the tide was turned in favor of the Christian church. It must be remembered, however, that, in spite of the long and exacting period of Moslem domination, the main features of the Christian faith did not differ in the church from those of the fifth century. This meant that the Jewish heritage as transmitted through its sacred Scriptures persisted together with that which was carried over and transmuted by Paul and others in the normative New Testament. This same tradition was held in the Greek churches which had creedal differences of slight variation and which ran its course more or less separately because of political fortunes.

Thus the fate of Judaism in the ongoing centuries of Western civilization was sealed: to surrender its treasures—its main contributions—to the two big competing religions, Islam and Christianity, both of which in time absorbed much of which it had gloriously to offer; and to be content with an identity within small and almost negligible minority groups. The rôle of Judaism as a religion followed a course much like that of later Unitarianism—which by being gradually absorbed by liberal Protestants contributed its characteristic ideas quietly and anonymously, continuing its own identity as small and unobtrusive minority groups.

Measured in terms of the long centuries which preceded it, Protestantism burst upon the scene almost overnight although there were warnings of the coming rebellion. It turned out to be a reformation that proved good both for the Roman church (acknowledged by the Catholic Church since Trent as the "Catholic Reformation") and for the plurality of Protestant offspring.

Through the Augustinian monk, Martin Luther, the Jewish apostle Paul came again to his own. Those who followed the path of this leadership carried on the stream of Jewish influence by maintaining the sacredness and the fully normative character of the Jewish Scriptures and the Pauline interpreta-

tion of the great Prophet of Nazareth, now long worshipped
by Christians as Lord and as an integral part of the Godhead
and as the One foretold in the Old Testament through Whom
comes ultimate salvation.

The other line followed a course which, in many respects,
was more like a genuinely Jewish renaissance. Wherever the
Protestant groups followed the leadership of Calvin and the
Calvinists, an even stronger consciousness of Jewish heritage
became evident. The Old Testament is dusted off and re-
studied and its normative character taken seriously. Calvinism,
in many respects (although, of course, Protestant), represents
in Protestantism the revival of Jewish traditional faith. The
Puritanism which became vocal in this sector strongly suggests
its affinity with the ancient proclamations from Mt. Sinai and
the tradition of the Law.

John Calvin's dream of a theocracy at Geneva (with, however, a representative government) is the new Israel dressed
in Protestant garb. Calvinists like the Jews of old regarded
themselves as peculiarly chosen, the true keepers of the temple of the Lord and appointed interpreters of God's will. The
absolute sovereignty of God was the theme song even as it
was of ancient Israel. Excommunication was a privileged pre-
rogative of the church for those who would not fit into the
chosen community, the elected of God. Even as in Israel offenders were put out of camp, so in Geneva there was to be
the same expulsion from the new Israel. Children were given
Jewish names: Abraham, Andrew, Daniel, Zachariah, Isaac,
Ruth, Esther and Mary, replacing the names of Catholic saints.
And when the heirs of those Protestant Israelites were privileged to name new settlements in America many of the towns
took on names of Israel: Salem, Bethel, Mt. Carmel, Kidron,
New Canaan and Zion. The Psalms remain the inspired hymns
of the church. What hymn writer dare stand up to compete
with David's songs? The Sabbath must be observed in truly
legal fashion as a day especially hallowed of the Lord (although perchance it was now the first day of the week). The

Old Testament was to be read and the stories about Israel and its Divine commission and experience must be learned, not merely as the prophets would have it but as the scribes prescribed. Gentile theological students must continue (the medieval way) to sweat through years of study of Hebrew (as well as Greek), certainly not for cultural attainments but in order to acquaint themselves first-hand as students of God's inspired Holy Word. (This, of course, became the continued practice of other educated non-Calvinist Protestant groups.) Tithing was the Lord's expectation as it was in ancient Israel and it was sure to bring its special blessings. The doctrine of predestination, with the help of Paul, went well with the doctrine of the peculiar call of a chosen people. Calvinism was a religion of severity and solemnity rather than of spontaneity and joy; the sin of Adam continued to impose itself with a holy curse down to each and every individual including those yet unborn. A philosophy of history there was in which the outcome is already fixed from the beginning even to the number of those to be saved. God's justice and exacting character were re-emphasized. The day of inspiration was long ago closed and no new novelty of doctrine was to be permitted. An ethics in which rules and regulations for detailed living were sharply set by ministers and with this a sensitive conscience was brought to focus. A Bibliolatry much after the pattern of Pharisaism-in-the-best-sense postponed the day of objective scholarship in Biblical studies. An organized effort of the church set clear the line of demarcation between regenerate saints and unregenerate sinners, thus marking the character of missionary efforts.

It is true that the mind of John Calvin was severe and that his thinking followed legalistic lines. It is not difficult to see, accordingly, how appealing the priestly type of religion depicted in the Jewish Scriptures would be to such a mind. But this is not the only reason, nor even perhaps the chief reason for Calvin's predisposal toward this ancient Jewish emphasis. Rather, it must not be overlooked that there was in him a deep desire to make Christianity a visible thing and the pattern of ancient Israel was already there to serve. Moreover, it was a pattern set by God which current Catholic practice with its alleged abuses could not match.

Calvinism became enormously influential in Protestant Christianity down to the present era; and in the lengthening shadows of Jewish influence—on the side of its institutional, sacerdotal and puritanical expressions—stretches into our day. Lutheranism, the strongest competing Protestant influence, together with the lesser groups which stressed (theoretically) the Pauline heritage and the freedom and release of mind to more spontaneous expressions, soon came under the spreading influence of Calvinism and, in America, at least, failed to carry through the implications of its own peculiar genius.

Modern Judaism has sought consciously to set its influence upon Western civilization in sharper focus in six ways. First, late in the last century the Reform group came to life. As its name suggests it conceived of the faith as sound in essence provided ideas become modernized: revelation must be conceived to be natural as well as unique; creation can operate through evolution; the chosen people can be chosen in the sense of being foremost rather than unique; Palestinian hopes may give way to common cause with sons of men in a sense of mission wherever fate has decreed one shall live; the Torah can be followed as a spiritual and moral guide but need not bind modern man to ancient mores; ceremonies may be kept but made modern.

Second, the conservative-reform group (a minority) would reform ancient Judaism only modestly: the retention of the Hebrew ritual, the keeping of many of the laws (such as feasts and fasts, more rigorous Sabbath observance, dietary rules and ceremonies). Third, the fundamentalist group which would hold to the old orthodoxy and make clear that it is still reasonable and binding; philosophical speculation to be subject to the Scriptures and tradition; the goodness of obedience to God's declared will; Israel remains the instrument of God's high purpose to teach men the only true way to God and to life; the dispersion is the work of God and the sense of mission is seen in it.

Fourth, the conservative group which began about the middle of the last century, a group today effective in their call for a return of the sons of Israel to the faith and practices of their fathers but at the same time sympathetic toward revisions in matters regarded as less essential. Fifth, the small but liberal group of reconstructionists (of recent origin) who see the Jewish faith as a civilization worthy to be preserved and of value to the total cultural life of mankind. Sixth, Zionism which only recently has come to its magnificent fruition by the turn of political events is a religious-political movement inaugurated during the last decade of the nineteenth century seeking to re-establish Palestine as the homeland of the Jewish people. Attracted to this cause were Jews of various schools of thought, from conservative to liberal, each with its own peculiar set of hopes but all having faith that the return will revitalize the whole cause of historic Judaism.[4]

It must be remembered that, as a whole, there is no one authoritative Judaistic religion today. There are rabbis who lead their groups by virtue of no apostolic succession other than that they succeed in convincing their followers that they are worthy interpreters of the ancient faith and culture. These range from the orthodox to the liberal. One factor which has contributed to a continued self-consciousness and, more or less, to a privileged sense of destiny has been the persistent habit of restricted marriages, a habit consciously striven for and eminently successful. No religious group in Western civilization can match this success—not even the Roman Catholic nor certainly the Protestant Christians who have sought to set up corresponding restrictions within their separate households of faith.

It is no part of this essay to predict the wave of the future. But the temptation is great enough, at least, to express an opinion if not a prophecy.

One thing seems clear enough: the new age in which we are entering will call for changes in religious thought far more revolutionary than any of the preceding centuries of reform. Intimations of such a revolution are to be seen in the swift changes now in progress throughout the whole cultural life of man: in technology, in medicine, in physical and biological concepts, in sociological areas of thought, in impending political reforms. Men's philosophies and religions move with much heavier feet—but they do move!

Religions need not aspire to become one other than in the appreciation of their fundamental and universal values. Judaism has a large share to contribute toward this end—especially in the prophetic stream of its heritage. So also have Christianity and Mohammedanism—to name only the three great Western religions. But such appreciation will not come from the priests of these religions but from the new prophets which each in time will produce. Already such prophetic voices have been raised but to heed them will take time—a long time if the changes come without too much external pressure and a short time if some cataclysmic experience (such as an even more hideous war) takes place.

The orthodoxies in each faith will not be expected to surrender. Only through liberal minds within each faith, receptive to the growing revelation of events, will there come the necessary leadership in the acknowledgment of values in the several households of faith, wider appreciations and the genuine spirit of *rapprochement.* Unity in essentials must naturally be expected in a world that is growing into one world; but differences in detailed theologies and practices, properly understood, will probably continue with more good than harm. A Christian need not give up his idealization of the Jewish Prophet of Nazareth as a revealer of God, nor the best in his tradition, nor the cultus which has sprung up around that Name and conditioned Christian devotees with strong emotional feeling. Jesus may well remain for those of the Christian heritage the Son of God and the Voice and Mediator of the supreme Way of Life. On the other side, the Jew need not give up his idealization of the best in his tradition and may well welcome the supreme idealization which others have given to the Prophet of Nazareth as perhaps the greatest which his own heritage has produced without harming his own strong feeling for monotheism and the greatness of the other teachers in his tradition. Nor need he give up the rich heritage of his cult-practices, feasts and festivals, around which center he holds ties of deep feeling and affection.

By whatever term we may call the revered saints of our faith, we may be reminded of the truth that a term or name does not make them qualitatively what they were or are to us. The variant Messianic concepts about which schisms have played so strongly in the past need not divide. All truly supreme religious prophets have more than a name to keep—they had a cause, a moral cause, which far exceeds in importance the names we give them. Jesus, it seems clear, was not bent upon setting up a new religion; rather, he was bent upon fulfilling the best in a hallowed tradition and leading it from more to more. This a liberal Jew might well accept and so may the Christian with a larger vision. On other points of interpretation there is room for variant theological and soteriological theories; but on the main issues Jews and Christians belong together in a closely knitted heritage—and not only they, but those of other faiths, also, who in their own heritage must have had their share of prophetic voices consecrated from beyond the veil.

FOOTNOTES

[1] The last major threat to *primitive* Catholic Christianity was that of Montanism which the Christian priests successfully squelched.

Christian Manichaeism with its rejection of the Old Testament came later but was not a serious threat especially since the towering Augustine, after tasting of it, came to disavow it.

[2] Clement made the extravagant claim that the Greeks had borrowed their best thought from Moses and the prophets!

[3] A striking example is the continued practice in ritualistic Christian churches of reading the Epistle first and then the Gospel after the pattern of the synagogue which consisted of reading first from the Book of Moses and then the Prophets.

4 For an exposition of Reform Judaism, Conservative Judaism and Reconstructionism see articles by their respective exponents in *Religion in the Twentieth Century* edited by Vergilius Ferm (Philosophical Library, 1948). Brief accounts of Orthodox Judaism and Zionism appear in *An Encyclopedia of Religion,* same editor (same publisher, 1945).

BIBLIOGRAPHY*

CRANSTON, RUTH, *World Faith.* New York, 1949.

EISENSTEIN, I., *Creative Judaism.* New York, 1941.

ENSLIN, M. S., *The Ethics of Paul.* New York, 1930.

FRIESS, H. L. and SCHNEIDER, H. W., *Religion in Various Cultures.* New York, 1932.

KAPLAN, M. M., *Judaism As A Civilization.* New York, 1934.

——, *Judaism in Transition.* New York, 1941.

KOHLER, K., *The Origins of the Synagogue and the Church*, edited by H. G. Enelow. New York, 1929.

LATOURETTE, K. S., *The First Five Centuries*, Vol. I of *A History of the Expansion of Christianity.* New York, 1937.

——, *The Thousand Years of Uncertainty*, Vol. II of *A History of the Expansion of Christianity.* New York, 1938.

McGIFFERT, A. C., *A History of Christian Thought*, Vol. I. New York, 1932.

* For recent bibliographies recommended by representatives of various Jewish schools of thought see the works cited in Footnote 4 (above).